The Compleat Phil Batt

The Compleat Phil Batt

A Kaleidoscope

by

Phil Batt

Bill - You are a great volunteer.

Best Wishes!

Phil Batt

2/26/02

Library of Congress Catalog Card Number 99-096227
ISBN 0-9677135-0-1 Paper Bound
0-9677135-5-2 Hard Bound

Additional Copies:
Contact
Eva Gay Yost
2638 N. Sea Cove Way
Meridian, Idaho 83642

Contents

Acknowledgements

In order to get the maximum flavor for this book; I needed to sort through 96 full file boxes of gubernatorial correspondence. It was also necessary to winnow out hundreds of weekly columns and reports of my activities for the past 35 years. This would have required more of my time than I could reasonably devote to it. I was rescued by my loyal former staff members who threw themselves into the task with great zeal.

Eva Gay Yost, who scheduled my activities when I was Governor, took charge of the whole operation. She prodded and pushed me and everyone else, did my typing, and made sure that every activity stayed on schedule.

Lindy High, my chief speechwriter, and long-time Idaho Statesman columnist, served as resident editor and grammarian, did the final sorting of my correspondence, and helped me through some knotty problems with my writing.

My two Rhodes scholars weighed in strong for the operation. Susan Bruns Rowe, Oxford 1989-91, is now an executive at Hewlett-Packard. She searched through the first boxes and then held a weekend sorting party at her home.

Valerie MacMillan, who has now returned to Oxford to complete her Rhodes studies, was also a staff member in my office. She consolidated the final efforts for the book.

Maggie Lawrence is a music teacher in the Boise Public Schools. She is a talented and prolific composer who helped get numerous grade school choirs to perform my Centennial song. She put "Centennial Idaho" and the "Jacque Elaine Waltz" into a proper form for publication.

Many members of my former staff volunteered to participate in the research. Included were Joanne Dick, Jason Kreizenbeck, Jim Yost, Dawn Kramer, Jeremy Pisca, Samantha Lawlis, Kathleen Trever, Edward Lodge, Amy Kleiner, Julie Pipal, Julie Robinson, Claudia Simplot Nally, Jeff Schrade, Calli Daly, Tana Shillingstad, Andrew Arulanandam, and Jeff Malmen.

All of these bright and dedicated folks are young at heart. Most of them are also tender in years, many in their twenties or early thirties. Several have already moved into important positions in industry and government service.

Early in my administration, I was criticized for having an inordinate number of young people on my staff. They sometimes needed to be reined in and corrected by a more experienced person (me), but they soon proved their mettle and we served the public well.

My guess is that several of these youngsters will be prominent on Idaho's economic face and in her politics over the next thirty or forty years.

But more seasoned folks also furnished a much-needed helping hand. My long time friend and prominent Idaho author, Louise Shadduck, helped me thin down my columns and save those that might be of interest to my readers.

The impeccable, and easily traceable, order of my records is a tribute to Ann Ingram and Tari Rice. Sometimes I groaned at their demands for orderly filing. I now see that it was worth it.

Jan Boles, archivist for Albertson College of Idaho, assembled my mementos into reasonable order and facilitated access of material for this book.

For the hundreds of hours of volunteer time donated by my former employees who are also lifetime friends, and for the support of my family, I'm deeply grateful.

Introduction

I met Phil Batt in the late 1960s, when he was a State Senator and I was a brand-new reporter for United Press International. Sometime after that, he and my father-in-law, then State Sen. Richard High of Twin Falls, competed for election as Senate President Pro Tem. Naturally, I thought High the better candidate, but Lewiston Morning Tribune columnist Bill Hall opined that the race was the rare example of a perfect choice -- a "happy flip," Hall called it. He wrote, in part,:

Both are conservatives...But they are non-righteous conservatives. They believe the truth in complex matters is so difficult to ascertain that they are unwilling to sit in moral judgment on others who come to more liberal conclusions...They keep their minds open, do their homework and vote with their heads rather than with their dogma. They are individualistic and unpredictable because neither believes that one approach is always the correct one...."

Senator Batt won and the rest, as they say, is history. More than a quarter-century later, he asked me to interview for a job in his new administration. Thus began four years of working for Governor Batt, acting as his specialist for health, welfare, education and related issues, and as one of his two main speechwriters. His other main writer was himself.

Governor Batt was a fascinating man, a good example of gap between perception and reality. In public, he often seemed stern and aloof; in private, he is a witty punster, a great mimic, and man of great compassion. He does two things at blinding speed: gets mad and gets over it. As governor, he took the lead in improving the technologies available to state government and to education, but as far as I know he never turned on the computer that sat behind his desk. In other words, people who knew the "public Batt" had an incomplete picture.

I always laughed when someone spoke of him as a "farmer," although he was a farmer (his license plate reads "Onion 1"). But he also was, and is, an author, a poet, a skilled musician, a writer, a demanding grammarian, and an eagle-eyed proofreader. (A family aside: my father, a musician, used to ask me what I thought about candidates in statewide races. When Phil Batt was running for governor, I asked whether Dad wanted to talk about candidates. "Nope," he said, "I'm voting for the clarinet player.")

At first, whenever he had a question of a staff member, the governor scribbled "See me" on the paper. Soon he told us that writing "See me" took too long, so he was shortening that to "SIMI." The SIMIs were frequent because Governor Batt prodded on a daily basis for a better performance. We dreaded picking up our draft speeches or letters and seeing the SIMI in the margin. That could mean a spelling or grammatical error or, worse, a non-sequitur or incomplete response, or worst of all, an inaccurate response.

A strict taskmaster, he was also quick to praise, often with handwritten notes. In fact, he was a prolific notewriter to people in all walks of life -- praising, criticizing, making suggestions, asking questions, offering reassurance.

Governor Batt carefully polished his image as a tightwad. He felt strongly that the public's money was not his to squander, and he guarded every nickel. But his penurious ways did not extend to his personal life. I've watched him speak in the morning about the need to slow government growth or cut back on spending, then write out a personal check in the afternoon to a stranger who needed help. "This is to buy your boy a bike for Christmas," he would say, or "I know you'll need new clothes as you go back to school." He always added that these were not loans, and that they were to be private -- between him and the recipient. As far as I know, that trust was never broken.

Governor Batt was also proud of Idaho's success in reducing the state's welfare rolls as part of its reform effort. To him, getting people off welfare was a way to improve their self-esteem. He made it clear that his goal was not to save money -- in fact, he suggested that any "savings" be plowed back into support for child care or medical services for poor children -- but rather to free people of dependence on government hand-outs.

He was frustrated throughout his term by Idaho's reputation as a haven for racist malcontents -- partly because it is not so, and partly because he spent his life putting actions behind his belief in equal treatment for all. His work with minorities was probably more significant than any of his predecessors. He was, and is, especially proud of the deep friendship and mutual respect that emerged between him and Idaho's five Native American tribes during his four years in office.

To some observers, Governor Batt's crowning achievement was obtaining workers compensation coverage for farm workers. He forced this issue through a reluctant legislature by using every weapon at his command. He was convinced the measure was needed to bring equity to a large segment of Idaho's population, but one that had little political clout. I remember walking into his office on the day of the final vote and telling him how proud I was to be a part of his team.

But he was subdued at what should have been a great moment: the signing of the bill into law. He said he had lost some lifelong friends over the issue, and he refused to join with those who were triumphant in victory. He wanted all of us to remember, he said, that the opposition came from those who acted in good faith, who faced enormous difficulties as they maintained their farming operations, and who had been mischaracterized and unjustly criticized during debate on the measure.

Governor Batt's decision not to seek re-election broke up a staff that had become a close-knit team with high morale. He was criticized from time to time for having so many youngsters in his office, a source of amusement to those of us closer to retirement age, but they added a lot of laughter and energy to the place. One of them, asked later what he had learned working in the office, replied that if he had the last dollar on earth in his possession, he'd want to turn it over to Phil Batt for safekeeping. I'd second that motion.

I suspect Phil Batt is among the last of the citizen-politicians, men and women with other lives for whom service in office is a duty and a privilege, rather than a career. He never mastered the art of the sound-bite. He said what he thought without asking for a poll. When he thought he was wrong, he said so without the cleansing spin so common these days. I was lucky to have been a part of it, and I'm glad Phil Batt let me share his experience.

Lindy High, September, 1999

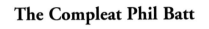

The Compleat Phil Batt

Chapter One—Life Story

I've been called a lot of things. Some of them are printable: The Little Giant; The Big Midget; Squeaky (for my voice); Machine Gun (for my rapid speaking style); Senator Butt; and Lucky Phil.

The latter is probably the most appropriate. I've taken a few lumps but, for the most part, fate has treated me amazingly well. I'm deeply grateful for my good fortune in life. I can say for certain that opportunity knocks more than once.

OPPORTUNITY

They do me wrong who say I come no more
When once I knocked and failed to find you in,
For every day I stand outside your door
And bid you wake, and rise to fight and win.

Wait not for precious chances passed away,
Weep not for golden ages on the wane!
Each night I burn the records of the day;
At sunrise every soul is born again.
Walter Malone

It was 1927, one of the worst of the Great Depression years, especially for farmers. My brothers and sisters had been sent to stay with relatives. It was my time for entering this world.

I was born in a small farmhouse two miles from Wilder. The house had an outside privy and no running water. It was divided into four rooms - the total area was about 900 square feet. One bedroom belonged to the kids. Two double beds filled it. The two girls got one, my two brothers the other for the 3 1/2 years I was there. I piled in wherever I could, mostly with my parents, I'm told.

I came several years after the rest. My father was 45 years old. Mother was 38, and I was, no doubt, an afterthought or an accident. But, in any case, my parents loved me dearly.

I had the best of all possible childhoods. My mother liked to dress me up and show me off. She would take me around and have me sing "My Old Straw Hat" to anyone who would listen.

I don't remember much about the old house, but I'm sure the primitive nature of it was not pleasant. The copper tub baths, using water brought in and heated, would have been tough for my older sisters.

I do remember, with clarity, one event - the hog slaughter. My father struck the doomed animal a mighty blow with a sledge hammer. While the porker lay stunned, our foreman slit his throat from ear to ear with a gigantic knife. In less than a minute, the hog was immersed in a vat of scalding hot water, the better to soften his bristles for removal.

At that instant, my Mom ran frantically from the house and herded me away from the grisly scene. So much for today's horror movies. I don't believe my psyche was injured by the real thing.

We moved from my country birthplace into the town of Wilder when I was almost four years old. Exchanging our rustic abode for a modern house in town was the epitome of progress. My father must have hit a lucky year in farming - it was probably a lettuce crop, for which the market gyrated wildly. He was able to purchase one of Wilder's finer homes.

My mother Elizabeth Karn Batt, was a sweet, sociable person. Although she deferred to my father in all economic matters, she had plenty to say about how the household was operated. She was an avid flower gardener and belonged to numerous social groups.

Mother's parents emigrated from South Dakota, via Salem, Oregon, to take advantage of the new homesteading opportunities brought about by the erection of Arrowrock Dam. In addition to grubbing out sagebrush and applying the newly-found irrigation water, Grandpa Karn was a talented inventor. His work in perfecting a grain binder helped revolutionize the harvest of small grains.

My mother's parents, Catherine and Edward Karn. Grandpa was an inventor as well as a farmer.

Grandpa Karn died about the time I was born. Grandma lived for another 30 years, mostly in a house right next to ours. Early in that period, when I was very young, Grandma got run down by a car while meandering across the main thoroughfare. I remember them placing her, bleeding, on a sofa. She said, "I'll be okay when I get my wits about me." She was laid up for a while, but I don't think the injuries were serious.

Mother had six siblings and they had large families. I spent a lot of childhood days and weekends visiting, and sometimes sleeping over, with my 30-odd cousins. They were, and are, a solid salt-of-the-earth group.

My father's parents both emigrated from England in 1879, as single Mormon missionaries. They were married in Salt Lake City. Grandpa Charles Batt was an irascible, religious gadfly. He renounced his LDS

Grandfather Charles Batt emigrated from England in 1879 as L.D.S. missionary.

religion and spent the remainder of his 97 years searching for religious truth and constantly debating it.

They homesteaded at Howe, Idaho, where they went broke, and then moved on to Salem, Oregon. Grandpa was a paperhanger, when he worked at all. Father and his two brothers worked as day laborers. They moved to the Boise Valley in about 1915. My father is reputed (as a laborer) to have helped lay the foundation for our Capitol building.

Grandma Batt died when I was only a few years old. Grandpa was given a small cabin outside Wilder. He and my father quarreled furiously. I remember, sadly, the times when my father would order the old man off our porch. "Get off my property," he would say, after Grandpa had goaded him until his explosive temper could stand no more.

My mother was totally engrossed in the Baptist church. I loved it and earned a lot of gold stars for memorizing Bible verses. The Baptists were absolutely convinced that theirs was the true religion. Mormons and

My parents, John and Elizabeth Karn Batt, 1947.

My sisters, Ruth (left) and Emma at inauguration ceremonies.

John, Jr., Jim and Phil. With John Batt, Sr., they farmed a large acreage at Wilder.

Catholics were considered misled; Methodists were tolerated but not totally embraced.

We had almost continuous card games at our house, and this required keeping an eye out for the preacher. The cards were swept out of sight whenever he was spotted, only to reappear immediately upon his departure.

Farmland around Wilder was being quickly developed from the sagebrush, and the town flourished. Still, the first grade was short of students. Three underage kids were recruited to help fill it out. I entered at 5 1/2 years of age. Miss Mercer was a tough, phonics-oriented teacher. No monkey business was tolerated. One day, a couple of kids were fighting in the hallway. She grabbed them both by the hair and banged their heads together. There was no more fighting.

School was a great experience for me, and the off-hours were even better. I soon formed a little gang of town friends. There were numerous vacant lots in Wilder, overgrown with weeds which towered well above our heads. We had well-developed paths and tunnels and we would play all kinds of secret games. The weeds and adjacent buildings were the home of giant spiders - one-inch black widows and garden varieties up to two and a half inches. It was fine sport to go into one of the nearby outhouses, pee on the webs across the holes, and watch those fierce spiders come running out.

Even at an early age, kids were expected to earn whatever money it took for penny candy and other extravagances. I ran errands, sold mail order magazines and anything else I could lay my hands on. Cattails were a hot seller. I'd pick them at their prime, color them in stripes or zigzags with crayons, then twist them for an artistic effect. When I presented them, along with some sunflowers, the old ladies would frequently purchase a few for 1 cent apiece, or as many as they wanted for 2 cents. I'd stay and visit and my hostess would often give me some lemonade.

I was shameless in my hustling, and I soon had several households providing me with pop and beer bottles, which fetched a tiny deposit upon return.

One memorable day I had several returnables, including a rare treasure, a 1/2-gallon beer bottle. I was on my way to the store when I encountered the preacher. We stopped to visit a minute, and the prized bottle slipped from my grasp and shattered on the sidewalk. The preacher allowed that this turn of events was unfortunate, observing that such bottles were, indeed, slippery.

Nearly all the proceeds from my enterprises went into penny candy. Our variety store had a large selection and you could get a little brown sack half-full for 2 or 3 cents.

Around the age of seven, I was introduced to fieldwork. My older siblings were at it nearly full time in the summer and I joined them intermittently. Sister Ruth, the oldest of our crew, made sure that the rest of us didn't goof off.

There were no real wages involved, but we did get a chance to earn a small allowance. One early job stands out in my memory. Our lettuce crop was being decimated by wireworms. There were no effective pesticides. We were given hand trowels with which to unearth wilting plants. We then destroyed the yellow marauders, that had been feasting on the lettuce roots. Others in the family received either a small hourly wage, or nothing at all. As I was a low producer, I was given a Prince Albert tobacco tin. I put the wireworms in it and was paid 1 cent per dozen. At the end of a short day I could net as much as 5 cents.

But my parents also allowed me plenty of free time. We played Kick the can, Hide and seek, Run sheep run, One 'o cat and carried on a wide variety of other activities.

I was envious of those who owned Monopoly games. When a set failed to appear at present-opening time, I decided to make my own. I think my parents bought the dice, but I made the rest from plywood scraps, paper, and cedar kindling wood (dyed with food coloring.) The statute of limitations now protects me from copyright infringement lawsuits.

One Christmas I got my number one wish - a set of boxing gloves. We hammered away with the large mitts. My cousin, Nellie, was probably the best. She could whip me and I was a year older.

I got hit by cars three times in a short period. Dad was admonishing me about running wild in town, when I tearfully confessed to the first knucklescraper at Wilder's main intersection. I didn't tell him about the fact that my foot was backed over while I was clamping on my roller skates, or of being knocked head over heels by a car entering my Grandpa's driveway.

Wages for adult labor in my early childhood were 10 cents per hour. I remember the pitiful stream of workers coming to our door and asking for a job - any job.

If my father weren't around, Mom was a fairly soft touch, and would generally give some kind of a handout. Dad wasn't that hardhearted, either - but if he were there, the itinerant would have to perform a good bit of labor around the place in order to be fed.

One magnificent summer my parents allowed me to become part of the contract pea-picking crew. The main body of this workforce consisted of genuine Gypsies (complete with moon and star-decorated tents, folk dances, and fortunetellers). They were augmented by a host of local children. We all gathered at the appointed place at 4 a.m., from whence we were transported from field to field.

I believe I was 8 years old. The pay was 25 cents per 30-pound hamper. Two neighborhood friends and I managed one hamper between us in about four hours. What a great feeling it was when we checked it in and blew the entire 25 cents at the lunch wagon on sweet rolls.

My father was determined not to fall back into abject poverty, and he tried all kinds of ways to turn a dollar. He bought some plywood and built a housing around a farm truck chassis. He then obtained the contract to haul the kids to school. I was forbidden on the bus, as I could easily walk to school. One day I sneaked on and was not discovered until the end of the line. The lecture I received still burns in my memory.

Dad bought and leased some farmland at Jamieson, north of Vale, Oregon, and farmed it long distance. During the summer he made the 110-mile round trip every day, sometimes twice, occasionally pulling a tractor behind his car - tethered by a rope. My two older brothers were assigned the task of riding those gyrating machines. It's a miracle they lived through it.

Potato harvest at Vale took about two weeks. We set up tents, and all the males moved to the Jamieson farm. My brothers ran the diggers. My assignment, at 9 years old, was to be the "bulldogger." The bulldogger followed the digger and, with bare feet, kicked the spuds out of the way so the tractor would not run over them next time around. The soil was cool and soft and the sociability of the spud-picking crew made for enjoyable work.

Our foreman cooked for us in our tent. It was his job to get us up, feed us breakfast, and have us in the field by 4:30 a.m. He slipped off to the tavern a couple of times, failed in his duties, was reported by my older brother, and received a tirade from my father which was, to say the least, unique.

I received $7 for the 14 days I spent in the tent and in the field. I was rich.

I remember those early years with great pleasure - watching the mules (chosen because of their small feet) pull the lettuce carts through the field; sneaking into the back of the cull lettuce dump truck at Uncle P.G.'s packing shed; savoring the slick, cool feeling when the load was dumped on a nearby field; or nursing an old truck along at two miles per hour while husky men loaded 60 pound potato sacks onto it. At the end of the field one of the crew would jump in, turn the truck around and adjust the accelerator.

One haunting memory is the totally destitute state of so many of the workers. They had nothing. They had to work, beg or starve. Wages were about $1 per 10-hour day. They had to produce or be laid off, as there was always a large pool of applicants waiting. One of our crew was in some disfavor with the foreman. A small gaggle of us kids started teasing him and finally got in a clod fight. He was fired, in spite of pleading for his job. I regret that incident to this day, as I was partly responsible.

First grade teacher, Miss Mercer's "Wranglers". I'm 3rd from left, front row.

High school play, "Cleaned & Pressed".

Things went well at school. I got to be part of Miss Mercer's "Wranglers," a cowboy singing group. (See Photo). My brother, Jim, started taking violin lessons. They cost 25 cents per week. My mother persuaded my father to buy me a small fiddle and I dutifully attended all of Jim's lessons, auditing them at no cost and squawking out the tunes at home. I found out much later that my father paid my older brother, John Jr., 25 cents per week not to take lessons.

I really liked school. I enjoyed the companionship of students and teachers, found the studies challenging and interesting, and I loved the music and plays and Maypole dancing. I sang a lot, played my violin, took up the Tonette and finally, at 12 years of age, started on the clarinet.

By the time another two years had passed, I was playing in the C. W. Steffens Dance Band. C. W. Steffens was my history teacher. I was the only young kid in the band, and we played in such sinful places as the Arena Valley Grange Hall. Most of the patrons stayed stone-cold sober, but a sizable contingent made frequent trips to their cars to have a few nips and improve their dancing ability.

When 1 a.m. rolled around, they'd sometimes pass the hat (literally), and keep the band another hour or two. That was fine with me, as the sandwiches were good and C. W. gave me a little money. Mother took a dim view of it.

My Uncle Roger had a large hop farm. This crop is unique. The vines are started onto strings made from coconut hulls and attached to an 18-foot high trellis. The hop "berries" resemble miniature soft pinecones. They contain lupulin, a yellow "pollen" which imparts flavor to beer. Hops required a large harvest crew; particularly in those days, when the "berries" were picked by hand.

I picked hops for my uncle and, after a few years, was advanced to "sack and water boy," driving a pickup through the hop yard. After I became more roadworthy, I hauled lettuce. Mules pulled the carts through the field, allowing selection of the ripe heads. The load was dumped, ladies rough-trimmed the heads, and men packed them into field crates. We then loaded the crates onto a flatbed truck and hauled them to my uncle's packing shed. If the market was hot, we worked 14 to16 hours per day. My buddies and I were probably 15 years old. We almost always grabbed a cold Pepsi (5 cents) as we went through Wilder. Those were glorious times.

But Pearl Harbor had occurred and the country was in great peril. It was during that time that the farm labor shortage brought reality to my sheltered world. Exposure to a wide variety of human beings showed me, for the first time, the eclectic, polyglot composition of the human race.

All able-bodied young men went to the service so the U. S. government brought in various groups to work on the farms. We had a large contingent of Jamaicans. Entire families came in. Those dark-black, beautiful people often sang and visited while they capably carried out their chores.

German and Japanese war prisoners were better workers. They were quick and efficient and seemed to enjoy the work more than their nighttime confinement. It was eerie to see our soldiers standing guard with their rifles in this free country. The Germans did their own cooking and the rumor around Wilder was that they were eating raw pork. As we were scared to pieces of trichinosis, we believed that those Nazis would soon be deathly sick.

The most reliable source of labor was the Mexican Bracero Program. Hard-working, single men were recruited in Mexico. They stayed in barracks provided by the U. S. government. This program laid the groundwork for the millions of Hispanics who have since come to this country, mainly for farm work. Today, a substantial and increasing number of these immigrants have achieved the level of education and training that permits them to reach their economic potential. They are a strong asset to Idaho.

Wilder was a small school. My graduating class numbered 31. That made for abundant opportunities for each of us.

I wanted to play football. I was too small until after I took a half-year hiatus to help on the farm. When I came back in my junior year, I made the team. As a senior, I became quarterback and captain. I weighed 126 pounds and my small hands could not grip the ball well enough to throw it accurately. We had a razzle-dazzle ground game, which earned us a share of the league title. One big kid did most of the work.

I debated for Wendell Willkie, who was the Republican candidate against President Roosevelt in 1940. Willkie didn't make much of a showing and neither did I. I also played the pantless victim in a school play, "Cleaned and Pressed." (See photo.)

The kids elected me their student body president. I was second in my class, scholastically.

Music was a big part of my life. I worked hard at becoming a clarinetist, competing in numerous music festivals, and finally holding my own in northwest competitions. I loved classics then, as I do now. I also formed my own dance band, playing the tenor sax and clarinet. We rented the Odd Fellows Hall in Caldwell and threw Friday night dances. They were a big draw for kids throughout the valley. The seven members of our band made quite a sum of money. We invested nearly all of it in music arrangements. We had a good dance book which mysteriously got legs after my departure for the Army.

The big war was on. My older brother John, Jr. went to the Army. After a couple of years Jim went, too. I stayed out of school one fall semester to help my beleaguered father haul his sugar beets to the receiving station. My sister, Emma, had been married only a few weeks when her husband, a lieutenant in the Army, was mowed down by 50-caliber machine-gun fire while leading his troops up the beach at Guadalcanal. Emma enlisted in the WAVES and served as an officer until war's end.

Brother Jim was engaged in fierce hand-to-hand fighting on Okinawa. Our own artillery, while attempting to give our troops a better chance, lobbed one too close, blowing off my brother's arm. That did it for me. As soon as I could qualify after my 17th birthday, I joined the Army Air Corps, hoping to become a fighter pilot and to avenge the damage to my family.

Due to missing a semester, I graduated from high school in midyear. Because I was underage, the Air Corps would not then call me to active duty. So they sent me to the University of Idaho under a special program until I became 18 years old. I got in about 5 months at the University before the Air Force called me up. While I was in basic training, the ghastly power of the A-Bomb was unleashed over Hiroshima.

I had been in the service less than 6 months when the war ended. I qualified as a clerk typist on my exams, and spent the rest of my military

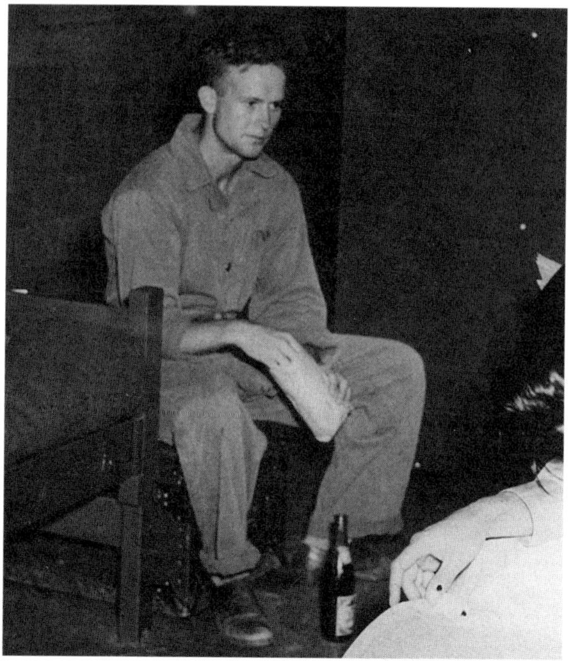

Private Phil Batt in basic training, Biloxi, Mississippi, discharged as Buck Sergeant eighteen months later.

Jacque's parents, Mary and Gordon Fallis. Gordon was a superintendent at a Washington water power plant near Spokane.

Phil and Jacque at U. of I. shortly before we eloped, December 1947.

career completing discharge papers for some of our great veterans. Lowry Field, at Denver, was my home for 16 months. What a beautiful city it was then, quite similar to Boise today. Denverites loved the servicemen. You could stand at the front gate on Sunday, and people would come by and take you to dinner.

After I served my hitch and was discharged, I told my father I was going back to the University of Idaho. He believed that the girls needed college, but the boys didn't. My two brothers were back from the service, so he reluctantly told me to "go get it over with."

It was great. I stayed in a dorm, and my G.I. stipend covered most of my cost. I cranked up another dance band and we got a lot of jobs playing for sororities and fraternities. I studied Chemical Engineering and found the material exciting, particularly the newly-found interest in the power of the atom.

I met a member of the Delta Delta Delta Sorority, Jacque Elaine Fallis, from Spokane, a beauty with an amazing sense of humor. We fell madly in love, and eloped in January 1948. Her parents were a little non-plussed, but quickly gave us their warm blessing. Gordon Fallis, her father, kept giving me an ever-larger share of the $50 bills he had saved for her college expenses.

We settled into a 12-foot trailer house at $10 per week. It had a bed, a table, and a hot plate. We ate, studied, went to school and enjoyed the pure bliss of having each other.

But tragedy struck less than a month later. My father got in a severe car wreck, which left him with limited strength and speech. He lasted 10 more years, but he wasn't up to par.

The farm operation had been expanding rapidly and management was critical. As my brothers had aborted their college careers, it seemed logical that I should, too. Jacque and I packed it up and went to the farm. It was tough for her, with less than a year to go to obtain her coveted degree.

But we made the best of it. John Batt and Sons, Inc. had just built a small house (1100 square feet) at a new location where we fed cattle. It was an ideal place for us, except that the cattle had first choice on a limited supply of water. We got the house and $250 per month. It was ample, but we watched our pennies. One weekend we bought a dozen live chickens. I whacked off their heads with a hatchet. (They flopped around like chickens with their heads cut off.) We hadn't learned much in those days, so we didn't dip the chickens in scalding hot water before plucking. The sun had set before we finished that chore.

Soon after, we obtained a dog and a donkey and gave up plans of returning to the University of Idaho. Our son, Bill, and oldest daughter,

Rebecca, were born during those years. Jacque gave ballet lessons to supplement our income.

Our family farm corporation was a profit-producing machine. We were highly competitive, not only with the rest of the world but between brothers and father. It gave each of us the highest satisfaction if we could bring in an outstanding yield or a good price, or facilitate any expansion of our operation.

My father regularly ignored the advice of his sons about when to buy feeder cattle and when to sell fat ones. He happily confounded us with his consistent market successes.

Jacque and I still longed for a little independence. Due to my veteran status, I was eligible to draw for a homestead on a U. S. Government project north of Rupert.

Some 10,000 veterans applied for those farms. Mine was the 7th name to be drawn. My father's pioneer spirit was piqued by this effort. I was surprised when he offered no opposition, and I was happy to get away from what I considered to be his domineering, wrong-headed authority.

Well, it was a nice farm - 113 acres, deep soil, good water. We built a house for $6,000, partly with our own labor. There were no TVs, or telephones. If it rained, we were stuck at home by the dirt roads. We didn't mind that at all. We struck up a warm friendship with our neighbors and enjoyed ourselves a lot. Our youngest daughter, Leslie, joined her two siblings. Our little family of desert rats did well. But it wasn't what I was used to. It was high country, and it froze every month of our first year there, capped by a tough freeze on July 22nd, which seriously reduced our spud yield.

After a couple of years, I decided that Dad had learned a lot and we moved back to Wilder. Our combined efforts flourished and each brother developed his own separate enterprises as my father's health declined.

I give my father credit for some of my good traits as well as my shortcomings. He taught me honesty, a direct and sometimes blunt manner, which I practice to a fault, and a belief that no permanent gain comes without hard work and perseverance. He also gave me an immoderate temper, which has not served me well at times.

But Dad believed all people should have a chance. One of his friends told him that he had given a ride to a permanent employee of our

Bottle feeding an orphan calf in our machine shop, circa 1950.

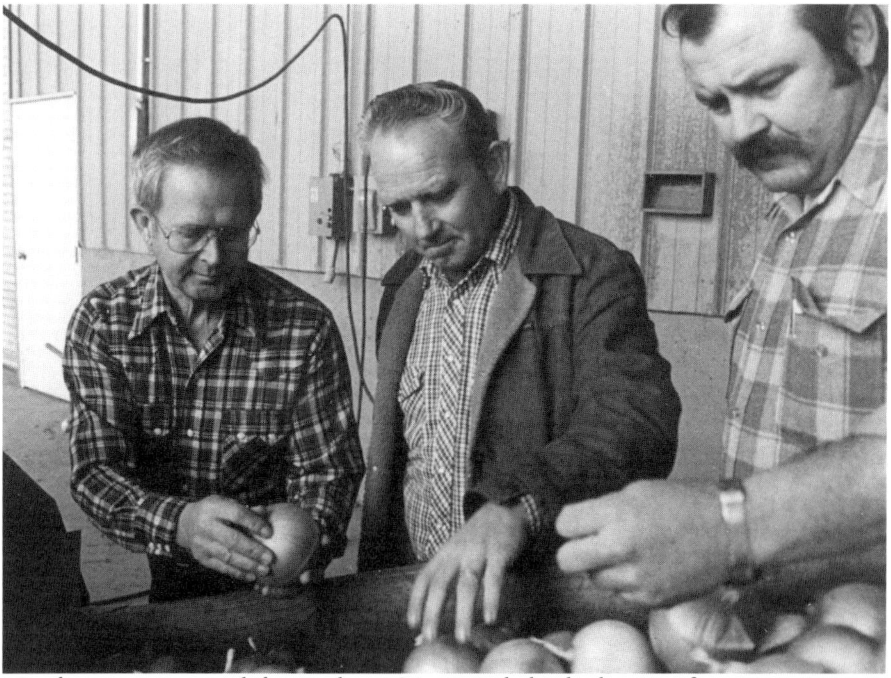

Grading onions at Holiday Packing Co., our wholesale shipping firm, circa 1980.

Another successful hike into the Owyhees with my son, Bill. Jet airplanes didn't scare the wildlife.

Jacque, ready to take off in air race with Mira Batt as co-pilot.

farm. The farmhand had vigorously denounced my father after being assured he wouldn't be quoted. My father's friend felt compelled to report it and gave his advice that the man should be fired.

My father said, "Forget it, he's entitled to his own opinion. He's been doing his job okay." That was the end of the matter. In the early days, a black man came seeking a job. No other farmer had seen fit to employ him. Dad gave him a job but kept him away from others to avoid "trouble."

My life changed considerably after he expired. Father had pretty much set the pattern for my working life from early childhood until his death. It was 1958 and I was 31 years old. I had a fine family and a good start toward a successful farming career.

It was a new era for my brothers and me. We split the family farm corporation and vigorously applied ourselves to our new career paths.

I became more appreciative of and attentive to my own family. Jacque, just as she has for all the 51 years of our marriage, welcomed new challenges and opportunities. We bought an 80-acre junkyard for $3,200, 'dozed the junk into the hollows, covered it over, drilled a well, built a house, and planted an orchard. We both became pilots and bought the first of three airplanes. After I had accumulated 60 hours of flight time (the minimum license time is 40 hours), we took off with our onion-growing friends, Kay and Mary Inouye, and flew to Miami, Florida. The trip was adventurous because of our greenhorn status. I wrote about it and sold the story to the Aircraft Owners and Pilots Association Magazine for $150. That's the most I've ever been paid for writing.

We had part ownership in three Piper Comanche airplanes over the next 25 years. Jacque served as President of the Idaho Chapter of the 99s, an international association of women pilots. During that time she participated in air races. Our joint travels took us all over the United States and at least five times into Mexico. We also explored western Canada.

One evening Jacque persuaded me to go to a Homedale PTA meeting. We were unaware that they needed a new president. I was elected by default.

Our bread and butter crop was hops. Some 99-1/2 percent of hop usage is for brewing beer (my Mother was a teetotaler and she used to claim that ours went for the other 1/2 percent.) Two domestic dealers and another based in Germany controlled almost all hop transactions between growers and brewers. It was unheard of for a grower to sell to a brewery and such action would bring high disfavor to both parties.

Well, in 1963, Jacque and I came up with about 1,500 bales of hops (200 pounds each), which we didn't have sold. We loaded some samples into our trusty airplane and headed for Colorado. We went into Coors Brewery, unannounced, and asked to see the purchasing agent. Bill Coors, who was in charge, was so intrigued by this audacity that he met with us personally and bought our hops.

The dealers were outraged and blackballed us forthwith. But Coors had immense power in the marketplace and swore to protect us.

Thus started a warm business relationship that lasted many years. Adolph Coors II, who was 90 years old at the time, greatly preferred hops grown in the Hallertau Region of Bavaria, Germany. Bill Coors sent me to Germany with two of his most trusted employees to see how we could produce similar hops.

We brought back some roots and set about propagating plants in two large greenhouses erected next to our own house. I ran experiments there, at Delta, Colorado, and at Bonners Ferry, Idaho. Although we eventually planted 135 acres of Hallertau hops on my farm, they were poor producers. Munich is on about the same latitude as the Canadian border. The cloudy weather is also similar to northern Idaho. The German hops at Wilder were suffering from too much direct ultraviolet sunlight, concluded Dr. Robert Romanko, who worked with hops at the Parma research branch of the University of Idaho.

He gave the opinion that German hops would produce better at Bonners Ferry. I started some experimental plots there, and frequently made the trip in our little airplane to oversee that operation.

Although Coors abandoned the experiment to Budweiser, that area now has over 1,500 acres of Bavarian-type hops.

The Coors organization also planted its first Idaho brewing barley plot on my farm. They then moved the operation to the Magic Valley, where they thought acreage would be more readily available.

My relationship with Coors was exciting and challenging. That progressive company demanded and expected the best. They treated me fairly, but were never extravagant. My relationship with the dealers was restored and it is now a common practice for a hop farmer to contract directly with brewers. (I sold out of the business in 1976. Hop prices are now in a disastrous slump, and acreage in Idaho is declining.)

During the late fifties, the Cold War had intensified to the point that it dominated public dialogue. A group of us young men started a political discussion group. We were fiercely anti-Communist and tended to be libertarian in our views.

It was decided that we would propose certain of our members for public office. One ran for mayor, another for the school board. My brother, John, Jr. was chosen to run for the Idaho House of Representatives. All were elected.

John was successful and highly respected by his peers. The press named him as an outstanding freshman. Some even said he would be governor someday.

But he didn't take to the job. He was stubbornly independent and found even the slightest compromise to be distasteful.

John quit after one term. I had only a mild interest in politics. Jacque had been working for Republican candidates for years, carrying on the strong conservative views of her parents. We decided I should give it a try.

On July 29, 1964, about a month before the August primary, a freak, tornado-like windstorm flattened 150 acres of my hopyard. I won't go into the horrible details, but the storm cut my yield in half - the salvaged remainder was of poor visual quality and the cost of rebuilding the 18-foot-high trellis was enormous.

The whole affair cost a great sum of money and just about wiped us out. I was already in hock at the bank, having expanded rapidly in previous years. It was a dark, dreary time for Jacque and me, but we clawed back. Our banker and our Coors relationship were vital in our recovery.

Immediately after the event, I knew what I was in for, and seriously considered withdrawing from the primary, which loomed a few weeks away. I decided to hang in and handily won one of Canyon County's six Republican nominations.

There was little time for campaigning due to the urgency of the farming disaster. Our strong county Republican organization did a lot for me in the general election. Running countywide, I placed fourth among the 12 candidates for the six seats, behind two Democrats.

The 1965 Legislature was historic, by anyone's standard. We enacted Idaho's first 3-cent sales tax, totally reformed our judicial system and, in special session, carried out the miserable chore of designing the first court-ordered reapportionment.

Until that time each county elected one member of our state Senate. Clark County, with a population of about 500, had the same power as Ada, with around 150,000.

Reapportionment brought out the worst of human behavior in a lot of incumbents. After all, it was political death for many of them. But we got the job done. An objective citizens' committee can better perform that important exercise. Idaho has adopted such a procedure. Hooray!!

In the reapportionment process, Canyon County went from one state Senate seat to three. There was an open Senate chair for the asking. Although I enjoyed the House, with its irreverent approach to legislating, I filed for the Senate. I had no opposition.

I spent a total of 15 years in the Senate. Practicing my own form of term limits, I never served more than six years in a row. I became majority leader during my second Senate term, served four years, and went back to the farm. After a two-year hiatus, I entered the Senate again, served four years as majority leader and two as President Pro Tempore. I was beginning to get serious about my political future and set about honing my oratorical skills.

In 1975 one of the Simplot enterprises put in a large turkey farm next to our homestead. There were thousands of Beltsville white turkeys penned next to us. They were on dry land and they liked to congregate along our boundary because of the cool sprinklers in the orchard.

I would go out by the turkeys and practice my speeches. Those tasty fowls didn't mind my staccato delivery at all and would crawl against the fence as I orated. Then I'd bang on my pickup door and they would gobble-gobble in unison. I would thank them for the applause.

Encouraged by such approval, I then took a shot at the lieutenant governor's spot. Governor John Evans had appointed Bill Murphy to that office. He was a fine man and we engaged in a high-level contest. Polls showed me far behind (my name ID was nominal), and my agency urged a dirty campaign ad, showing side-by-side pictures of me as the vigorous young comer and Bill Murphy as an over-the-hill politician. I refused to let the ad run. It was then that I started my practice of driving a "Battmobile." The first was a 1973 pickup, well broken in (109,000

Battmobile #1, 1978.

Reluctantly posing as King Kamehameha at Republican Convention in 1980. Daughter Rebecca holds first Batt bumper strips for 1982 campaign.

Battmobile #2, 1982

Frankie (Killer) Garrett, my neighbor, embraces me after NBC declared me the victor over John Evans. Late returns reversed that order.

miles) and it bore the marks of a long and honorable farm career. My campaign colors were yellow and green. The old truck was green, so we added yellow flying bats, augmented with baseball bats. It was eye-popping. I won in a squeaker because of innovative campaigning tactics such as that, which drew a lot of attention

About that time, after a 25-year hiatus, I rekindled my interest in the clarinet. Pianist Louie Ventrella put together a rag-tag quartet for legislative parties. But the big opportunity was to join the incomparable Gene Harris for Tuesday night jams at the Idanha Hotel. For a person

With President Ronald Reagan and Senator Steve Symms.

with limited talent, I've been fortunate to sit in with some of the best. In addition to Gene Harris, I've played with Scatman Crothers, Chet Atkins, Lionel Hampton, Gib Hochstrasser, Bill Watrous, Buddy De Franco, and various symphonies and dance bands. What a privilege!!

It was time to go up or out in politics and I filed against John Evans for Governor. He had served six years and was at the height of his popularity. The national elections went the Democrats' way and my party ended up with a net loss of 10 Governors' seats. I made a lot of mistakes, but still came within 1% of unseating Evans. I believe that the fatal blow was a comic book depicting "Big John" dangling as a puppet while the union bosses manipulated the strings. It was printed and distributed by "friends." I denounced it but it still cost me dearly.

With Vice President George Bush and, left to right, Senator Jim McClure, Senator Steve Symms, Batt, Representative George Hansen, (V. P. Bush), and Representative Larry Craig, 1982.

A more substantive issue was the ominous deficit building in the state's finances because of a recession in our economy. The Evans administration refused to face up to this shortfall during the campaign. I predicted we would be $65 million short of balancing our budget. (It turned out to be $70 million.)

John Evans said no such shortfall would occur.

I gave the opinion that sales taxes might have to be raised unless we drastically cut school aid. This alienated the anti-tax forces and alarmed the citizens along the Oregon border.

Governor Evans said there would be no raise in sales taxes, a promise he later abandoned. Shortly after the election, the governor proposed, and the Legislature passed, a "temporary" 2% increase in our sales tax.

In any event, John Evans was re-elected. I congratulated him, and said that he was my governor, too, and that we should all support him. John did a creditable job and he and Lola have been gracious friends.

At the time I got out of the hop business, I established a small wholesale onion packing shed. It has enjoyed slow and steady growth. We grade and ship to wholesalers throughout the nation and abroad.

After my defeat by Governor Evans, I concentrated on the farm and packing shed. A couple of years later, an open state Senate seat appeared again. I decided that another legislative stint would help me forget my "close, but no cigar" Governor's race. I was elected to the state Senate in 1984 and 1986 and re-entered leadership.

Cecil Andrus had served as governor from 1970 to 1977 when he left to become a Cabinet officer under President Carter. In 1986, he once again won the governor's chair. Governor Andrus and I have always maintained a cordial relationship since the late sixties when we served together in the State Senate.

Shortly after he resumed the office, his Health and Welfare Department prematurely started up a new electronic data processing system. This elaborate computer system crashed and burned. Clients were not receiving their medical or welfare checks. Employees were quitting in despair.

I wasn't overburdened with duties so I volunteered to help Governor Andrus sort out the mess.

He put me on special assignment without pay. (I couldn't be paid by both the legislative and executive branches.)

I set about my work. I traveled the state for a month, interviewing about 100 people. I then formed a small group of private industry experts, and called in the computer vendor and the Health and Welfare executives. We knocked heads together until we reached a feasible repair solution. It cost the state several million dollars but it worked.

Toward the end of my 1987 Senate term, Governor Andrus proposed a nominee for the Transportation Board. That particular appointment required a Republican. The GOP discovered that his nominee had not only contributed to Andrus and Evans, but also to John Kennedy.

When it became evident that the Senate would not confirm his proposed appointee, Governor Andrus decided to withdraw the nomination.

I was tiring of the Legislature and I asked the Governor if he would like me to be his substitute nominee. He decided he would, so I resigned my Senate seat and joined the Transportation Board.

It was a challenging and interesting assignment. My main contribution was forcing a realistic assessment of what highway projects might be funded during the so-called "Six Year Plan." The Board had been promising two or three times as much as could be done. We came back to reality.

In 1990, Idaho Republicans endured their worst election results in decades. We lost both congressional seats and control of the State Land Board. The state Senate was tied 21 to 21 with Lieutenant Governor Otter keeping tenuous Republican control, through his tie-breaking votes.

We Republicans had become sloppy in our organizational work. I volunteered to serve as State Chairman and was accepted. After I resigned from the Transportation Board, our new team went to work. We held self-assessment and motivational workshops across the state, concentrated on what united us, and determined what divided us. I threw myself into this effort with great gusto, traveling to countless meetings and recruiting effective precinct committee members. We gave the Democrats no safe seats, going for outstanding Republican candidates in every corner of the state. The result was accelerated success in the next two elections. In 1994, we elected Republicans to nearly every major office and enjoyed the largest ratio of Republican Legislators in the nation. In 1992, we gave George Bush his highest percentage vote. Ross Perot nearly beat out Bill Clinton for second choice. It's not Idaho's fault that we have a defective President.

But how could we claim to be a Republican state when Democrats had occupied the governor's chair for 24 years? In 1992 we started casting about for a candidate who could capture that elusive political prize. I came to the conclusion that I had the best shot, despite the fact that I would be 67 years old at the start of the term.

Jacque and I had strong reservations about the campaign, but we jumped in and gave it our best.

Appearing with Larry Echohawk, 1994.

It appeared that John Peavey would be the Democrat nominee. I felt confident that I could beat John, whose idealism often hampered sound judgment. I settled down to the primary contest among four good candidates.

My confidence was severely dented when Larry Echohawk entered the race. Peavey deferred to Echohawk, and pundits declared that it was all but certain he would become the first Native American Governor. Early polls showed him beating me by 40 points in a trial heat.

Mr. Echohawk attracted nation-wide attention. He received large sums of money from Indian gambling interests in Connecticut. He was also assisted by Robert Redford and Dustin Hoffman. He was written up

Debating Larry Echohawk and Ron Rankin in Coeur d'Alene, 1994.

in national publications and had his picture taken while jogging with Bill Clinton.

Well, this is a natural set-up for a fall in Idaho. Larry was a good man, but he believed his own press releases. He was proud of his association with the President and his destiny in trailblazing for Native Americans.

A group that was backing my candidacy bought billboards showing a picture of President Clinton and Echohawk together with a slash through it and adding "Not For Idaho."

Larry protested loudly, calling it dirty politics. I had not been consulted nor had I approved the billboards. However, I responded by saying that he could use one of the numerous pictures I had taken with Presidents Reagan and Bush and do anything he wanted with it, including advertising with a slash.

He made some other serious errors. I was holding a press conference on the Capitol steps; Echohawk and his entourage came up in several cars. As they screeched to a halt, the candidate bustled through my group and demanded the microphone, claiming that I was distorting his record. That outburst gained me a lot of votes.

Mr. Echohawk is a devout Mormon. Thus he felt comfortable in carrying out a fund-raising event on church property in Salt Lake City. LDS faithful in Idaho were angry and did not hesitate to disavow such a practice.

Larry Echohawk attacked my own personal finances and demanded that I release my tax returns. He falsely accused me of living off farm subsidies. I reluctantly (for privacy reasons) released the returns. They showed a large gain from the sale of a farm. They also showed that I had given generously to charity. The farm community was not pleased by that whole affair. They felt as if Mr. Echohawk were attacking farmers.

In the meantime, we went about the business of running an effective campaign. Our organizational work was incredibly strong. My years of party service evoked a maximum effort from my troops. My campaign staff was composed mostly of bright young people led by the incomparable Jeff Malmen. They were brash and sometimes careless, but with their stamina and enthusiasm they danced circles around the opposition.

We plugged away. Aided by Echohawk's mistakes, and enjoying a strong national Republican year, I was handily elected.

I will deal with an appraisal of my service as Governor in another chapter. I will forever be indebted to Idahoans for the confidence they have shown in my political judgment for over 30 years.

Chapter Two—Service as Governor

Receiving the oath of office as governor of the State of Idaho in a heavy snow storm.

My family at the inaugural ceremonies: Left to right, back row; Phil, Jacque, Bill Batt and wife, Cathy Naugle, Leslie Batt-Corbet and husband, Tom Corbet, Rebecca Batt-Hart and husband, Randy Hart; front; grandchildren Max Batt, Jacob Corbet, Anna Batt, Lindsey Corbet.

Greeting Velma Morrison, et al, at inaugural ball.

Gene Harris (left) and Bill Mitchell (right) present a framed copy of "Jacque Elaine Waltz" at inaugural ball

I was astounded when I was elected Governor. I knew I had a fighting chance by Election Day, but the most recent public polls still showed me trailing Mr. Echohawk by a few points.

Nevertheless, I had already given considerable thought to possible appointments and to a crackerjack transition team. We settled into the task of assuming the responsibilities of the Chief Executive of Idaho. Governor Andrus was most gracious and facilitated my succession to the office as much as he could, considering the change in the ruling political party after 24 years.

He gave us ample office space on the first floor of the Capitol Building. We had only $15 thousand to spend for the two-month transition period, so we got by with three paid staff members. I had access to a complete set of transition books, which are prepared according to law. I took them home and read them in the evenings. I put in about 70 hours per week during the transition.

Inauguration ceremony, 1995, Governor Bob Smylie and Lu, Governor Cecil Andrus and Carol, Jacque and Governor Phil Batt, Governor John Evans and Lola, Governor Don Samuelson and Ruby.

Defending nuclear waste agreement at Twin Falls with demonstrators from both sides in the background.

Photo: Twin Falls Times-News

Mail came in by the box, heavily laced with résumés. I was looking for people with extensive experience in management to be my department heads. I also wanted those pivotal employees to be frugal with the taxpayers' dollars. The pool of such executives is limited because most qualified folks are already working at high-paying jobs.

But, with due diligence, I was able to select outstanding cabinet members and they served me well throughout my term. I had to make only a few changes after the initial appointments. Our watchword was **thrift.** We initiated hundreds of cost-saving measures and, through attrition, reduced the total number of state employees. After four years, total state government employment was less than when I took office.

We were careful, however, that we did not compromise state services. My first admonition to all who worked with me was that the only reason to have our jobs was to serve the people.

With Senator Mike Crapo 4,000 feet underground at nuclear waste repository in Carlsbad, NM. Room 7 was readied for Idaho's first shipment, which has now been received.

Enjoying a friendly game of golfsticks with Cecil Andrus who was crucial to the Nuclear Waste Agreement.

The media did a thorough and, for the most part, fair job of reporting my performance as Governor. I want to mention only a few of the critical decisions I made and the actions I took during my term.

The most widely examined, and the most important to Idaho, was the consummation of an unprecedented agreement with the federal government concerning the storage of nuclear waste.

The nuclear waste issue hit me right between the eyes. Governor Andrus had obtained an injunction limiting the number of shipments of spent naval fuel rods into Idaho to 19 over an approximate 18-month period. Normal shipments could not resume until an environmental impact statement could be completed. Under a court stipulation, an additional eight loads could be shipped, however, if there was evidence that our national security was being compromised. U. S. Secretary of Defense William J. Perry declared that such an emergency existed. Governor Andrus had challenged the validity of that declaration in court.

When I was in office less than two weeks, Admiral Bruce DeMars and his entourage flew in from Washington, D.C. in their own naval airplane.

They presented me with a compelling case that our defense capabilities were being jeopardized. They claimed that the aircraft carrier Nimitz would soon be out of service if its spent fuel rods could not be unloaded on schedule. They also said that a great number of Navy servicemen would be out longer than their six-month promised sea duty, if the refueling operation was not done on a timely basis.

I believe that Congress would have soon dictated our acceptance of this small amount of spent fuel rather than to idle any ships or submarines. However, I admired Governor Andrus' actions that got the attention of both the Navy and the Department of Energy, and that generated almost universal support among Idahoans.

The eight loads were only a fraction of the larger question regarding our responsibilities to accept nuclear waste. I wanted to face up to this dilemma and work out something favorable to our state. There was no plan in place for a permanent disposal site for the naval fuel. Military waste was excluded from the proposed repository at Yucca Mountain in Nevada.

I told the Admiral that, if he and the Secretary of Defense would lobby Congress to include military spent fuel in the proposal for Yucca Mountain, I would accept the extra eight loads. We signed a formal agreement with those stipulations. It should be noted that the military waste is now designated for that Nevada facility as a result of that temporary agreement.

I received skunk cabbage from nearly every quarter. I must say, gratefully, that most of the media reported that series of events objectively and editorialists offered little criticism. But it was a tough time for me. It tested my mettle as a new governor, and ground me down a bit. That's why I'm only five foot six today.

The larger question of the resumption of regular shipments remained before us. Some 90% of Idahoans did not, and do not, approve of the storage of nuclear waste above Idaho's precious aquifer at the Idaho Nuclear Engineering and Environmental Laboratory (INEEL) near Idaho Falls.

I count myself among that 90%. But I was not handed a choice of accepting or rejecting waste. I could continue a battle in federal court (a suit we would have soon lost) or I could deal realistically with our limited options. I chose to address this perplexing situation head on, based on facts instead of emotion.

The facts were these: INEEL was already the home to some 1550 shipments of spent nuclear fuel rods, both military and commercial; enough transuranic waste (plutonium contaminated waste) to fill over 300,000 barrels; scores of pits of uncontained transuranic waste (i.e. the notorious pit #9) working its way down through the soil; 2 million gallons of high-level liquid waste (the result of processing Navy fuel rods and nuclear bomb materials earlier); debris from the Three Mile Island nuclear catastrophe; and a wide array of other waste. The high-level liquid waste was being held in aging underground tanks. Traces of radiation had been found some 200 feet below the surface of the buried transuranic waste. These materials posed a much higher threat to Idaho than adding a reasonable number to our inventory of spent fuel rods.

The INEEL was also the premier U. S. laboratory for nuclear research. It was the home of the first prototype reactor for electrical generation from the atom. The pioneering scientific work done there has led the way for the creation of nuclear power plants throughout the world.

Its importance to the Navy could not be overstated. The U. S. Navy did a great deal of practical experimentation at INEEL, examining and testing spent fuel rods. This resulted in an increase in the useful life of naval fuel rods for propelling subs and ships from a few months to 20 years or more, greatly enhancing our naval superiority and reducing our quantity of waste. The Idaho facility served as the womb for the Nautilus - the first nuclear-powered craft in the world. The Navy also trained submarine crews, using a life-like model nuclear submarine. Naval personnel carried on numerous experiments and training, both nuclear and non-nuclear. INEEL was, and is, a vital part of the Navy.

All of the naval spent fuel rods are at the INEEL. It would take multi-billions of dollars, as well as many years, to move this operation elsewhere.

Elsewhere in the nation are some 90,000 shipments of spent fuel rods from commercial generating plants. Nobody wants them. The federal government has taken title to these and has guaranteed a home for them. Our federal Department of Energy was casting a covetous eye at INEEL.

The State of Idaho was engaged in a lawsuit regarding the shipment of additional waste to Idaho. I don't underestimate the importance of this legal action, carried out by Governor Andrus, to our state. It set the stage for my agreement.

The lawsuit called for an environmental impact statement regarding further shipments. The U. S. Department of Energy (DOE), during the negotiations, announced a preferred option which would have resulted in 1,940 additional shipments of spent fuel rods to Idaho. No concessions to Idaho were offered.

Most of the legal advice I could obtain painted a dim picture of our chances of winning the lawsuit. In fact, a Federal Appeals Court upheld our right to continue the negotiations only by a two-to-one vote.

But we had a strong factor working in our favor. The U. S. Navy was desperate to unload spent fuel, which had been backing up at ports and in submarines due to the Andrus lawsuit.

There was little doubt that Congress would order us to take this naval fuel in order to prevent a deterioration of our defense capabilities. Yet, the naval authorities were anxious to avoid a forceful imposition on Idaho because of the public relations damage that would ensue.

Hence, the Navy put tremendous pressure on DOE to strike an agreement with me. Time was running out before we would have suffered a court-imposed requirement to accept the 1,940 shipments. These included the naval fuel over the next 30 years; 170 shipments of spent rods from the "Atoms for Peace" program which belonged to the U. S. but had been used in foreign countries; 244 shipments of commercial spent rods from the Fort St. Vrain facility in Colorado; and 524 from Hanford, of various configurations.

We held negotiating sessions at several spots throughout the U. S. At one of those sessions, held in Minneapolis, I received separate phone calls from Senator Larry Craig, Senator Dirk Kempthorne and Representative Mike Crapo.

They all told me the same story. They were temporarily holding Congress at bay, but an overwhelming bipartisan majority was ready to require us to take the naval fuel now and for all time. They urged me to settle our case immediately. Even with that renewed urgency to negotiate, we nearly lost the agreement in Minneapolis. I finally walked out of the meetings and told the DOE and Navy folks that I could not meet their demands and that I would see them in court. It was then that they came forward with most of the concessions. After further meetings, I was able to obtain the following stipulations:

1. The total shipments will be reduced from 1,940 to 1,133 over the next 30 years. As nearly half of the 1,133 shipments are naval fuel, we accepted only about 600 shipments over which we had the slightest chance to stop in court.

2. Cleanup of dangerous high-level radioactive liquids will be accelerated. This material is being converted into a solid form for eventual shipment from the State.

3. Our 300,000 barrel equivalents of transuranic waste (60% of the entire U. S. inventory) will be shipped to the Waste Isolation Pilot Plant (WIPP) in New Mexico, starting in April, 1999.

4. The Three Mile Island debris will be moved into superior storage.

5. All spent fuel rods, now held in water tanks, will be brought above ground and converted to dry storage.

6. $30 million will be distributed to Idaho for use in creating new job opportunities in Eastern Idaho.

7. None of the huge mountain of commercial spent fuel rods, accumulating at nuclear power plants around the nation, will ever be brought to Idaho, including those from Fort St. Vrain as proposed by DOE in the 1,940 shipments.

8. All high-level spent fuel rods now stored in Idaho plus the 1,133 additional shipments, will be placed in dry storage, prepared for shipping containers, and then removed from Idaho within 40 years.

9. Failure to remove waste from Idaho as scheduled will cause all incoming shipments of DOE material to stop and fines of $60,000 per day will be imposed.

10. The Superfund Agreement, which included digging up buried transuranic waste, preceded my administration, but it was referred to in my agreement and ratified.

The above measures mean that an additional $3 to $4 billion will be spent at INEEL because of the agreement.

Most of Idaho's previous officeholders, federal and state, had expressed their concern about the threat to our aquifer posed by storage of nuclear waste. The U. S. government had made empty promises to Frank

Church, Jim McClure, John Evans and Cecil Andrus, to name a few. The story was always the same - Idaho was a temporary storage and the material would eventually be moved to a permanent repository.

Governor Andrus finally had enough. He stopped a shipment from Colorado and demanded a court review of the environmental impact to Idaho from these materials. His tough stance helped lay the groundwork for this agreement. Nevertheless, with his annoying flair for one-up-manship, he couldn't resist criticizing, in his recent book, the penalty provisions provided in the agreement.

I must tell my friend Cecil that I got every ounce of flesh that I could get. If the Navy had not been in a bind, we could not have come close to the deal we made.

The U. S. Justice Department was aghast that the federal government was making these huge concessions. DOE Under-Secretary Tom Grumbly finally told me we could not continue to negotiate, even with the persistent prodding of Admiral DeMars of the Navy. We held the agreement together by the skin of our teeth.

Inevitably, I received scathing criticism from a number of sources. The emotional nature of the question was ready-made for political exploitation.

Former state Senator John Peavey saw it as an opportunity to propel himself into the governor's chair. He, and other Democrats, started a petition drive to annul the agreement. There was an aborted attempt to recall me from office.

The proposed cancellation of the agreement did reach the ballot. It was known as Proposition 3. A full-blown, well-financed campaign developed on both sides of the issue. Things looked bleak for a while. Strong emotional support for revoking the agreement overwhelmed me at first.

Celebrities joined with anti-nuclear activists and hundreds of concerned citizens in support of Proposition 3. They held frequent Statehouse rallies.

But when it came to factual discussion, my opponents had little to offer. By revoking the agreement we would have left ourselves wide open to becoming the nuclear waste dump of the nation.

A series of formal debates was held. And after each one, support for the agreement and for the defeat of Proposition 3 grew stronger. Shortly before the election, I appealed personally to the voters, telling them I had done the best I could do, and that the agreement was vital to Idaho. They sustained me by a wide margin. Time will prove the wisdom of their action

---

I had promised property tax relief during the campaign. I persuaded the legislature to repeal one-fourth of the School Maintenance and Operation (M & O) levy. That move impacted our general fund $40 million (this amount has now grown to $60 million annually). It was all we could afford, and made for tight budgets.

But it accomplished its purpose. Limitations on property taxes such as the One-Percent Initiative were popping up every election. The One-Percent Initiative would have decimated the ability of local governments to finance their necessary operations. But even worse, it would have been almost impossible to implement. The county commissioners would have been forced to decide what portion of the remaining proceeds would go to each taxing district. It was a potential gold mine for the lawyers.

Passage of such a Draconian measure would have seriously upset our balanced 3-legged taxation system consisting of income, sales, and property taxes. My property tax relief program prevented much more drastic proposals from becoming law. In addition to the M & O relief, we capped increases, in all property taxing districts except schools, at 3 percent annually plus new construction. Some of the local officials still gripe a little, but there has been a precipitous drop in individual tax complaints.

Critics of my property tax relief program predicted that we would be forced to raise other taxes. I made it clear that I believed our basic tax structure would generate sufficient funds. Now that our tax receipts are regularly exceeding projections, it appears that my case has been made.

I recognized that our available funds were tight and proposed only thrifty budgets. As I am a believer in limited government, I had no problem with this.

However, in order to provide as much state financial aid as possible for schools, I searched for ways to bring in more money under our present tax structure. Our Tax Collection department was woefully understaffed. Out-of-state taxpayers sometimes would show Idaho income on federal returns, but would not even file an Idaho tax form.

I talked the Legislature into beefing up our department. It was a hard sell but we prevailed. Already, after the first year, we collected $17 million above the cost of the additional personnel. This figure could go much higher.

Also at my urging, the State Land Board proposed altering our investment provisions to allow our multi billion dollar assets to be invested in higher-yielding instruments. This could bring us $30 to $60 million more per year when it is fully enacted. The voters overwhelmingly approved this proposal last election.

Unfortunately, the drafters of the proposal included some unrelated questions, and the Idaho Supreme Court threw the measure out. It can, and will, be corrected and our general fund will receive a healthy boost when it becomes law.

I've been a farmer for 50 years. I have worked alongside my employees and I know of their vital contributions to success in farming. I've established profit-sharing plans and paid bonuses when possible. I have also, voluntarily, carried workers compensation insurance for most of that 50 years. (I also voluntarily carried unemployment insurance before it became mandatory, but found that, due to federal rules regarding exempt employees, none of my employees were eligible for payments - I wasted 2 years of premiums.)

In reviewing my political activities, I can honestly say that I have been consistent. I've always been tight with the money. I've favored only a minimum of restrictions on free enterprise. One of Idaho's major strengths is its relatively unfettered entrepreneurial spirit.

At the same time, I have strongly advocated equal treatment for all our citizens. I authored and championed our first comprehensive civil rights bill and have stoutly defended our Human Rights Commission. If society requires field toilets for construction workers, but makes an agricultural worker walk a mile to an open ditch in order to relieve herself, something is wrong. I've pushed for such facilities and adequate housing for farm workers, and gave urgent testimony for dedicating a holiday to Martin Luther King Jr. at a time when it seemed doomed to failure.

I helped form the Hispanic Commission and have worked hard to make it successful.

Before 1996 there had been numerous attempts to require workers compensation coverage for agriculture employees, none of which were successful.

I decided to give it my best shot. Some farm organizations argued that an industry in economic trouble should not be further burdened. They claimed that liability insurance and medical coverage was sufficient and that an injured worker could sue to recover damages. In practice, few farm workers had the finances or the knowledge to institute a lawsuit.

I know from personal experience that workers comp is valuable to the employer as well as to the worker. I made no promises other than I would work to hold premiums down. Workers comp rates were reduced by more than 25% during my term.

This was the only legislative matter in my 4-year term for which I appealed privately to numerous lawmakers asking for support.

Public approval for this effort surged after a tragic accident maimed an uninsured farm worker. The Ada County Farm Bureau and the Idaho Potato Growers Association, at the urging of my key employee, Jim Yost, decided to back my workers comp bill. That support helped turn the tide. A number of legislators, led by Representative Bill Deal and Senator Dean Cameron, took up the cause, and argued forcefully for its adoption. After lengthy hearings and some acrimonious debate, Idaho lawmakers adopted my proposal.

It was a bittersweet victory. I lost some lifetime farm friends and was branded a liberal by some former supporters.

I don't accept that label. I'm a governmental tightwad and I despise overregulation. Nevertheless, our free-market system will not function properly if people are denied fundamental rights because of their race, religion or occupation. If that belief damages my conservative credentials, so be it.

Probably the most pleasant surprise I had during my governorship was the warm friendship I formed with our five Native American tribes. In my campaign travels, I was struck by the grinding poverty that was apparent on the reservations. Shortly after I took office, I met with a delegation of tribal leaders. They were wary of me and a little hostile in their approach. They wanted to know if I was planning to establish an "Indian Desk." I told them that I would personally be their Indian Desk and that we would meet on a regular basis. For most of my term we met monthly, and I grew to deeply appreciate the fine human qualities of such leaders as Ernie Stensgar, Sam Penney and Marjorie Zarate. These and other tribal officers are selfless in their approach, desiring only to improve the lot of their fellow Native Americans.

I happen to believe that legalized gambling is a poorly conceived idea. No wealth is created and profits are merely transferred from a loser to a winner. A number of social ills invariably permeate big-time gambling centers, such as Las Vegas and Atlantic City

Thus, I find myself at odds with the tribes over "gaming." We have never settled the question as to whether their activities are legal in Idaho. Tribal leaders argue that their casinos are only carrying out a function similar to our state lottery (which I also think was a mistake). The state's legal officers claim that our Constitution specifically prohibits the electronic machines found in Idaho's Indian casinos.

I've always believed in settling questions instead of leaving them up in the air, so I asked for a court determination. But it's not that simple. There are questions of jurisdiction. Federal courts are the only effective venue. Similar disputes have surfaced all over the country and courts have ruled for the tribes more often than not. Neither side in Idaho has pushed hard for a legal resolution.

In the meantime, there has been no question about the spectacular economic changes that have occurred on the reservations.

Tribes, which were previously mired in despair, have achieved a remarkable transformation. Schools and school attendance have dramatically improved. Unemployment rates that had run from 50 to 80% are now down to manageable figures. Profits from the casinos have been used almost exclusively for beneficial projects.

I believe most folks in the state want to leave this situation alone. The voters overwhelmingly approved a constitutional amendment only a few years ago banning just the type of machines now operating. Yet I think today a majority would favor allowing the tribes to take advantage of this short-term opportunity to become participants in Idaho's economic success. I'm reluctantly siding with that majority. I hope the tribes don't ride that vehicle too long. It will probably run out of gas.

Nothing irritates me more than the continuing assertion that Idaho is a haven for racists and bigots.

We do have a handful of oddballs who get far more than their share of publicity. These include the Nazi-loving Aryan Nations at Hayden Lake. That pitiful band of 20 or 30 does incredible harm to Idaho's national image. Periodically, journalists from New York or Paris or L. A. or Dallas come in, do a story on the Nazis and then go back home to make money off putting down Idaho.

Lindsay Nothern, my communications director at the time, spent an afternoon with a German reporter whose technique consisted mainly of citing another distorted article as the "source" of her own coverage. Nothing Lindsay told her seemed to make a dent in her thinking.

I call it drive-by journalism. It's a cheap and easy way to get wide readership. While highlighting this despicable group, the writers ignore widespread racial intolerance and violence in their own states and countries. More reporters than supporters attend the puny parades and public events of the Aryan Nations - and the "Idaho story" being told is an unattractive and untruthful one.

Two years ago, The New York Times did an inaccurate, false and demeaning article on Idaho's image. I rebutted it point-by-point in a letter, but the paper would not deign to print an opinion of a governor from a backwater state such as Idaho.

My reasons for wanting to set the record straight were based on something more than a public relations effort. I met with representatives of Hewlett-Packard, which has a printer manufacturing plant in Boise, and listened as those business leaders explained that they were having difficulty recruiting some talented people to work in Idaho. Even the Newsweek article, naming Boise as one of the preeminent high-tech cities in the nation included mention of our reputation.

Tribal leaders at our final monthly meeting (left to right): Terry Gibson, Shoshone-Paiute, Duck Valley; Delbert Farmer, Shoshone-Bannock, Fort Hall; Velma Bahe, Kootenai, Bonners Ferry; Ernie Stensgar, Coeur d'Alene, Plummer; Sam Penney, Nez Perce, Lapwai; Reginald Sópe, Shoshone-Paiute.

Caldwell, Idaho, Governor Alberto Cárdenas pictured with Idahoans whose roots are in Jalisco, Mexico, the governor's home state.

It hurts Idaho in many ways when what people think of us elsewhere is that we mainly excel at growing potatoes and harboring bigots.

I dismissed the suggestion by H-P and others that we sponsor a nationwide ad campaign to refute false impressions about Idaho. I thought this tactic might draw even more attention to the bad image being created by these malcontents. Such a campaign is again being considered and it may have merit.

Nonetheless, I believe we made considerable progress during my term, both with our image and, just as importantly, with improving our general tolerance and concern for the well being of minorities.

I took the Aryans to task in their home territory of Coeur d'Alene. (What a burden for that wonderful place.) The enthusiastic reception I received proved to me that the Nazi venom has not spread beyond their own wretched crew.

In addition to creating an effective dialogue with the tribes, I initiated a dynamic effort to better the lives of Hispanics. Our Hispanic Initiative has coincided with the emergence of a flood of new Hispanic leaders. These young people have become well educated and are serving as role models for the thousands of Hispanics who are not reaching their economic and educational potential.

The success of the initiative rested with the Hispanics themselves, who started by identifying the issues that were of most concern to them: education, substance abuse, crime among youth, access to services and so on. Then, over the next year, my department heads worked hard to see what each agency could do to make sure Idaho's largest minority had ample opportunity to improve itself. All Idahoans have a stake in this.

Midway through my term, Hewlett-Packard invited me to travel to Guadalajara, Jalisco, Mexico on their corporate jet. As H-P has a large component plant at Guadalajara, the plane makes the trip frequently.

Idaho had established a sister-state relationship with Jalisco, but it had never been formalized. I met with Governor Alberto Cárdenas to sign the formal documents.

Governor Cárdenas and I hit it off from the start. A large percentage of Idaho's Hispanic population has roots in Jalisco. My intimate acquaintance with this group intrigued the Governor.

He is a member of the opposition party (PAN) in Mexico. Governor Cárdenas is the antithesis of the power-hungry, corruption-riddled politicians who have hobbled Mexico's progress for far too long. He is determined to elevate his people, through free enterprise, from the mire of poverty in which they find themselves.

Governor Cárdenas returned my visit in 1998. He brought an entourage to Boise where our Commerce Department gave them an outstanding reception. He visited Jaliscans throughout the Treasure Valley and included an inspection of the fine low-income housing project in my hometown of Wilder.

The governor informed us, with profound sadness, that some 1,600,000 former Jaliscans had emigrated to the United States, and that he has visited perhaps a dozen states to check on their progress.

Governor Cárdenas stated, unequivocally, that Hispanics were treated better in Idaho than he had observed in any other state. In view of this, he said, Jalisco wished to contribute $50,000 toward the completion of the Hispanic Cultural Center in Nampa.

I was so impressed by this heartfelt and generous gesture that I promised I would submit a request to the legislature to match his gift. The legislators met, after I left office, and decided that they could not grant such an appropriation.

Governor Kempthorne recently completed a highly successful trade mission to Guadalajara. He received the $50,000 gift from the state of Jalisco, which has now been matched by Hewlett-Packard. Governor Kempthorne has indicated that he will again ask the legislature to give financial aid to the cultural center.

There is a long road ahead before Idaho's Hispanic population reaches its economic potential. But a new confidence and pride swells through that community. I am concerned that our Hispanic Commission, which has been well focused in the past, might become preoccupied with lobbying for so-called "rights." The commission will do more good if it sticks with encouragement for better education and job training than it will in building bigger budgets for specially designed programs. I, along with most Idahoans, support opportunity, but not special treatment.

My long time colleague, former state Representative Jesse Berain, is now vice-chair of the commission. Gladys Esquivel, who has provided practical leadership for Hispanics for decades, is the chairperson. I now feel confident that this agency, under such outstanding leadership, will effectively improve the status of Hispanics

I worked hard at trying to improve our tarnished national image. My efforts with farm workers got national attention in the *Wall Street Journal* and *Governing* magazine. I welcomed the all-black National Brotherhood of Skiers to Sun Valley. These talented skiers were pleased with our hospitality and they are talking of a return visit.

I've never felt that protection of our environmental excellence should be a partisan issue. Few Idahoans are willing to suffer unnecessary degradation of our air, water or scenic wonders.

Yet we know that we must continue to use our assets in a practical manner if we are to provide employment and recreational opportunities for our citizens.

Many of our businesses, particularly the large ones, make an impact on our air and water while carrying out necessary procedures.

National and state governments over the past several decades have promulgated standards for air and water purity. Our state Division of Environmental Quality, under criteria set by the federal Environmental Protection Agency, is charged with enforcing these standards.

There are two ways to gain this compliance. One is to assiduously hunt for violations, levy large fines and shut down certain operations. The other is to work closely with businesses and to help them in complying with federal and state regulations.

I chose the latter method. It doesn't bring in as much fine money, but it doesn't throw people out of work and hamper our economy either.

I had my share of critics. I maintain that the proof is in the cleanliness of the environment. Both air and water quality continued to improve under my watch.

But I was no patsy for the potential polluters either. Big business floated a scheme early in my administration to carry out self-audits and to be immune for any violations they brought forward. I demanded amendments, which insured that DEQ would set the rules. I also required a 3-year sunset clause. This act was never used because of the tough compliance we required. I refused to renew it at the end of the trial period.

The federal Endangered Species Act brought the Idaho economy into direct conflict with the need to protect certain plants and animals. The most prominent question concerns recovery of acceptable runs of our magnificent native salmon and other anadromous fish. There was a great deal of support for flushing additional Idaho water downstream in the Snake River to improve passage of these fish. The impact on Idaho's irrigators and other water users would have been devastating. We resisted this. Later studies indicate that increased flows would have little, if any, beneficial effect on the anadromous fish.

There is still considerable speculation about the efficacy of breaching or modifying the four lower Snake River dams in order to facilitate fish passage. I stated that certain basic questions about this matter needed to be answered before I could back the effort. They have not yet been answered:

1. Would removal or modification ensure recovery of the species? Although a preponderance of research indicates that such action would be helpful, fish scientists are far from agreement about long-term benefits.

2. What would be the economic losses to existing benefactors of the dams from removal? I don't mean a cavalier estimate, but a true comprehensive compilation of the impact.

3. Who will pay for those losses? Users should not be expected to go bankrupt voluntarily. The state can't pay; Congress would have to appropriate the money.

All in all, it appears to me that dam breaching is a long way off, if it occurs at all. In the meantime, we must continue in other remedial

Jacque, Phil and Sniffer led off dog walk for 1500-2000 dogs in 1997, 1998 and 1999.

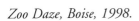

Zoo Daze, Boise, 1998.

efforts: cut down on harvest; improve passage through the dams; minimize predation; improve hatcheries and barging.

I'll have to say that this problem was among the most frustrating and intractable of any I faced in office.

I believe we did better with Bull Trout. This threatened species has a wide habitat in Idaho. I aggressively developed a plan to prevent further deterioration of the stock. We appointed citizen advisory groups throughout the state to recommend remedial action. Some 50 projects have been carried out, including the construction of a critical fish ladder at Kirby Dam near Atlanta. We addressed inadvertent harvest problems and altered environmental standards to keep the water temperatures in our streams cold enough for healthy fish. Bull Trout are thriving in some Idaho waters. I believe they will soon be at improved levels throughout Idaho.

I'm not a fan of greyhound racing. A surplus of racers is bred. The fastest survive to compete; the rest are destroyed if they can't be adopted. Horror stories about abuse and neglect abound. Whether they are all factual has been debated. There is no doubt that some dogs suffer needlessly.

In any case, I unsuccessfully opposed the authorization of dog racing when I was in the Legislature. As I predicted, rosy promises of economic Nirvana failed to materialize.

A drive to prohibit this activity arose in northern Idaho. I backed the effort and live racing came to a close in 1995. As a necessary compromise, we allowed simulcasting of dog races to continue for 3 years. My dog, Sniffer, helped sign the bill.

When the 3-year term was about to expire, an attempt was made in the Legislature to extend it. I made it clear that I would not approve such a bill. Since I left office, simulcasting has been extended indefinitely.

After 35 years of intermittent service in our beautiful State Capitol, I view it as an old friend. But, like the author, it's a little worse for the wear.

I set up a Capitol Restoration Commission to figure out what refurbishment needs to be done to this irreplaceable gem, and to find the funds to do it. Governor Kempthorne has continued this initiative and the Commission is already making some progress. The goal is to finish the restoration by 2005, the year when the Capitol will be 100 years old.

Most people don't know that, by custom, the governor doesn't visit the third or fourth floors of the Capitol during a legislative session without an invitation from the Legislature. Thus, when a legislative committee is appointed to wait upon the governor and to escort him to the legislative chambers for the state-of-the-state and budget messages, it is for a necessary purpose.

My office received complaints from callers who were upset that their soap operas were preempted by the once-a-year TV presentation of the state's health and its plans by the governor.

I am a University of Idaho alumnus, although I never earned a graduate's robe. I am an enthusiastic booster and I'm proud that the university is the cornerstone of our higher education effort.

Yet, when it became apparent that exciting engineering opportunities were on the horizon for Boise State University, I decided to back a stand-alone engineering school for the Boise institution. This brought a storm of protests from U of I partisans.

Micron Technology and other high-tech industries convinced me that prospective electrical and microtechnology engineers were missing out on a chance for a participating partnership geared for the future.

Micron proposed putting $6 million into an engineering building on the BSU campus if we would let the engineering school stand on its own. (Micron also put up $5 million for our first public/private highway project. We built a freeway interchange near their plant.)

The U of I has a nationally renowned engineering school and was offering degrees through its satellite on the BSU campus. Vandal alumni were aghast at the thought of a competitive school in Boise. I caught a lot of heat from my U of I friends.

In fact, my office was deluged with mail, phone calls and even personal visits. Those contacts were divided between BSU boosters and unhappy U of I supporters.

Part of the campaign against the BSU program seemed to be based on the misunderstanding that this was an either/or proposition. Idaho would have engineering programs at Moscow or at Boise, but not at both places. Like many other issues, this one was too often seen in black-and-white terms rather than in terms of what might serve Idaho's students better over the long term.

Nevertheless, the creation of a stand-alone Engineering School at BSU has proved to be a rousing success. It has reached accreditation status ahead of schedule and is providing valuable engineering degrees for hundreds of students.

In the meantime, my dear old Alma Mater at Moscow continues to attract a record number of students to its enviable engineering program. There are winners all around.

Academics are important and we are justifiably proud of Idaho's well-run higher-ed system. However, vocational education is crucial too, as some 80 percent of the jobs don't require formal academic training. I changed the thrust of the annual Governor's Cup Golf Tournament by directing the proceeds toward vocational education.

We netted nearly a half-million dollars during my 4 years in office. This allowed 81 Idaho students to take 2 and 3-year courses in health care services, mechanics, computer technology, and a wide variety of other fields. Most of the recipients told me they would not have been able to finance this effort without our help. I'm grateful to the participants and to the Idaho based corporations that contributed most of these funds.

I've touched only on the highlights of my administration. Idaho led the nation in accomplishing a welfare reform, which removed large numbers of our citizens from welfare dependence and turned them into to jobholders. We combined our Labor and Employment Departments, putting to rest some of the unnecessary quarrels between management and labor.

Soon after I took office, and on the recommendation of the Department of Health and Welfare, I reorganized the Council on Teenage Pregnancy, appointed mostly new members, and charged it with promoting an abstinence-based message. This was more restrictive than in the past, and I wondered whether it would be able to do anything worthwhile.

To my surprise, the council members embarked on an attention-getting, memorable, upbeat campaign that both encouraged parents to talk to their youngsters about sex before it was too late, and that also warned teens of the long-term consequences of early sexual activity. The tag line - "Sex lasts just a minute, but being a father (or mother) lasts a lifetime" - had high recognition ratings when teens were asked whether they had seen and recalled any of the ads. Idaho's teenage pregnancy rate has dropped markedly.

I met with committee chair Skip Oppenheimer of Boise just before I left office so that I could thank him in person for the hours and hours of time he devoted to this effort, often with no public recognition and a lot of hard work. He and his colleagues are typical of the hundreds of Idahoans who volunteer their time every day on these thorny issues

---

I negotiated for and helped form several new state parks. Previous governors had demonstrated foresight by seizing upon the opportunities to create state parks. Governor Smylie, in particular, took a lead role.

It is difficult, because the money is not there for expansion. Yet, a lost opportunity will diminish the state forever. I decided we could not afford to pass up these wonderful state assets. We took on Lake Wolcott and Cascade Reservoir Parks and expanded Ponderosa at McCall, one of the state's most popular parks. Also, we accepted responsibility for Big Eddy Marina on Dworshak Reservoir. We matched private donations and helped build a pioneer interpretive center at Three Island Crossing near Glenns Ferry.

But the biggest prize of all was obtaining Box Canyon Springs near Buhl. This spectacular canyon contains a huge waterfall fed by underground springs. There are numerous species of plants and animals in an unmatched, picturesque setting.

This unique treasure was in private ownership and there were plans to cap off the springs for a trout-raising enterprise.

Earl Hardy, the owner, was a hard-driving, successful businessman. He had sunk over a million dollars into foundations for a fish farm, when our Division of Environmental Quality refused his permits.

Mr. Hardy felt as if he had been singled out for unfair governmental treatment, claiming that others in similar circumstances had obtained permits.

Lawsuits were filed and a bitter legal struggle took place. Some environmental groups unfairly cast Mr. Hardy in the role of a heartless despoiler of Idaho's treasures.

Earl Hardy asked me to take a helicopter trip, at his expense, to look at the property and to see how he had been pinpointed for abuse. By the time I set foot back in Boise, some environmentalists were claiming I was involved in a sellout and reporters gathered for the hanging of me and Mr. Hardy.

What actually took place was that I told him how I was awestruck by the canyon and that we must find some way to share it with the public.

He was never adamant in his opposition but his pride was deeply hurt. For a long period of time he would not submit to any negotiations.

Toward the end of my term, Earl Hardy's health went into a serious decline. With the help of my environmental specialist, Jim Yost, we appealed to Mr. Hardy's sense of destiny. He finally offered to part with the property for $20 million dollars.

After intense dickering, I got him down to $5 million. We found $3 million of the money from Idaho Power Company, which it pledged as mitigation for some dam relicensing. Another million came from fines paid by DOE for environmental infractions at INEEL. The remaining million was pledged by the Nature Conservancy, a private organization that has done a world of good for Idaho and elsewhere in the nation.

My time as Governor of Idaho was rapidly ticking away. Finally on December 31, 1998, I signed the agreement with Mr. Hardy. Shortly afterward, at 4 p.m. on New Year's Eve, a crew came in and changed the locks. I was out of business, but Earl Hardy had come through at the eleventh hour. He and his family were pleased that they could add this masterpiece to their many civic accomplishments.

Mr. Hardy died only a few weeks later. Idaho is the richer for his legacy.

Midway through my term, I was informed that, if I played my cards right, Idaho might be able to obtain title to the only unspoiled camp spot of the Lewis and Clark Expedition.

Plum Creek Timber Company, among its vast forest properties, had title to a 160 acre plot through which meandered Glade Creek. It is only a few miles from Lolo Pass on the Idaho-Montana border. Meriwether Lewis wrote about the camp spot in his journal.

Remarkably, the Plum Creek firm, through the foresight of some key employees, had spared the area from logging or development.

In order to do its part for history, the company agreed to part with the 160 acres, which encompassed the Glade Creek Campsite, for the appraised price of its value for timber. This amounted to only $250,000 and is a steal for that historic jewel. The Idaho Heritage Trust, a private-public historical preservation group, immediately agreed to pony up the money. I put the deal together. Now, for only the cost of maintenance, Idaho's Park System and Transportation Department will be able to host the most interesting spot on the Lewis and Clark trail.

After the deal was made, we had a celebratory dedication. Stephen Ambrose, the pre-eminent Lewis and Clark chronicler, was the featured speaker. He is the author of "Undaunted Courage," the finest of many Lewis and Clark books. What an immense sense of history he infuses into the area! On the day of the formal transfer of the land from private ownership to the state, I flew to Missoula, where I met Mr. Ambrose, and then together we drove back into Idaho for the ceremony. All the while, Mr. Ambrose pointed out landmarks and recounted their significance to the Lewis and Clark exploration - a true example of a "hands on" history lesson. Idaho and the entire nation owe him a debt of gratitude for bringing that incredible journey to life again.

In a poignant moment at the ceremony Sam Penney, present day chairman of the Nez Perce tribe, spoke of the importance of protecting the spot. He emphasized that actual history should be faithfully reproduced, including the involvement of his Nez Perce forebears.

Members of the Expedition of Discovery, under Lewis and Clark, had been on the verge of starvation and defeat when native Americans provided them with care and comfort and helped them on their way.

I believe that Chairman Penney was reflecting on the events that later befell the tribes after they had accommodated the Expedition. The Glade Creek site also marked the path of the retreat by Chief Joseph shortly before he gave up the fight in Montana.

Chairman Penney's call for an accurate rendition of history at the site is most appropriate.

When I was on the campaign trail in 1994, I sensed the profound disgust of the electorate regarding widespread juvenile crime. Our system was not adequately addressing the problem. Hardened young thugs were maiming, raping and looting Idahoans; and then receiving only perfunctory punishments. Juvenile criminal records were being held in such secrecy that school and law enforcement officials often did not know of the odious backgrounds of most of these criminals. Many times they would be returned to school without adequate warning of their potentially dangerous behavior.

I promised to reform juvenile justice. After I was elected I proposed moving it from its niche in the Health and Welfare Department to a correction agency.

Representative Celia Gould, Senator Denton Darrington and other prominent legislators accepted the challenge and set up a new Department of Juvenile Correction. It is an expensive process, but it is worth it. Young punks can no longer hide behind their youth while making life miserable for our law-abiding citizens. The department is also sensitive to the need to give those offenders, who wish to get back on a useful path, a chance to do so.

Correction is costly in the extreme and I set out to see what I could do about containing these escalating expenditures.

I formed my own "Committee of One" to deal with our burgeoning prison population. I spent over one hundred hours listening to advice from judges, law enforcement people, prosecutors, correction officials, and other experts in criminal behavior and punishment. My recommendations resulted in more realistic sentencing and parole proposals and helped decelerate this unmanageable growth. But the last Legislature added more mandatory sentences, further denying the judges the opportunity of using independent judgment. This ensures that we'll put even more people in the pen. Reversing the trend I started toward alleviating our prison crunch is, in my opinion, a mistake. We are surely smart enough to address this problem without imposing mandatory sentences for an increasing array of crimes relating to addiction.

I later undertook another "Committee of One" review of Idaho's alcohol and substance abuse problems and their relationship to the state's growing prison population. Almost everyone with whom I spoke, from police officers to counselors, agreed that locking up drug or alcohol abusers does not solve the problem for the offender or for society. But treatment and rehabilitation are costly. Ada County is trying out a "drug court" where the offender receives treatment in exchange for pleading guilty to his crime. If he relapses, he serves his time. This may be the option of the future.

Violent crime has decreased in our nation in recent years. Although Idaho had an increase in 1998, our crime rate is low. Let's not whack ourselves over the head by increasing our incarceration rate.

One of the most difficult decisions I had to make concerned the execution of a prisoner. Donald Paradis was on death row after being convicted of the first-degree murder of Kimberly Ann Palmer.

Mr. Paradis had always stoutly maintained his innocence. Under our legal system only the Pardons and Parole Board has the power to commute a sentence. The governor can only veto its recommendations.

After years of news media attention and high-profile advocacy for his cause, capped by a feature article in *The New Yorker*, Mr. Paradis was successful in persuading the board that there was enough doubt about his guilt to change his sentence from death to an absolute life term.

The case was then put in my lap. I cancelled a week of appointments and devoted my entire attention to the matter.

I am an advocate of the death penalty. I believe most of those prisoners on death row should be executed for their ghastly crimes. So I went into my deliberations with a skeptical attitude.

Mr. Paradis was a member of a group of Spokane bikers who were drug dealing criminals. They were among the least desirable characters of all the northwest people. There was no question that among this group the foul murder was committed.

Mr. Paradis' contention was that he was not present when the killing occurred in Spokane, but that he did help transport and abandon the body in Idaho.

Bill Mauk, a long-time critic of mine who later became chairman of the Idaho Democrat Party and still later ran for the U. S. Senate against Mike Crapo, represented him.

Mr. Mauk is not my bosom buddy. Mr. Paradis was one of a group of unsavory characters. Nevertheless, I gave them a week to plead their case.

The question involved some disputed evidence as to whether Miss Palmer was alive when she was dumped in a creek in northern Idaho. I met with the victim's mother. She was convinced of Mr. Paradis' guilt, and urged me to carry out the death penalty.

But I finally concluded that there was substantial doubt about whether Mr. Paradis killed the young lady. I sustained the Parole Board's decision.

Another prisoner has now pleaded guilty to the murder. He insists that Mr. Paradis was not involved. I'm glad I didn't order his execution.

Idaho is a conservative, hard-working state. The belief that each should pull his share of the load, and that all employees should earn their pay, is strong throughout our 20,000 state employees.

Early in my term, I visited every working unit of state government and attempted to converse with as many employees as possible. They were most appreciative of these visits. I ended each with a free-wheeling discussion. They were naturally interested in receiving a fair wage, but they were more concerned that their work was not appreciated. I believe I elevated the status of state employees. I hope so, because they deserve it.

Many of them wrote to me after my tour of their departments. Here are excerpts from one such letter:

"Dear Governor Batt,

Thank you for coming to visit us yesterday!! In the 18 years I have worked in state government, a governor has never visited my office

.....I hope you don't interpret our 'reserve' (in the conference room) as lack of interest. On the contrary, we were all somewhat awestruck and speechless by your sincere interest in state employees.

I look forward to continued service in state government under your leadership..... Again, thank you for your gracious visit. Sincerely, ..."

An example of a dedicated public employee is Clive Strong, chief deputy in Attorney General Al Lance's office.

Mr. Strong served in the same capacity for Larry Echohawk.

Clive is widely regarded as one of the foremost water rights attorneys in the state.

During the hottest part of our battle for the governorship, Attorney General Echohawk put out a news release. If he were elected, he said, he would name Mr. Strong as his chief-of-staff. It was a shrewd move, as I was eating into Echohawk's lead by declaring him to be soft on protecting Idaho's water.

After the election, Al Lance decided to keep Mr. Strong as his chief deputy. I was a little chagrined by this, as I would be asking for advice on crucial matters from my opponent's proposed chief aide. Clive Strong and I had a frank conversation. He declared himself to be a professional who did not engage in political decisions. He told me that he could make far more money in private practice. If I wanted him to quit, he said, he would consider it. I didn't ask him to leave and I'm glad I didn't. Clive was helpful to me as we worked through nuclear waste, tribal water rights, the Snake River adjudication process, grazing leases, and the Earl Hardy Box Canyon Springs negotiations.

Army National Guard maneuvers between Boise and Mountain Home, 1996.

St. Anthony, 1997, General Kane, Governor Batt, Colonel La Frenz in front of Blackhawk helicopter.

I see why Larry Echohawk wanted Mr. Strong as his chief aide. He's a skilled mediator and a smart, hard-working state employee.

We had a destructive forest fire and three major floods while I was in office. At least we didn't have pestilence, if I exclude certain critics.

During each of the disasters, I spent a lot of time on the scene. Those who lost homes and otherwise suffered major damage are pleased to know that the state cares about them. General John (Jack) Kane, our National Guard Adjutant, and I usually traveled in a Blackhawk helicopter. It is a great way to see the overall picture and to get into places which are hard to access. I used to joke that I felt like General Halftrack, with my special place in the 'copter.

President Clinton visited during the aftermath of the worst flood. I was impressed by his obvious heartfelt concern. I later remarked to a member of my staff that Clinton was doing what he loved best: sharing my pain and handing out federal tax dollars.

The floods had a disastrous effect on the finances of counties and other taxing districts. I made the decision that the State would be responsible for the local matching share needed to qualify for federal aid. Idahoans throughout the state applauded that decision. We are truly a united people when it comes to helping our own.

Inspecting flood containment near Cataldo, 1997.

President Clinton visited Boise to assess flood damage.

Batt with key employees, Lindsay Nothern and Jason Kreizenbeck, Alaska, 1998.

I made some mistakes. Others are more than willing to point them out, so I'll leave it to them. In general, I believe I did a good job.

My personal approval rating grew steadily while I was in office, reaching well into the eighties toward the end. I knew that such a high level would not be sustained, but I was confident I could be re-elected.

I would have been nearly 76 years old by the end of my second term. I'm in good health now, but nobody can be sure when severe physical ailments will set in. Serving as governor is a rigorous occupation, involving long hours and a lot of mandatory meetings and travel. Unlike my hero Ronald Reagan, I didn't have a large personal staff that would allow me to rest frequently and lighten my schedule. I wouldn't want such a staff.

Therefore, Jacque and I decided to call it a day. It's been a marvelous experience and I thank Idahoans from the bottom of my heart for the opportunity.

Fourth graders from all over the state visit the Capitol. Whenever I could, I welcomed them into my office. I estimate that I hosted at least 50,000 kids in my four years in the office.

I gave all of them the same basic drill. I thanked them for coming to visit their Capitol Building, which I always described as the most beau-

KIDS, KIDS, KIDS!
Phil Batt estimated that he invited 50,000 kids into his office during his 4 year term.

LEARNING LAB

tiful in the entire United States. I then asked them to look around this "magnificent, spacious" office which belonged to each of them as much as it did to me. I told them that a person could serve there only as long as the people wanted him or her to. The electorate could vote the governor out and elect a new one at any time.

I told them that, if they applied themselves, one of them could be Governor. (I also told them I made $85,000 per year). Their eyes would light up, and I could tell they were inspired. They would cluster around the desk and we'd take a picture.

And I was telling them the truth. Any one of them can reach that high office. It is the strength of our system that the people rule through their vote. Nobody has a cinch on being elected and nobody is eliminated from the chance. I'm living proof of that.

I was elected to be the Governor of the best state in the country, which is far and away the finest in world history. My life has been blessed with good fortune but this one tops it off.

Butch Otter and me racing elephants at Shrine circus. I won because the fix was in.

With Reverend Billy Graham at a Boise crusade.

With Justice Sandra Day O'Connor, Law School Dean Vincent, and President Bob Hoover, Uviversity of Idaho, 1997

Editorialists and columnists were never shy about pouring it on me when they thought I needed admonishment. They were usually correct and I believe that I profited from the more constructive critics.

As my term progressed, their appraisals took on a mellower tone. And, at the end, I received widespread approval.

Presenting Idaho's highest honor, a Distinguished Service medal, to Vernon Baker at Orofino. Mr. Baker also has been awarded the Congressional Medal of Honor for heroic actions in battle.

Glade Creek dedication, author Steven Ambrose, Governor Batt, John Taylor. (Idaho Heritage Trust)

Herewith are excerpts from some of the editorial comments, most of which came after I declined to seek a second term:

Idaho Press Tribune - November, 1998

Four years ago, an onion farmer from Wilder laid the foundation for his four-year term as governor.

Phil Batt tackled his job like a pit bull. He sank his teeth into several issues and quelled debate on others. He chopped out excess state jobs, drafted an agreement with the federal government on nuclear waste in eastern Idaho and kept his promise to cut property taxes.

In short form, he managed the state without chaos. We saw growth. We saw change for the good. He challenged us. He served us.

He made Canyon County proud.

Twin Falls Times News - June, 1996

When Phil Batt beat Larry Echohawk for the governorship (against all odds and most conventional wisdom, including this newspaper's), the word that most people attached to him was "transitional."

But Batt has turned out to be anything but a footnote.

He has settled Idaho's long-running battle with the Energy Department over nuclear waste shipments to Idaho - something Andrus never managed - and he seems to have neutralized the political fallout.

And he ended the state's 79-year-old farmers' exemption from workers compensation insurance, a feat that "Governing" magazine recently called, "Idaho's version of Nixon going to China."

And through it all, Batt has become indisputably Idaho's most popular statewide politician, despite a stump style that you might expect from an onion farmer from Wilder.

Idahoans want competence, integrity, candor and an absence of pretense - all of the things that Batt represents.

One of the governor's favorite words - used often in his public discourse - is "honorable." In a political sense, that's a term from another generation, and it speaks volumes about both the man and his vision of his job.

"Honorable" means honest, but it also describes intent. To act honorably is to follow where the facts and the public interest lead you, whether or not that conclusion fits your ideology and your preconceptions.

For that reason, Batt is one of the very few politicians who will admit from time to time that he was wrong - not misinformed or misled, but mistaken. That goes a long way with an electorate that is weary to the bone of politicians' excuses.

But most remarkable of all has been the fact that the first two years of the Batt administration have been among the least partisan in Idaho postwar history. Who could have predicted that education and farmworkers, two bedrock Democratic constituencies, would have fared so well on Mr. Republican's watch?

That's because Batt senses what most people feel: Political labels don't matter very much in Idaho, and who gets the credit doesn't matter at all.

What Idahoans do want is state government that is as competent as they are, presided over by someone whom they feel instinctively that they can trust.

That's Phil Batt, and right now, he's in his prime. We are lucky to have him.

Randy Stapilus in Rexburg Standard Journal - December, 1998

Earlier this month, I bumped into Gov. Phil Batt, and he said he was planning to release soon (and did, soon after) a summary of his four years as governor. It would present him in a more favorable light, he said, than many others were likely to do.

He's still smarting, it seems, from the occasional criticism that comes with the job of chief executive, which he referred to when he announced he would not run again.

It's a little sad that the outgoing governor's sense is that attitudes about his governorship seem to be so negative. I doubt that they are, especially since Batt pulled off a feat unusual in electoral politics: He kept getting better in office, and the attitudes people had about him kept on improving too.

...Over time, piece by piece, he whittled away at the state's problems. It has to be said that the jury isn't yet in where the nuclear waste issue is concerned; Batt's ultimate state-federal agreement has many more years to run before we can truly know for sure how well it works. But it seems a good start, does at least provide a clear benchmark for progress, and won consensus support from the voters. Not bad.

That may not even be among Batt's best achievements, when it's all done. If in the next few years the explosive - insane - growth in Idaho's prison population begins to be curbed, Batt will deserve a large chunk of the credit. He went out on a limb politically several times, on prison sentencing and on drug offender policy, running counter to the standard conservative "lock 'em up and throw away the key" approach. He was alone in doing it, but his gutsy stand may start to turn others around.

As a state senator Batt was renowned for his work on behalf of minorities, and here too he may leave a big mark. He turned around what had been ice-cold relations with the state's Indian tribes into something approaching genuine cooperation - no small feat. And the state's farm workers will get worker compensation insurance, in no small part because Batt was governor. It wouldn't have happened at all but for Batt.

Phil Batt leaves a state in condition as good as he found it when he took office, and a little better off in some respects. History may treat him better than he thinks.

Moscow-Pullman Daily News - January 1999

Four years ago, Phil Batt swept into office in a GOP landslide that made him Idaho's first Republican governor in a quarter century. He left on an upbeat note - the same affable onion farmer who served his state in various capacities for over 33 years.

Batt, a pillar of the state Republican Party for decades, came from eight terms in the House and Senate, four years as lieutenant governor and a stint as state party chairman.

In other words, Batt was more than prepared for the job. Which is why many admirers in both parties wondered what happened to Batt early in his term. He wasted the first two years - attempting to right ancient wrongs, dour in nature, and ill tempered with anyone who crossed him - especially the media.

But Batt finally came back to square one - ending his governorship reminiscent of the well-respected politician who served the Gem State so well over the years. His sense of humor returned and, once again, the real Phil Batt was among us.

Batt can take pride in his accomplishments, especially the kudos received from Idaho tribal leaders who were highly complimentary of the governor in his dealings with the tribes on several potentially volatile issues.

We also point to Batt's efforts for farm workers, who for the first time, are covered by Workers Compensation. He attempted to combat the state's white supremacist image by establishing the Governor's Hispanic Initiative in 1996, as a way to help Idaho's largest minority identify its own unmet needs and come up with ideas to improve the quality of life for Hispanics.

The out going governor also worked to streamline the Idaho State Tax Commission - cutting the backlog of appealed tax cases in half and installing computer-assisted mass appraisal for counties.

But Batt-watchers on the Palouse remember him in a lighter vein as a featured artist at the annual Lionel Hampton Jazz Festival. Batt has hit the stage a couple of times with Hampton and his New York Big Band, performing like a pro on the clarinet - an instrument he's been playing since a kid.

Batt noted in a recent report on his four-year tenure as governor of Idaho, "History will judge what I did or did not accomplish." He wrote, "I believe most public opinion will conclude that I faced problems head-on and without equivocation."

The Oregonian - December, 1998

As Idaho Gov. Phil Batt prepares to retire Dec. 31, Latinos and Native-Americans are lauding him as a humanitarian, a diminutive man at 5 feet 6 inches who championed the cause of the little guy.

Latinos are particularly grateful for Batt's leadership in prodding the 1996 Legislature to extend worker's compensation to farm workers, ending a 79-year exemption for about 40,000 workers.

"We have made more progress under Gov. Batt than we've had in 24 years," said Dan Ramirez, executive director of the Idaho Hispanic Commission.

Tribal chairmen met monthly with Batt, discussing education and business issues. "My own dream is to have a national model here in Idaho of tribal and state governments working together with mutual understanding," Coeur d'Alene Tribal Chairman Ernie Stensgar told Batt in the group's final meeting last month. "You have begun to make that dream a reality."

Stensgar said Batt's assistance has led to a number of strides in education, economic development and in access to state government. "In the four short years of your administration, the Coeur d'Alene tribe has created hundreds of jobs, developed facilities that serve our Indian and non-Indian public, generated economic growth that impacts an entire region and created educational opportunities that were never before dreamed of."

Dan Popkey in The Idaho Statesman - December, 1998

Add my voice to those showering praise on retiring Gov. Phil Batt.

We met in 1987, when I was covering my first legislative session. Batt, then in the Senate, was among a handful of real movers in the Legislature.

But he treated me with kindness, explaining how things really worked. He took his job seriously, but had an incisive wit he happily shared.

Now, after he has saved the Republican Party from self-immolation and had a successful four years as governor, I must say I'm going to miss him.

I'll miss Batt's intellect, his ability to cut to the heart of a problem, and his humility.

Despite his lofty office, Batt never got imperious. When I arrived for an interview Monday, his door was open - as it usually is when he's not in a meeting. When I left, he was making arrangements for lunch at the weenie cart.

When I asked if he gets "weepy" about leaving, Batt shot back: "Oh, hell no. This is just another phase in my life. I've never felt that I had to be governor."

Unlike many politicians, Batt sees mostly shades of gray. When he decided on something - like extending workers compensation insurance to farm workers or his nuclear-waste deal with the feds - he was workman-like, not high and mighty.

I watched Batt closely on those issues. I was in Twin Falls in February 1995, when he went to defend the nuke waste deal. An effort to recall him was under way, and he expected a tough crowd. "I knew I was in the soup," he said.

But he won them over by saying he believed he was following the best course. Later, despite actor Bruce Willis' promise to make Batt a 7-Eleven clerk if he didn't overturn the deal, voters agreed.

On workers comp, Batt overcame his concern about state intervention because he believed it was just plain wrong to exclude the poorest of workers, most of them Hispanic.

Reform had failed many times, but Batt's lobbying of lawmakers made the difference in 1996.

"That's the one issue I really did some cranking on," he said. "I'd just call 'em in and say, 'Do you think you can help me on this one? I understand the reasons for being reluctant to. And I don't relish making people angry on this, but I think it's something that needs to be done. Can you help me out?'"

Lawmakers were persuaded.

Now that he's leaving, Batt concedes he cherishes one modest perk - a bit of real estate next to the Capitol steps with his name on it.

"Yeah, I will miss my parking space," he said.

Tim Woodward in The Idaho Statesman - 1997

Idaho won't remember Phil Batt for getting laughs with his pet mynah bird.

We won't remember him for his eulogy to the victims of the Kellogg mining disaster.

Or for admonishing state workers to keep quiet about his charitable contributions.

That was the Phil Batt that didn't come across as governor. The governor Idaho will remember is the Wilder farmer with the funny voice. A man who quietly did his job, occasionally stuck his neck out on principle and retired to the farm to play his clarinet and mind the hops and onions.

Those who know him well saw a more complex person.

"I don't think the average Idahoan ever knew the real Phil Batt," said longtime friend and fellow legislator James Risch.

"He'll be remembered as governor because that was the highest office he attained, but we shouldn't forget the rest of his life in public service."

Much of that was in the state Senate, where his wit was a local legend.

"He had a pet mynah bird he'd bring right into the senate," said former legislator H. Dean Summers. "He taught it to say bad things about Cecil Andrus."

Andrus, a Democrat, was governor much of the time Batt led the Republican dominated Senate. Batt's work in the Senate won praise from both parties.

"He probably never did anything in public life as well as he ran that Senate," said former senator Perry Swisher. "He was swift and efficient. He ran it like a steam engine."

Idaho Falls Post Register - January, 1997

....In Idaho, Batt's own Medicaid reform task force considered expanding upon a federal policy by denying benefits to some legal aliens.

Batt, whose place in history may end up revolving around his four-decade-long crusade for human rights, will have none of that:

"I do not think it is in our best interest to deny basic medical services to anyone," Batt said. "...Nor do I believe we should ask our schools to shut the door on any child, be they alien or citizen. There can be no benefit to Idaho society to have within its borders children declared to be pariahs - uneducated, unhealthy and shunned.".....

Mtn. Home News - September, 1997

Gov. Phil Batt's announcement last week that he will not seek reelection to a second term did not particularly surprise me.

I've known Phil since I was a kid, and watched as he entered politics and rose to become one of the most effective leaders of the Idaho

Legislature I've ever seen. Things were a lot smoother and a lot saner than they are now, when Phil was there quietly cracking the whip to keep his party in line and under control.

When he was lieutenant governor I was one of the first to suggest that this quiet, humble man would make a great governor.

...Privately, he always had a dry wit. If you didn't know him, sometimes you'd think he was serious, until you saw the twinkle in his eye and realized he was pulling your leg.

But, his wonderful humor aside, Phil was always dead serious about his duties as an elected official.

He always had the ability to work out compromises that left most people happy, and he cared about the people of this state as much as any person I've ever met.

Because Phil was one of those rare politicians that come along only once in a lifetime, a man who cared not for the power of his office, but for the ability it gave him to serve the people. He was always a public servant first, and a public official second.

When Phil replaced Andrus, he faced a number of major issues, none of which were bound to satisfy everyone, although he is the type that always wished he could. He tackled them head on and, in my opinion, succeeded.

.....So when Phil decided not to run again, it was no great surprise. He'd done the jobs he'd set out to do. He wasn't looking for immortality.

Boise Weekly announced its annual "Best In Class" selections. It whimsically included a category for "Best Ex-Governor."

Boise Weekly - 1999

No offense, Cece, we think you're the cat's pajamas, but we also think it's time people gave Phil Batt his due. The reason we like Phil Batt is the same reason everybody else does. Phil Batt - whether he's in the governor's chair or the barber's chair - is the same guy, an onion farmer from Wilder who had a knack for politics, despite a disposition that would suggest otherwise. He was thin skinned. He was not pretty. He wasn't a great speaker. In short, he was like most of us. What he had was a very solid sense of who he was, making decisions he thought were best for the state, at times regardless of who agreed or disagreed with him. Lord knows those decisions weren't always popular, and they weren't always right, but most of the time they came from a sincere belief in purpose. Since he's been out of office, Batt's been gracious enough to give Cecil Andrus a lot of credit for how he dealt with nuke waste issues and feisty enough to remind the Kempthorne administration - and everyone else - that a recent jump in child immunization rates came because of the work on his watch.

Thanks, Newsies, I always did love ya', even though it sometimes wasn't evident.

Chapter Three—*Letters*

Immediately after I was elected in November 1994, an avalanche of mail started pouring in.

I had less than two months to select my cabinet and staff, prepare my State of the State address and budget, and generally get to know the ropes of state government from the chief executive's perspective.

Therefore, it was physically impossible for me to answer the mail in a timely fashion.

People had written because they wanted a job for themselves or someone else, or to talk about their pet programs or heartfelt concerns and they hoped to beat the rush in getting that information to me first.

It bothered me to delay anybody's mail, as I had always been prompt. So, after I took office and had a staff, the mail became a top priority. From that time forward I learned about the blood, sweat, and tears of the state through the eyes of thousands of constituents.

I inherited a good tracking system, which properly logged in and classified the mail. I then had it forwarded to my desk where I scanned every piece of it. I also checked each reply before it was sent from my office.

I averaged a couple of hours a day on mail-following procedures. That's a lot of time, but I believe it allowed me to keep my finger on the pulse of Idaho.

There were an abundance of form letters and publicity campaigns such as mailing in pop cans in an attempt to gain immediate attention. We learned to quickly discount such efforts and move on to serious correspondence.

Unanswered letters were few in number. Everything else was read, discussed, followed up on, and responded to. We set a deadline of two weeks for an answer and seldom violated it. Sometimes I asked an agency director to compose an answer, but much more often I replied from my office.

There were, of course, basketfuls of letters regarding anadromous fish, nuclear waste storage, welfare reform, school facilities, and other major interests, but what surprised me was the wide variety of topics where people exercised their right to "tell it to the Governor." For example:

...my wife and I were on Freeze Out Hill at approximately 6:30 a.m. leaving Emmett Id. & heading for Boise to attend a meeting. We saw an object moving from west to east at a slow speed app. 40-50 mph & 150 ft high. It was very colorful and about the size of a bus...We would like to speak to someone in your office or military as I'm sure they would like to know more about what we saw. I'm sure it would be a national security issue if it isn't ours.

I just finished listening to the local news, learning how you had declared three counties as disaster areas. This letter has to do with a subject, which of course is not a natural disaster, but is in itself, a major disaster for Boise. That being the so-called B(oise) S(tate) U(niversity) parking control....

We read quite often about the population growth causing a shortage of potable water and too much sewage...If all the present toilets in houses were removed and the ones used in recreational vehicles installed in their place, it would save approximately 3 (three) gallons of water each time the toilet is flushed...A lot of women would complain, but dishwashers should be outlawed too, as they are water wasters.

(From a student) I'm writing this letter in regards of the income coming in for education. We're the future. Education

is one of the most important things we need...The part that needs the most help is the lunch! It is not even real meat! The drinks are so small you can't wash anything down....

This letter is to inform you of something special! Please be informed now and hereafter, that Every Child Should Have It's Mother's Maiden Name!!...

I would like to call to the attention, of the correct individuals, who are responsible for the menu, at the Pocatello Senior Citizen Center...The complaint that I am hearing is, they are serving Ham too frequently...The most favorite and popular meal at the Center is Turkey and Dressing. As a child I recall eating fish loafs frequently. Perhaps Tuna loaf with creamed peas. Salmon would be nice, however, because of the expense, I think Tuna would be fine. Also, beef, chicken, and turkey pies with vegetables....

(Writing about her mother's neighbors, a woman complained that the husband) would place his hand on his ear, each time he left his residence and drove past the picture window of my Mother's home. This has gone on for a long while. His wife...does this to me each time that I run into her. Yesterday, while returning from a walk, as soon as she saw me, she placed her hand on her ear...I am bringing this to your attention so that you can correct the situation!

Dear Sir: I believe that fish eating is a form of meat eating. Yours faithfully...

I am writing about the practice we have of changing our clocks twice a year...There is no way we can save daylight or time...I know there are many more important things to work on while you are in session, but please consider getting back to the old time and staying there... (I'm for it!)

I do not think the speed limit is enforced well enough on my street. On Desert Avenue the speed limit is 35 miles per hour. Most motorists go faster than that though, and it presents quite a hazard to pedestrians and bicyclists. A good solution might be speed bumps.

I am writing to you because I'm damn mad at someone who is shipping potatoes with the Idaho label that are not up to par. The G&T brand is the first one in 3 months where we did not find green under the skin or red centers in the potato. Someone is sabotaging the good name of Idaho and I want you to clobber them. (Maybe I could persuade Dan Quayle to settle this.)

From time to time I was criticized for devoting so much of my presumably precious time on the mail. But it's the best way to get a handle on what people were thinking about, even if the news wasn't always pleasant. And my staff assured me that they liked being able to tell callers that, yes, they could write to the governor and, yes, he would read their letters himself. The time spent reading mail was not wasted.

Of course, some of the letters were painful to read. People wrote about losing their jobs, or losing their children, or losing their faith in government. Some included appeals for help, but often the writer just wanted me to know how bad things were. One man serving a life sentence without possibility of parole asked me to allow him to donate his heart to his ailing brother, adding,

...Being locked up for the rest of my life, is a waste of the taxpayers money and I'm just taking up extra bed space for some crazed killer...

I forwarded that letter to the Office of the Attorney General, who advised the inmate that I could not honor his request:

> *...Governor Batt cannot authorize your death. You are serving a life sentence, not a death sentence, and for anyone to take your life in order to remove your heart and donate it to your brother would amount to homicide in this state.*

Another inmate, a woman, wrote to ask me for a pardon so that she could be released from prison and begin a counseling program. She mentioned her grandparents, both of whom I knew. It pained me to have to turn down the granddaughter of people whom I liked and admired.

Nevertheless, I received my share of letters thanking me for taking care of certain problems and for providing good service. One letter came from the mother of an Idaho inmate who had been returned to Idaho after a period of incarceration in another state.

> *No matter what anyone else says, we love our boy. Thank you for bringing him home to us.*

I sent her a handwritten note, which said, in part,

> *Thank you for a most touching letter. I think all of us in society must not forget that each of us is a human being subject to frailties. I am wholly supportive of the need for society to jail those who break the law. However, to place these inmates out of state puts an extreme burden on the loved ones. I am working hard at bringing all our prisoners back into the state and, also, to reduce the need for placing so many folks in our prisons.*

The writers weren't always kind, however. That's all right. Being governor makes you fair game.

> *If your religion is about promoting discord, intolerance, and abuse of power, then you will certainly be a saint. In my book, you're a scoundrel.*

This letter is by way of letting you know that we do not agree with your out-look on making the Mini-Cassia area bow down to making our community a Mexican culture community. You don't need to expect the white people to vote for you in the next election...if this is the attitude that you are going to take. We will get a petition against you or whatever it takes to see that you don't have a chance to make us live in a community where nothing is done to protect the American way of life and they get away with this type of thing.

Well, by golley gov, looks like you may have gotten in over your head...I understand you were a good farmer. That is a good respectable job. But don't sell the farm. You may need it.

I would just like to state that you are just another wolf in sheeps clothes. Those that act and say the things you do expose yourself to all of us "Patriots" across this nation...I would suggest that you take the time to read "all" of the Aryan Nations website. Maybe, then, you might see the "big Picture."

One young man, a fourth grader, straddled the fence, telling me the bad things he'd heard about me, but still offering support:

Some of the kids in my class think you let Nuclear Waste in Idaho but I don't. I know your a good guy. Its local gossip and if I was old enough I'd always vote for you as governor. I know your a busy man and all but if you get a chance and you want to write back I'd be so happy I'd put the letter in a frame and hang it on the wall.

This letter, warts and all, came from a young woman who managed to get most of her facts, spelling, and grammar wrong in one brief note:

I...am currently worried about my environment quite a bit due to the company ASARCO. Besides the point, that due to your irresponsible company ASARCO -- you are funding that is going to ruin beautiful Montana and Idaho, you do have many factors that effect you and your decision, such as unproven water treatment process, an ulined talings impoundments, and no ramdation bond which I do believe is a pontentially big mess!! But you dont mind as long as you get money in your pocket right?

To which I replied:

I would not ordinarily respond to such an inaccurate and insulting letter as yours, but here goes: Nearly all the campaign money from mining companies went to my opponent.. ASARCO is planning to mine in Montana. We have no jurisdiction and no authority to stop the mine. I have made it plain, to Montana officials and to ASARCO, and to the U.S. government, that we have strong concerns about the purity of Pend Oreille. All we can do is monitor the waste and we have agreed to do that with ASARCO paying for that process. You can be assured that we will do everything in our power to protect our beautiful lake.

Another frequent complaint had to do with funding "cuts" for various agencies and programs. Far too often, an agency that did not get what it asked for would complain about a reduction -- and its users would begin to write to me -- when, in fact, the reality was that the increase was not as much as hoped for. This letter was typical:

I have recently read that the state aid for public schools has dropped 4% in the past decade..We're weakening our future public by reducing the money given to public schools. What can be done about this horrifying change?

In response, I tried to set the record straight:

> *I did not recommend a cut in education. I proposed in my executive budget -- and the legislature passed -- a 2.3% increase in education funding for FY1998. A decade ago, the state general account appropriation for public schools was $343 million; for FY1998, the state appropriation is $705 million. I don't know how anyone could consider this a "decrease."*

I received a batch of notes arguing in favor of restoring wolves, grizzlies, and other wildlife to Idaho. The messages came from California, Florida, Wyoming, Virginia, Texas, Oklahoma, and Florida. To the man from Torrance, Calif., who concluded his letter by writing "There are many, many reasons to continue with wolf, grizzly, and bison reintroductions in North America, and NO sound reason to eliminate them," I scrawled in the margin, "How about introducing a few in Torrance?"

I generated my own note to actor Bruce Willis, one of the major bankrollers of a movement to void the agreement I reached with the U.S. Department of Energy to remove, over time, all federally-owned nuclear waste from Idaho. In one of his interviews on the topic, Mr. Willis promised that he would see me clerking at a 7-11 Store. That comment inspired the manager of a local 7-11 to send me an employment application, and inspired me to send this note to Mr. Willis:

> *Dear Bruce:*
> *Thanks for making a movie in Magic Valley*
> *If you have a spot for a 7-11 clerk, I'd be interested in a try-out.*
> *Phil Batt*

Mr. Willis did not answer my letter.

Martina Navratilova was much nicer. The tennis star appeared in Idaho shortly after the death of her dog, and a rude spectator shouted some mean comments about the loss of her pet. I wrote to apologize, and to tell her of the recent death of my own dog, Sniffer. To my surprise, she wrote back:

> *Thank you very much for your note. Apparently Sniffer was as special to you as K.D. (Killer Dog) was to me. I wish you all the best in your public as well as private life.*

People wrote to me about their most intimate problems, their mounting fears, their most pressing concerns. Some of the letters pulled at the heartstrings. This was particularly true of letters from custodial parents who were not receiving the child support to which they were entitled. Shattered families wrote by the hundreds. Women, some of them married twice, three, or four times, wrote of the difficulties of trying to raise children when the ex did not send the child support as expected. The divorced men wrote that they were being denied legal visitation privileges. The kids were always caught in the middle, witnesses to or victims of physical and mental abuse. These letters were a strong argument for welfare reform, which brought dignity, self-esteem, and respectability back to hundreds of broken homes.

One of the most unusual requests came from a high school student who wanted to go to the prom, but apparently was nervous about asking for a date. He gave me the name and address of the young woman in question, and asked me to do the heavy lifting for him. I complied (the names that follow are fictitious):

> *Dear Anne: I don't know you and I don't know Bruce. But Bruce asked me to ask you if you will go to the prom with him. I am impressed, however, by somebody wanting a date enough that he would ask me to write a letter helping him out. I am hereby doing so. However, we all know the old story about Priscilla and John -- so, I hope Bruce follows through by "speaking for himself."*

I don't think I ever heard the end of that story. I hope Anne said "yes" and that they had a great time together.

All requests were not that easy to fill. This letter came from a man who had been thinking about career opportunities:

> *I want a job that I can do and that will not cause me to have health problems. The only thing I can think of would be to be the state executioner. Please don't get me wrong. I am not morbid or anything. I do not pretend to judge people, but if their convicted of a horrible crime and been sentenced to death I think I could pull the switch. I don't think I would let my family or friends know what I do if I had the job, but I think I could handle the job. Of course, I hope I don't have to keep real busy.*

Often writers were not aware of the diversity of opinion on an issue. People would complain that I obviously wasn't reading the mail -- or listening to the public -- because I was not doing what the writer wanted me to do. The fact is that Idahoans are rarely of one mind on any issue.

On Indian gaming, for example:

> *Dear Governor Batt, I am enclosing an article from the paper. It describes the very reason I oppose gambling. Too often I see people at the checkout counter at the grocery store buying lottery tickets, but they look like they should be buying milk, bread or shoes for their children...I hope you will do what you can to stop all gambling in our state. Too many people can't resist -- always hope to hit the "big one."*

> *Dear Governor Batt: I'm writing to you to let you know what I think of the gaming facility of the Coeur d'Alene Tribe in Worley, Idaho... Now since the Coeur d'Alene Tribe has started the gambling they have produced jobs and are able to take care of their families & themselves. They aren't on welfare, which the tribe should be glad that they can support them-*

selves. Jobs and education have benefited from that. What's wrong with that?

One thoughtful letter I received was from a young man concerned about proposed legislation that would open juvenile records to public scrutiny:

I have been in trouble a lot of my life. I have been through drugs, gangs, and in and out of correctional facilities. I have recently had a baby daughter, and she forced me to realize that I am not only hurting myself but the ones I love. I have recently got my GED and High School Equivalency and have recently taken my SATs to get into college. When I found out that the law might be changed I was shocked. I am worried about my future employers stereotyping me as something that I am not any more. I don't understand what the point of this is, so if you could send me a reply it would be much appreciated.

I replied that the law was not retroactive and so his records would probably not be open. Still, his letter made me think about the constant tension between protecting the public and protecting the right of the individual. I certainly wished him every success in his effort to turn his life around.

My advice to anyone who wants to be governor is this: If you want to make everyone happy, find another job. I can't think of many issues during my four years in office that had unanimous support. Whatever I did, whatever I said, there was always someone who objected to it. Even my personal interests were open to critics:

While I understand that it may be important for you to put the business of state government on hold to support Republican party activities, I am concerned that your trip to the Republican Convention in San Diego may have been at taxpayer expense. Please confirm that you either billed accrued vacation time or were not paid for your labor hours for this trip, and that your travel expenses were not paid out of public funds.

And my response:

Even the Governor is entitled to vacations now and then. I chose to spend some of mine at the GOP convention. Taxpayers did not underwrite the cost of my travel. I used personal and campaign funds to make the trip.

On occasion I initiated correspondence on my own, as when I wrote to Marty Schottenheimer, head coach of the Kansas City Chiefs, early in 1998, after the Chiefs lost a playoff game to Denver:

I'm a Denver fan and particularly fond of (John) Elway, so I always root for them. By the 4th quarter, however, I was on your side, mainly because of you. You personify what the game should be about - honesty, hard work, careful planning - above all sportsmanship. I hope you put no stock in any critics who say you and your teams fold up in the playoffs. You have an excellent team and you are a standout among the cry-baby, exhibitionist coaches for the sensible way you lead your team.

Coach Schottenheimer wrote back:

Many thanks for your recent letter... You certainly understand the tremendous effort that an organization expends in pursuit of a championship. While we came up short, this was one of my most enjoyable seasons.

Some of the best letters came from the youngest writers. They wrote to sympathize after the death of my dog Sniffer, they wrote as part of a homework assignment, they wrote to thank me for letting them tour the governor's office, and they often wrote to comment on the same issues their parents were writing about.

> *Dear Governor Batt: Idaho does not have a state dog. I know not many states do, but I think Idaho needs one. We have a lot of raccoons so I thought a hound would be appropriate. A red-bone hound or the black and tan hound are two suggestions.*

> *Dear Governor Batt, Your last name is awesome! Our class is learning about bats...I used to think bats were gross and ugly, but now that I know how useful they are I enjoy them.*

> *Dear Phil Bat. I went to the Capitol on Monday the 9th of March, I saw you...My birthday is July 30. I was born in 1988 so I am nine. You are 71, right, that is what my teacher thinks, but you look like you are 50 or 60.*

> *My concern is that I would like to get a tatoo. I am only eleven, so because of my age I need a parent signature. I think that is not fair because my parents won't let me get one. Anyway it's my body...I think you should lower the age at least two years. People mite want to get a tatoo when they are younger. P.S. Please write back.*

The letters, faxes, and e-mail continued at a steady pace until about a month before I left office. Then they slacked off precipitously. I suppose people assumed I wouldn't be there long enough to be of much help to them.

As usual, the public was perceptive.

Chapter Four—Batt'n the Breeze—The Early Years

Shortly after my first Legislative session in 1965, I wrote an opinion piece on the issue of property taxes. The Caldwell and Homedale papers agreed to print it, and it got some attention. By 1975, I was up to writing one each week, typically for a dozen or more papers statewide. A total of 28 Idaho newspapers used them at various times. Some irreverent wag labeled my efforts the "Wilder Wipe." More visionary critics called it "Batt'n the Breeze."

I've lost that first column, but I do have most of the 400 others. Some I wrote with great seriousness, on topics from racism to global economic policy. Mostly, though, I was lighthearted, from the time I issued a rallying call to short people to when I took on the burning topic of waiting-room magazines. Bill Hall, Jay Shelledy and John Corlett were among those who helped me develop my writing style.

Reading those columns, sometimes more than 30 years later, is an interesting experience. I might change a few if I had the power but, as Omar Khayyam said, "The moving finger writes; and having writ, moves on; nor all thy piety nor wit shall lure it back to cancel half a line........." Still, I've had the same stand on most issues throughout my political life. I've tried to be historically objective about which ones I've excerpted here; there are some "wipes" along with my home runs. I've also given my later perspective on those same topics and offered context where necessary.

This one was among my first in 1965. I hadn't yet learned brevity in writing so I had to cut about half of it out.

LOVE LETTERS FROM UNCLE SAM

It all began on a warm June day in 1964. I was opening my mail when I came to a routine release from my senior Senator in Washington, D.C. Brushing aside an urge to put the letter in the round file, I proceeded to see what he had to say. The release concerned the availability of government publications and assured me that if I would just check those items I would like to have, my good Senator would "see that it is promptly handled."

A close perusal of the list brought home to me just how much my government was concerned with my welfare. #L501 was entitled "The Old House-Borer." As my house was only eight years old I passed this over, pausing when I reached "Silverfish and Firebrats - How to Control Them." This one was a little strange so I centered my attention on "Eat a Good Breakfast," supplemented down the list by #050, "Cooking With Dried Egg." By this time I was overwhelmed by the good things Uncle Sam could provide for me but, suddenly, I had a twinge of conscience. If I sent for these publications, some poor taxpayer would have to provide the money to pay for them.

I decided to be firm with myself, so I took pen in hand and answered my dear Senator. After complimenting him on certain actions, which I considered to be beneficial to the country, I said,

"I don't think the other taxpayers in this country should send to me or any other farmer a bulletin on "Carpet and Rug Repair" or "Ornamental Shrubs for the Southern Great Plains." Neither do I think that one taxpayer should furnish for another a leaflet concerning "What to do when your freezer stops" or "Ways to cook rabbit" or "Food for the young couple." A bulletin on "Federal Baloney" might be interesting. Please send me a copy if you have one."

This incident caused me to wonder if my government would always be so concerned with my lot in life. I have saved all my federal "junk mail" from that time until this. It occupies two large files and has convinced me that Uncle's love is here to stay. I'll touch on some of the highlights...............

Last year the gentleman from the first district (now deposed) dispensed to me a whopping two-pound classification of soil types in Gem

County, Idaho. This was interesting, but I have no farming interests in Gem County nor do I contemplate having any. My second district Congressman evidently felt inadequate after this performance because, for his next "Congressional Record" release, he sent the whole day's proceedings instead of just the one column which pertained to him.

I am called upon by the U. S. Crop Reporting Service to make reports on the prospects of the various crops. Occasionally I have some reason why I don't send these reports in .... The compilator then sends a form marked in red - "Second Request." If this fails, he sends a reporter forty miles to my farm to obtain the information personally. I still can refuse to cooperate if I wish, but I am not afforded that option on the next problem. For some two years, under the auspices of the census bureau, I submitted a monthly form telling how many employees I had, how much they were paid, how many hours they worked and what they were doing. Refusal to cooperate in the census could have resulted in severe penalties. The form had twelve pages and included such questions of national interest as, "How many vegetables did you raise for home use?" I completed that tome after a five-hour struggle. Alas, an enumerator came to my home and started from scratch.

My farm operations entitle me to various goodies from the government. These are dispensed through the Agricultural Stabilization Service and I also receive their monthly ASC Canyon Farmletter. This tells me what I must do to qualify for federal support on barley or to receive "cost-shares" when I lay a cement ditch. To help the recipient forget that his tax dollars are helping to finance these programs, the Farmletter adds bits of humor such as this one from the Goose Creek Gazette:

"At the Odd Fellows" picnic Sunday, Mrs. Murchison won first prize in the ladies' rolling-pin throwing contest. She threw her pin ninety-nine yards."

"Mr. Murchison won the one-hundred yard dash."

They also give homely advice on this order:

"If you meet anyone without a smile-Give them one of yours!"

Well, you get the point. While Uncle Sam may be an ardent suitor, he is fickle. He clues me in on the damages of smoking, yet he subsidized the tobacco industry. At least he does not change his methods with time.

When he was handing out stiff penalties to violators of the Volstead Act, during prohibition, he was distributing pamphlets giving detailed directions for making hooch from such things as pumpkins and parsnips.

All in all, his correspondence costs me plenty of money as a taxpayer. While we decry the free ride we give the junk mail peddlers, we let the biggest one of all go on his merry way. So please, Uncle Sam, no more love letters.

If I'd stop paying attention to such trivia, the world might be a better place.

My interest in racial matters has always been strong. Yet, I have never advocated arbitrary quotas to redress imbalance between races. From an early column:

QUOTA CRITIC

July, 1975

Wilder - Of all mankind's baser modes of behavior, I believe that racism is the worst. It is the prime cause of a majority of wars. It causes fist fights, murder and fear. Perhaps worse, it causes millions of people to live in degradation and hopelessness.

I co-authored and was the prime mover for the creation of Idaho's Human Rights Commission. It took a lot of compromise and persuasion to get this bill passed. I also resigned from the Elks in protest of their "white only" regulations. After that clause was eliminated I asked for reinstatement, but received 14 blackballs, a new record. So my interest in the subject of race has not been without its price.

With that background, I would like to state that racial quotas are for the birds. The Equal Employment Opportunity Commission, through its affirmative action program, continuously seeks to force employers to hire set percentages of their employees from minority groups and women. The intent of this may be honorable, but such action has no place in our free society.

Capitalism will not work properly unless every person is assured free access to its opportunities. It is most proper for the government to prohibit discrimination in hiring practices under the guarantees provided by the Fourteenth Amendment to the Constitution. But when quotas are introduced, these same guarantees are twisted and the process becomes grossly unfair. If 10 jobs are open and 10 persons from one race are the most highly qualified applicants, they should get the jobs. Race should be totally ignored, either for rejection or acceptance of a prospective employee.

Discrimination based on sex, although deplorable, has not degraded its victims to the extent of that based on race. Most male chauvinists love and respect women even though they sometimes treat them unfairly. Obviously, it is a problem but, again, I don't think quotas are the answer. Time after time, the courts have held in favor of women who have wrongly been denied jobs. Penalties are severe. Employers will soon break the habit.

A recent study aimed at Boise State University concluded that women have not been given a proper percentage of the high-paying jobs. Maybe so, but if I were a female member of that working force, I'd rather make my case for higher pay on my ability, instead of relying on a slide rule to make my position for me.

Recent court decisions have ruled quotas to be invalid. In fact, the jurists are now rightfully recognizing that reverse discrimination occurs when "minorities" are given preference. My optimism regarding future fair job treatment for women was not justified. The struggle continues today. I had the privilege, as governor, of appointing Idaho's first female Chief of Staff, Tana Shillingstad.

During most of my political career, Republicans have dominated the legislature in Idaho. Our Congressional delegation has varied with Republicans doing better, overall. However, Cecil Andrus and John Evans kept Democrats in control of the Governor's chair for twenty-four years. All in all, Republicans have had a slight edge and now are in firm control. But that situation can, and will, change.

In 1975, John Corlett of the Idaho Statesman wrote that Republicans were in decline. In response, I wrote the following:

STILL KICKING

July, 1975

Wilder - John Corlett, writing in the Idaho Statesman, has just announced for the umpteenth time that the Republican Party in Idaho is in shambles. John regularly reports on the moribund condition of my party. If his assessments were correct, we should have long ago faded into obscurity.

.....It is true that all political parties have experienced a decline in loyalty, in Idaho as well as nationwide. I believe that this trend will be lengthy and those parties will have to be innovative to attract enough finances to function.

It does little good to wail about interfactional disputes. Republicans have a penchant for doing this, fanned on by a willing press... This cannibalistic trend has been going on for a long time. I ran for state chairman several years ago, but was roundly defeated on the basis of my "liberality." I resolved then that no one would run me out of the Party, if I wished to remain. Time and reapportionment have allowed me to enjoy a good position in the Party today.

The parties, in order to be successful, must make room for various creeds and philosophies. While the tent must be large there is, obviously, a limit. I believe that a basic difference exists between the two major parties. Republicans believe in closely limited federal intervention in our affairs. We abhor the loss of freedom and waste of money that comes with most federal programs. Some Idaho Democrats share this reluctance, but their national counterparts seem to think nothing of spending us into bankruptcy through costly, unsound programs.

Political parties are going through a tough period. It will likely last for a while. Republicans are equipped to ride it out as well as any party.

And so today, my advice to Idaho's beleaguered Democrats is: Don't give up. Your party will rise again from the ashes - just as the Phoenix did. Talk to each other, minimize your quarrels, maximize the areas where all factions agree. Hey, wait! Why am I trying to pull you out of a hole. I spent a lot of time and effort putting you there.

There was never a better university president than John Barnes of Boise State University. He was frugal, innovative and smart. Yet I couldn't resist taking him on over football tickets.

LOBBYING WITH TICKETS

September, 1975

Wilder - Even the poet's pen can't capture the electric excitement of Idaho in autumn. The farmers are going full-speed trying to bring in the harvest ahead of the weather. The hops and onions are a little light, dashing once again the hopes of making a fortune. But that disappointment is balanced 10 times over by the privilege of working with Idaho's rich soil.

In other areas, the forests are in full flower and the fish are getting fat. On campus there are fun-loving freshmen - and FOOTBALL.

Dr. John Barnes, president of Boise State University, is one tough hombre. When I received my free football tickets last year, I wrote him a letter returning them and roasted BSU in the press. He received that treatment in stony silence, neither commenting nor answering my letter. I have received offers from all three universities in the past, but no one has the class of BSU.

This year, after offering me tickets to all home games, Dr. Barnes informs me that such gifts will be reported under the Sunshine Act. But he follows with this line: "While we certainly do not consider this to be lobbying, we do wish to work within the legal framework as we understand it."

Now why would they give me tickets if it weren't lobbying? Maybe they like the color of my eyes. At least this year they didn't offer me free swimming pool privileges.

I'm sure I'm no purer than most people but, long before Watergate and Sunshine, I eschewed the practice of receiving gifts for public service. My first chance was the Christmas after I was appointed to the Potato Commission. Our advertising agency presented me with a Vandal blanket. I returned it and indignantly informed the agency that my favors were not for sale. They replied they had never been turned down before. The same agency has had the account for some 35 years. I'd say they had the situation well blanketed.

Anyway, I had my own Vandal blanket and made the trip to Moscow annually to shiver through Homecoming. I can still sing "Go Vandals Go" and say "Wait till next year" with the best of them.

I was never a pusher for the new enclosed stadium. Six to eight million dollars is a lot of bread. But football will have its way, sweeping aside all obstacles, including the legislature. It won't seem right trading my frigid seat in Neale Stadium for the antiseptic atmosphere of Kibbie Koliseum. It's probably a good thing, though. A person could freeze to death during those late season games if they took away his specially-prepared coffee.

Alas, now we Vandals go to play some of our "home games" at Washington State University in order to follow some nonsensical attendance requirements necessitated by moving to a bigger league. Count me out. Have we no dignity left? I wouldn't go to WSU if John Barnes escorted me there personally.

During one of those rare times when farmers' wheat prices rose to a profitable level, the cost of a loaf of bread rose like the yeast within it. As a self-appointed farmer's defender, I wrote the following.

IN DEFENSE OF FARMERS

March, 1976

Wilder - The scenario of the wheat fiasco is hard to believe. The price of wheat went from about 4¢ to 7¢ per pound. The newspapers started carrying stories of predictions that bread would soon be selling for $1.00 per loaf because of the wheat prices. The facts are these: About .6 of a pound of wheat of goes into a one pound loaf of bread. The big price rise in wheat added 2¢ to the cost of such a loaf. Since then, wheat prices have dropped back near their former levels. What has happened to the price of bread? It has risen steadily. Why? Because the salaries of the people who sell the bread are a bigger cost factor than the wheat itself.

Sure, food prices have gone up. They went up 64% in the last 20 years. But in that same period housing went up 67%, medical care 125%, and average wages 142%. Leave the farmer a free hand and you'll continue to get a bargain.

Now a loaf of bread that sells for $1.50 brings the wheat farmer about 3¢.

All of us dog owners are experts, and I proved it with this rather illogical column.

COUNTY POLITICS

June 25, 1976

Wilder-I now leave the relative security of commenting on state and national affairs to plunge into the dangerous waters of county politics. The recent doggy actions of the Canyon County Commissioners deserve some scrutiny.

After July 1, a dog owner in the county will be required to buy a dog license for his pet. If the dog sets his paws on the neighbor's property he will be whisked off to the pound. If he starts barking, his owner can be fined.

To my amazement, I find that all this was done on the commissioners' own motions, without the benefit of a public hearing. Some changes in the statutes appear to be in order, but that is another subject.

The new regulations were precipitated by the destruction of livestock by roving bands of dogs. I favor the elimination of such marauders, but I maintain that a sheep will be no less dead if he has his throat slit by a dog wearing a license.

The license provisions are only incidental to the rest of the act. It is really a county leash law. Fido will be just as apt to do his job on the neighbor's lawn while sporting his new collar as he was without it.

But, of course, that is the advantage of the new law. Neighbors have always quarreled. You used to have to wait until his kid threw a rock through your window before you could give your neighbor his just desserts. Now you merely wait until his dog starts barking and you can get the SOB in a peck of trouble.

Not a cent of the proceeds will be used to take care of stray dogs, even though the only such shelter in the county is desperately in need of funds. The money will further bloat the sheriff's budget, which has already increased close to 150 per cent in the four years he has been in office. Now he'll really be able to zoom down on those dogs while milk trucks and others continue to run the stop signs in Central Cove flat out.

It is a classic case where government is called upon to solve problems that are essentially private in nature. The law will not serve any great public purpose. It will merely increase the size of the government.

It won't be long until you have to have a license to part your hair. Come to think of it, if you do that for money you have to have one now.

My dog, Sniffer, became the first dog of Idaho when I was elected Governor. He signed bills, freed the greyhounds, and led parades. May he rest in peace.

Throughout my political career, I've held out-of-state traveling to a minimum. The benefits Idaho obtains from national and regional conferences could be put in your eye and you would never feel it.

Back in 1976, I tried out a national legislative meeting to see if we were getting our money's worth out of our dues. I don't think we were.

THE COUNCIL OF INCONSISTENCIES

July 2, 1976

Wilder - It was an ill-starred journey from the start. My plane was late. I chose the wrong hotel - nine blocks from the meeting. I walked into the bar in the lobby, only to be evicted for not wearing a tie. Deciding to scour the rest of downtown Denver, I found a veritable sewer of adult book stores, strip joints, and body shops. So, off to my room to watch the same re-runs on TV that appeared in Boise five years ago.

It was a regional meeting of the Council of State Governments. Idaho sent five delegates. I agreed to go for the purpose of evaluating the desirability of our continued membership. I am unable to make that recommendation. If we dropped out we would lose our representation. However, I would hope some of the ridiculous positions taken do not reflect the wishes of our great state.

The resolutions passed are a model of inconsistency. Here are some of them:

- The federal government was asked to increase its spending on Title 20 social services program above its $2.5 billion limit. Yet it was also asked to ease the restrictions on how the money could be spent.

- The government recently ruled that welfare payments would be reduced to those states that were guilty of a high rate of overpayment and other errors. The CSG objected to this.

- The CSG called upon Uncle Sam to establish a National Health Insurance Program. But they insisted that the states incur no cost. They asked Washington, D.C. to again shoulder the load, but to give flexibility to the states in administrating the program.

- They asked for "technical assistance" in administering the Medicaid program.

- They urged Congress to provide "adequate financing" for accelerated research into recycling and other resource-conserving options.

- They asked the Farmers Home Administration to be "more aggressive" in providing government subsidized credit and that programs for housing, planning, sewer and water facilities under the Rural Development Act not be terminated as proposed by the administration.

- Expansion of student loans to families earning up to $25,000, from the federal coffers, was promoted. Due notice was taken that most of the loans have been defaulting. At least that defined it for what it is - another call for uncontrolled federal spending.

Yet the CSG had the effrontery to decry the recent huge federal deficits. They maintained that the growing national debt is causing "inflation, lagging economic investment, excessive interest rates, and resulting unemployment."

Even the village idiot can see that the two positions are contradictory. The states turn out to be the same as any other lobbyist: asking for more services but a reduction in the bill.

Most of the sessions I attended were devoted to perfecting methods of borrowing money. For many of the states that is a matter of utmost concern as they are deeply, maybe hopelessly, in debt. Fortunately, we in Idaho are not. Our constitution prohibits deficit spending.

It may well be that we should forego attending conferences with our high-spending counterparts from other states and concentrate on our own limited business.

A longtime project for the CSG has been to encourage uniformity in state laws. A film was shown called "Pointless Diversity." It bemoaned the cost to business caused by differing state laws. Yet I believe that one strength of state governments is the adoption of laws fitted to their local situations. It would indeed be pointless to change our laws to match New

York's merely for the purpose of consistency. Idaho's membership in the CSG is probably pointless.

The question still exists today. The legislature spends over $100,000 yearly on national and regional dues. The Western Governors' Association conferences ($35,000 per year for dues) often provide useful dialogue and information to Idaho. I can't say the same for the National Governor's Association ($60,000 per year for dues). However, we would be classed as oddballs if we dropped our membership and it does provide some personal acquaintance with the President.

This column is nearly 25 years old. The generation gap was more like a yawning chasm. The Kent State student shooting and Haight-Ashbury were in the news.

A FRIGHTENING, HONEST GENERATION

No generalization is worth a damn, including this one - H. L. Mencken

July 9, 1976

Wilder - Even so, I will generalize by saying our young adults are the most unfairly maligned of any generation in American history.

They have been guilty of asking us to do strange things such as to protect our remaining natural resources, to provide true racial equality, and to get out of a war that we did not have the national unity to win. Sometimes they have marched in protest. Occasionally their voices, like their music, became unbearably loud. But nearly always, in the best tradition of the democratic system, their case was presented without violence.

We encouraged them to be inquisitive, to take the status quo apart and put it back together better. We did this hoping that their talents would be applied to increased technology and to make the good life better. When these same methods were used to attempt to rearrange the system we were dismayed. But this generation was doing us a valuable, probably an essential service. We could not continue mindlessly to expand in a material way without assessing and repairing the basics of the republic.

Most of our revolutionary forebears were young people. They concerned themselves heavily with theory. One of the lines of the constitution held it to be self-evident that all men are created equal. Yet our black population never really got into our mainstream except during the last 20 years. And who carried their banner? The young people again.

Some of their causes have been unsound. The drug scene is probably the worst, but it's time we listened carefully to some of their ideas. Do we need to spend most of our higher education treasures on academic disciplines when most of the jobs do not require that training? Do we need stringent uniform building codes when simpler modes suffice for simpler living?

Most young people would say no.

President Kennedy said, "The torch is passed to a new generation." Until the assassin's bullets cut him down he kept his promise. His administration was infused with youthfulness. We didn't have to embrace his programs to admire his vigorous approach to government. Politics and politicians are at a low ebb in public esteem. Our best hope to correct this lies with the youth of our nation.

"Our youth now love luxury. They have bad manners, contempt for authority; they show disrespect for elders, and they love to chatter instead of exercise. Children are now tyrants, not the servants of their households. They no longer rise when elders enter the room. They contradict their parents, chatter before company, gobble up their food and tyrannize their teachers." -------Socrates

The difference in perspective between generations is as old as life itself. Fortunately it's not as pronounced today as a quarter century ago. We're paying more attention to our kids and that will improve life for everybody.

The debate concerning an official residence for the Governor goes way back. Here are a few of my thoughts long before I entertained gubernatorial aspirations.

HOME SWEET HOME

August 2, 1976

Wilder - Governor Andrus is exceedingly popular. If a politician is brave enough to criticize the chief executive, he should be prepared to defend his remarks from all quarters. Even so, I understand that the Governor puts his trousers on one leg at a time and has other human qualities, including the commission of occasional errors in judgment. As a member of the loyal opposition, I have been know to grab up a big stick and start beating him with it.

I lose my enthusiasm for that task, however, when I read some of the unfair and petty potshots that are taken at him occasionally. One of the most recent concerned a patio which was built onto his home....

The state of Idaho has not seen fit to provide an adequate place for its governor to live in. The house (it would be grossly incorrect to call it a mansion) which we now provide was probably one of the best of its day. But that day has long since passed. The mere fact that the dwelling had no patio indicated its age. How many fine homes have been built in the past thirty years without one?

At any rate, it was reported that the governor was building a "two-storied patio" at the grand cost of $10,000; that proper building procedures had been circumvented by the declaration of an emergency, etc. Balderdash! The fact is that Mrs. Andrus had been saving maintenance money for several years for that project. The two-story aspect came from a drop down a stairs of about five feet from one level to another; any excessive cost was derived from state building requirements rather than bidding procedures.

My only misgivings came from putting any more money into the old place because I'm thoroughly convinced we need a new one. But I certainly don't blame the first family for wanting to make the house functional while they live in it.

The debate has gone on and on. When the legislature balked at providing me a housing allowance, I bought a house. The State purchased it from me a few months later for the same price. I presumed I could buy it back, providing that my successor didn't want it.

We ran into a conflict-of-interest problem in the bidding procedure. I had to vacate the house. The state of Idaho is now selling it for less than I was willing to pay. The whole thing is a mess. Idaho is one of a handful of states without an official residence. We have over one million dollars set aside, plus a magnificent lot. I suggest we buy or build a nice place for $300,000 to $600,000 (but not a mansion) and get the problem behind us.

It has been one of my pleasant duties in life to defend short people. So I said:

ONE FOR THE LITTLE PEOPLE

August, 1976

Wilder - Now I know how the women libbers feel. Also the black militants, the senior citizens lobby and all those other people who do all the bellyaching.

We short people are now the victims of outrageous discrimination. The director of the State Insurance Fund has prescribed a minimum height of five feet, eight inches, for newly employed firemen. Attorney General Kidwell, after extensive research, backed him up. How Wayne Kidwell could betray his own kind is beyond me. He is only five feet six inches, having attained the same height I did. That's the reason we see eye-to-eye on most issues.

The case came about when a five feet seven inch applicant was hired as a firefighter in Nampa. The Director of the State Insurance Fund informed the City of Nampa that the fireman was not eligible for employment.

The Nampa Fire Chief defended his action. He said that Shorty had performed well and that in certain situations a small individual was an asset to a fire-fighting team. That's good judgment. Obviously he could climb through a smaller window, but he could probably also hop into his boots more quickly and take up less space sliding down the firepole.

However, the President of the Idaho Paid Fireman's Pension Association swayed the AG with his argument. He said, for example, that if four people carry a piece of equipment at shoulder height, a shorter person in the group may be required to carry the object at head level, increasing the stress on him and ruining the team effort. I say, a pox on that argument. I've been able to slide the load off on the big guys all my life. All a shorty has to do is to act like he's carrying more than his share of the load.

Anyway, if the average applicant is five-foot ten and they enforce a minimum of five-foot eight they should top out at six feet in order to keep the load even. Instead they placed the maximum at 6 foot 6 inches - another victory for the tall people. But don't feel like you've won the war. We midgets don't give up easily. You'll hear from us again.

Short people unite! We will rise again! But only to a modest height.

My dear friend Jim Yamada taught me some important lessons.

SAYONARA

September 10, 1976

Wilder- The best word to describe Jim Yamada was gentle. Yet I felt, deep inside him, was a tiger on a leash.

Pearl Harbor found Mr. Yamada operating a nursery near Portland. He was given 48 hours to sell out and get out. He never gave me details of how he complied with that devastating order, but comply he did. He did tell me about his surreptitious trips back to Portland. He would drive all night, taking care of his affairs in the darkness and lead-footing it back so that the sun would shine on him in the Boise Valley, where he was not subject to arrest. He was the epitome of a law-abiding man and those trips were probably some of the few exceptions he ever made.

The United States felt that its very survival was in jeopardy. In view of the times, the actions taken against our Japanese-American citizens can be understood if not justified. My sister was widowed after a marriage of two weeks when her husband got his on Guadalcanal. She joined the Navy. My brother left one of his arms on Okinawa. I was as virulent a Jap-hater as the rest, helping to gang-tackle a Nisei football player on an opposing team and eagerly awaiting my 17th birthday when I could sign up and help sink the Rising Sun.

The venom had gone from my system by the time I started farming with Jim Yamada. But my conversations with him served not only as a cleanser for that abominable congestion, but also to improve my tolerance in general. He would admonish me mildly when I indulged in criticism of nearly anybody, coming on a little stronger when I would rip into my father. An edge would come into his voice and the tiger would strain at its leash when we discussed the internment of the Japanese-Americans. But he always kept it under control.

Jim had fought back in the most effective way he could find. During the period of their fall from favor, he and his counterparts worked tirelessly through the Japanese-American Citizens League. They set out to prove that they could excel at exemplary citizenship. When a Nisei youngster took up a musical instrument, he rehearsed until he was outstanding. The Japanese-American kids took honors in debate, writing, acting, and scholastics. You name it - they could do it better, because they practiced and practiced and practiced. Almost never was one of their race involved in trouble. They worked at whatever they were doing with a dogged determination and, for the most part, they overcame their stigma.

Yamada threw himself tirelessly into all kinds of community activities. He was a joiner and doer. When he had his second heart attack, he was forced to give up his successful farming operation. He went to school and became a realtor, rising rapidly in their professional organization.

Last week they buried Jim Yamada. My one-armed brother helped carry the casket. They said that Jim's damaged and diseased heart played out on him. It was one the biggest hearts of all and it first broke on December 7, 1941.

In retrospect, I should not have ever accepted as understandable the incredible crimes committed against our Japanese-American citizens. Thanks, JimYamada.

My interest in race has been pervasive. This piece from December 1976 was, no doubt, too sanguine about progress in the South. But the premise was correct. They were ahead of us in coming to grips with the need for racial harmony.

SPEAKING TOGETHER

Wilder - My mother loved every single soul. She reminded me frequently that all God's children were created as equals. She was equally determined that all would be allowed to hear the teachings of her own church. If I earned a dime from extraordinary household chores, she encouraged me to put it in the missionary box. Thus, I contributed to the conversion of the heathens of darkest Africa. My mother didn't have much to say about the American Negroes. I got the impression that they were basically a happy lot, as long as they were Baptists.

My father believed in equal opportunity. But his interest in black people centered around the "Amos and Andy" show. He probably would not have considered Earl Butz's infamous description of colored people to be too far off the mark.

I personally saw only two or three blacks in my life before 1945 when I was sent to Biloxi, Mississippi, to take my basic training in the Army Air Force. [With the exception of Jamaican farm crews brought in by the government during the war.]

I was appalled. "Colored folks" stepped deferentially off into the gutter to allow white people free passage on the sidewalk. Buses would not move until blacks scrambled to the rear of the vehicle. There were separate restrooms, separate entrances to the park as well as separate service establishments of all kinds.

I visited Ocala, Florida, in 1960. There was still a separate section in the telephone book for "colored." Even black obituaries had a section of their own at the end of the page.

Now, in 1976, I took my third southern tour. I stopped in Alabama where Rosa Parks decided her feet were too tired to move to the back of the bus and where Governor Wallace stood in the doorway of a school in a vain attempt to stop integration. I had lunch in Selma, where blacks chose to face fire hoses and police dogs rather than to give up their bus strike. I drove through Hattiesburg, Mississippi, where Charles Evers was gunned down during a freedom march, and then spent several days in New Orleans, where the population is predominately black.

What did I find? I found two races basically at peace with each other. A black man carrying one end of a rug and a white man the other, chatting animatedly as they went along; two waitresses, one white and one black, slapping their sides in laughter as they discussed the boyfriend of a third; a white college student asking a white bus driver directions to TCU without results, and then being courteously and efficiently straightened out by a black passenger; a white saleswoman demonstrating a sewing machine to a black customer, with their common interest in the subject creating a bond of excitement.

What I didn't see was any hatred. Obviously there are still problems. There are only a few blacks around the fancy night spots - not because they're unwelcome, but because of economics. It will take a long time before that disparity is corrected. Louisiana still has the only separate white and black teachers association in the nation, but they are voting on a merger today with passage certain. There is almost uninhibited conversation between the races. They have faced their own private Armageddon, and they have both come out stronger for it. They are going to make it.

We in Idaho could take a lesson from them. I didn't see any of the mutual disdain that often hangs over racial relations here. The militant Chicano and the uncompromising white need to face reality. We are both here to stay and we will always have our own weaknesses and differences. The oppressive curtain of hate will not solve anything. We need to start speaking to each other.

Since that time we in Idaho have made good progress. Racial prejudice is still here, as it is everywhere else. But I believe we are taking practical steps, both public and private, to deal with it.

Legalized gambling is a will-o-the-wisp economic undertaking. I opposed this activity early on.

ON GAMBLING

December 24, 1976

Wilder - Let's roll the dice and see what we can come up with on the subject of legalized gambling. A special interest group is proposing an amendment to our Idaho State Constitution to permit certain forms of gambling.

Our Attorney General has said, the constitution notwithstanding, that Idaho residents are eligible to compete in "Reader's Digest" type contests and receive the prizes if they are the winners. I don't know if any Idaho residents have been paid, but there is a legal cloud over such activities. Most of us would like to correct this. I also don't think a group of people should be subject to arrest for playing cards in a motel room. The Boise police could more adequately protect the public in some other endeavor.

Yet, I will vigorously oppose major changes in our constitution and/or statutes concerning gambling. The economic benefits and growth to be obtained by legalizing gambling are insignificant compared with the damage which would be done to our public safety and other personal freedoms.

Las Vegas has the dubious distinction of having the HIGHEST crime rate in the nation. But even if that is of no great concern, the atmosphere is phony and stifling. Do we really want to turn Boise or even McCall or Sun Valley into a huge carnival? We're justly proud of the quality of life in Idaho. Would we seriously dilute that quality for a roll on the roulette wheel? Better to go visit Nevada when one gets the urge; not bring Nevada here.

A state lottery is also under consideration. The argument for this function is based on innate human frailty. Due to the fact that most people like to gamble occasionally, it follows that the State can extract a painless cut. In the states that have a lottery it hasn't worked out that well. Some are finding that overhead and advertising are eating up nearly all of the take. In others, the Mafia has found ways to counterfeit the tickets and skim off the cream.

The fact is that gambling is a weak crutch for a state to lean on. For every dollar taken in through this vehicle, we would pay a larger price in environmental, aesthetic and moral values. We have the finest place in the world to live in now. Let's not sacrifice it on the crap table.

As you will see in another chapter, I'm ambivalent about tribal gambling. Yet, I think the whole concept is wrong.

OUT WITH THE XXX

January 6, 1977

Wilder - It's a new year and a time for introspection and attempted self-improvement. I've written this column regularly for about three years now. Most of my subjects have been in a light-hearted vein or transitory nature.

A few have dealt with philosophy concerning continuing social problems. One of those related to the proper role of government in trying to control pornography.

I concluded in that column that government would be well advised to ignore that social aberration. I pointed out that no one was being forced to patronize porno shops.

Bolstering that argument is the difficulty involved in defining pornography. Even with a continuing effort, lawmakers and courts have not been able to come up with a workable definition as to what degree of graphic sexual display should be tolerated by society.

But recent events have convinced me that my thinking has been faulty. 1977 was the year when exploitation of children for pornography was widely reported. That disgusting practice, which ruins many young lives, is deplored by everyone.

It is also becoming apparent that unchecked tolerance for pornography results in increasingly baser concepts. The depicting of "normal" sexual scenes no longer meets the competition. Brutality and abnormality are now the rule. The result is the total debasement of human dignity.

Moreover, it cannot be denied that whole sections of urban areas fall into complete decay when pornography is not curtailed. Organized crime is becoming increasingly involved. That cancerous element of society doesn't care who its victims are: children of all ages; women who are held in slavery to both prostitution and pornography; and of course, the gullible patron who provides the cash.

Attempts to at least mute these unsavory practices through law will never be easy. In fact, those laws may never be very effective. But I now agree with a Boise psychiatrist who said that the difficulty of the task should not prevent society from making the attempt. The recent practice of ignoring pornography and hoping it will control itself or go away hasn't worked.

This column from January 1977, is one of my favorites because of the pleasure derived from our collective effort to rescue the young lady. The connection with anti-violence is tenuous, but I submit it anyway.

VIOLENCE

Wilder - Last night I watched a TV special on "Violence in America." After three hours of exposure to killings, maimings, rapes, assaults, fistfights, car wrecks, and various other aggressive acts, I was numbed and sickened.

Why do we love violence? Among the plausible explanations is the pioneer evolution of the country. Also on the list of causes is exposure to violent entertainment in sports, TV, and movies. Our rapid technological advances have no doubt created an appetite for excitement, which spills over into the dangerous anti-social behavior that permeates our society.

Whatever the causes, the effects are devastating. We seem to be caught up in a macabre dance, feeding on more and more violent entertainment and behavior until we inevitably collapse and die.

We must reverse this trend. For starters, we need to crack down harder on lawbreakers. But discipline alone will not cure our ills. We already have our prisons crammed full. Our courts have such a backlog that justice is never served in many instances. Rules and regulations don't help much either. The family viewing hour concept for TV, the rating system for movies, the legal attempts to close porno shops have only resulted in round after round of increased violence and degenerate behavior.

What we need is to collectively shed our veneer of insensitivity and let our natural love for each other prevail. This phenomenon occasionally surfaces.

Two days ago, I was inching along the glare ice of State Highway 19 near Caldwell. Ahead of me, a pickup spun around once and then stopped, hanging precariously over the incline. The young lady driver, no more than 20 years old, slumped over the wheel. She was sobbing uncontrollably.

About fifteen cars stopped. Their occupants arrived at the scene impatient and interested only in clearing the road. But, upon seeing the plight of the driver, a change in mood came over the whole group. Suddenly they cared.

A jovial but authoritative type assigned a driver to replace the shaken girl and called on everyone to heave-ho. In a few minutes, the shiny new pickup was back on the road.

But nobody was in a hurry anymore. Each one waited until the girl regained her composure to drive. Even then, they were reluctant to leave. The milk of human kindness was flowing. Finally, amidst a chorus of hearty goodbyes, the gathering broke up.

Violence and antisocial behavior lost that round. Human decency won. It can and must prevail in the future.

Now, in the wake of school shootings, dragging people with pickups until they are dead, beating "different" people to death in Wyoming, uncontrolled road rage, and other outrageous acts in defiance of decency, nobody questions the degeneration of our collective behavior. We have the ability to come to our senses. Will we do it?

During the worst part of Idaho's eight-year drought, government solutions became an insult to our collective intelligence.

BUREAUCRATIC ADVICE TO FARMERS

May 20, 1977

Wilder - Some of the governmental advice being distributed nowadays would make good material from Johnny Carson's Tonight Show monologue.

The various agencies seem to be trying to outdo each other in providing tips to farmers that will allow them to survive the drought.

I propose that we give an award to the bureaucrat who comes forth with the most inane advice for farmers.

There are lots of potential winners. For instance, there was the irrigation specialist who expressed his concern that the recent rains would give the farmers a false sense of security. Then, possessing inferior brainpower, the clods would likely not water in a timely fashion later on.

Another gem advises the farmer to plant his most fertile acres when he decides to leave some idle. It seems most unlikely that he would do this, without governmental advice, given his history of preferring low levels of production. Being a good citizen, I left 80 acres of sand and rock out of production, but dutifully planted my best ground.

There are so many good ones. The winner so far would have to be this one from the Soil Conservation Service: "Know how much water is being delivered to the field. This will give an indication of how long to irrigate."

An amazing piece of advice! Even though the poor sap has ordered the water, he is not likely to know how much there is until an agency reminds him that he should find out. That's probably the best one since OSHA advised against stepping on manure because it might be slippery.

Won't it be a shame when we get back to normal and have to do without these immortal proclamations? Then the farmer can resume his old game of proving that he is the most efficient producer in history, primarily because of his ability to adapt to changing circumstances such as low-water years.

During my inauguration ceremony, a tremendous snowstorm blanketed the proceedings. It was the end of the drought! Now three floods later and with a record snowpack in the mountains, I'd like to figure out how to convince God that we've had enough.

It seems such a short time since I turned 50. That is more than 22 years ago. Herewith are the thoughts I presented at that time.

LIVING 5 DECADES

May 27, 1977

Wilder - Some random thoughts on reaching the half-century mark: I used to think that people who sat around a lot were lazy. Now I find that contemplation is a rewarding way to spend one's time.

There are several things that are important for me to do before I die. Some of them I've already done. I've picked up as many beer cans along the road as I threw out before I got to know better; helped carry more people to the grave that it will take to carry me; cleaned more fish than I'll ever eat; milked my share of cows; mowed the requisite number of lawns.

Other projects I'm still working on: Calling on as many old people as I want to call on me when I'm old; planting as many trees as I've cut down; lifting my family's spirits as many times as they have lifted mine. Others in the offing: writing as many thank-yous as need to be written; shooting better golf than former-Governor Andrus; smiling more times than I frown; staying in good physical shape.

I want to learn to accept criticism easier; to listen better; to give the opinions of my political opponents fair consideration (this one will be hard).

"Some worthy goals I'll never make: Giving as many rides to hitch-hikers as I received when I was a kid (too scared); doing my share of the housework (too lazy); thanking God as many times as he has blessed me (impossible).

I'll run another inventory when I'm 75.

Here are my thoughts on one of my most dependable critics.

THE BLESSINGS OF A CRITIC

June 5, 1977

Wilder - Just when I thought nobody was bothering to read my column along comes Harold Miles to the rescue.

"Gibraltar may crumble/ the Rockies may tumble/ they're only made of clay; but my faithful critic is here to stay."

Most things in life are undependable. Fame and fortune, riches and good health - they're all transitory. Only a few items are sure, like death and taxes - and my faithful critic, Harold Miles of Nampa.

What Mr. Miles lacks in accuracy, he makes up in gusto. Apparently he is warming to his task, because his prose is becoming more ornate, his invective more pronounced, his utter contempt for me more apparent.

But Harold is giving me far too much credit. I felt more comfortable when he merely looked upon me as a lackey for the power company. Now he depicts me as "assuming the role of knight errant astride a coal-black steed with a double-barreled shotgun over one shoulder and a coal pick over the other."

I used to tend to the mules on the farm when I was a child and they weren't so bad. But horses? We've never been able to hit it off. While my kids were growing up, I suffered through three horses. All they want to do is stomp on you or bite you. I finally made a deal with horses. I don't ride them and they don't ride me.

And I would never think of shooting a shotgun from the back of my steed, particularly with one hand. It would be suicide.

Mr. Miles seems concerned about my designs on a governor's mansion. At the rate government functions operate, I don't think it is likely that we'd have a mansion built in time for the next governor to inhabit it. In the unlikely event that I ran for the office and was elected, I would cheerfully accept whatever abode is offered. The taxpayers have poured almost $200,000 into the old house over the last five years. I'm not sure any economy is effected by refusing to build a new one.

My critic also jabs me for supporting the econometric simulation computer energy study passed by the recent session. If Harold will check the record, he will find that I voted against that study. I was the only one of my party in the Senate to do so.

But I am nit-picking. It's not important that Mr. Miles should be factual. He's been at it too long to change his style. The main thing is to hang in there and prove that there are constants in life.

It's comforting to know that as surely as day follows night my faithful critic will keep me informed of my shortcomings.

Mr. Miles has passed on to his heavenly reward. Thankfully, others took his place - John Peavey, Beatrice Brailsford, and Bruce Willis to name only a few.

Mr. Willis, as you will recall, appeared on the Capitol steps to denounce my efforts in solving the nuclear waste issue. He said that I would be thrown out of office for signing that federal court settlement agreement. The mighty Bruce Willis would not return my phone calls nor answer my mail when I attempted to address his concerns.

As a total non-expert in foreign affairs, I probably should not have been preaching. But it is appropriate today to review our obligations to the oppressed of the world.

LET'S KEEP OUR BEACON BRIGHTLY SHINING

July 30, 1977

Wilder - It's easy for a President to attract criticism concerning his conduct of foreign policy. There are plentiful sources: the opposition party, heads of state, political columnists, delegates to the United Nations.

President Carter is being awarded skunk cabbage from all these quarters for his remarks about human rights behind the Iron Curtain. Some of the wailing is to be expected. West European diplomats are prepared to toady to the Soviets because they may have large communistic constituencies to deal with in upcoming elections.

But the chorus of displeasure coming from within this country amazes me. Should we really close our ears when freedom-seeking Hungarians cry out in anguish as Russian-built tanks roll over their unprotected bodies?

Shall we studiously avert our eyes when accounts are published of the latest attempt to breach the hideous Berlin Wall? Not guard dogs, not machine gun nests, not concrete ditches, nor expanses of freshly plowed ground deter oppressed East Germans from trying to escape and often dying in the attempt.

Must we remain mute when the tyrants in the Kremlin refuse to allow their subjects any criticism of their system, or a free vote, or a chance to travel about? Shall we just label it a naughty prank when those despots bang their shoes on their desk at the Untied Nations and shout that they will bury us?

What if France, in 1776, had said, "We mustn't upset England," instead of sending Lafayette? Wasn't "détente" just as important then?

It is reported that only twenty percent of mother earth's population lives under the semblance of a free government. Are we satisfied with that percentage? Shall we stand by and let it shrink to the six per cent portion within our borders?

This country needs no wall to keep its people in. The only practical use we would have for one would be to keep illegal entrants from coming in to enjoy the incomparable benefits of a free society. Contrast this to the armada of rafts and homemade boats that flee the paradise of Cuba, or the gallant attempts to scale the Berlin Wall or the long lines of emigrants waiting in vain to leave Russia.

President Carter is doing the only thing humanely possible by encouraging these poor wretches to hold onto their ray of hope. If this action angers some of the lords of the Kremlin, that's just too bad. It couldn't happen to more deserving people.

Please note that President Carter's successor, Ronald Reagan, overthrew the Soviet Union without firing a shot. But both Carter and Reagan were forceful and consistent in deploring that slave state.

Ideas are more potent than rifles. We should have stuck to diplomacy rather than thrusting our bombers into the complicated Balkan situation without either defining our purpose or devising a plan to win.

We farmers do a lot of griping. But we have a wonderful occupation.

A GOLDEN TIME FOR FARMING

August 12, 1977

Wilder - From August through November is the golden time of year for farmers. Not in the economic sense, because present farm prices are at disastrously low levels, but in the essence of the reason why we chose farming for an occupation.

The deep pleasure obtained from watching grain come out the spout of the combine has little to do with the check which the mill will eventually write. It is the culmination of the year's effort: of drilling the grain seed; of tramping in gopher holes to contain irrigation water; of controlling the weeds; and of anxiously wondering if the meager supply of water would allow the kernels to fill.

But the best is yet to come. The onions have been doubling in size every two weeks since the fourth of July. The farmer becomes awestruck daily when he stands in the early morning light and observes the miracle of growth during the past 24 hours.

The hops are now hanging heavily from their 18-foot trellises. The annual guessing game has begun. It's amazing how an experienced hop farmer can be off 20% in his estimate of yield. The only way to tell is to run the vines through the machine.

Sugar beets seem to add an inch of circumference every day. Potatoes have finally let up on their astronomical demands for water. The scent of mint oil permeates the air. It's the only crop that smells like money.

The rest of the crop year will have its share of headaches: cut off the water at the right time; find enough labor which has been plentiful all year but which will evaporate during harvest; keep the machinery in repair; stall off the creditors; pray for good weather.

But through it all, the true farmer will do a lot of smiling. Nobody else can share his feeling of accomplishment. His thoughts are already turning to next year. The Lord and the banker willing, he'll try it again.

There were 50 million American farmers in 1900. Now there are only a couple of million. We're going through another cull-out period right now.

ON DEFENDING UNREGULATED FARMING

August 15, 1977

Wilder - Some of the preservationists will argue that any change imposed by man upon his environment makes the world a less desirable place to live. As a farmer I'm prejudiced, but I'll argue that transformation of desert land into irrigated farms not only feeds the country, but also improves the landscape.

Lizards and scorpions and jackrabbits are interesting, but it would be improvident to leave the whole thing to them. And neat rows of vegetables present a pleasing view to most observers.

It takes a dry year to appreciate the prescience demonstrated by our forbears in planning and obtaining approval for irrigation projects in Idaho. Arrowrock Dam, on the Boise River, no doubt flooded out some good fishing as well as a spectacular canyon, but it was the cornerstone of the agricultural industry that has allowed Boise Valley to flourish. ...

I can vaguely remember when the town of Wilder celebrated the 25th anniversary of the coming of water. The big kids were given blue and white crepe paper streamers and went running through the streets depicting that precious flow.

No such celebration was held for the 50th anniversary in 1960. It is highly unlikely that any future fete will honor this event. The impact of irrigation on our economy is taken for granted and the beneficial aspects of dam building are under question to say the least.

During the last critically dry year, in 1936, my father took me along when he bought water from marginal farms in order to keep his land in production.... I believe my dad leased the entire water right from forty acres for $100.00 that year.

That same annual right today would go for around $4,000. Every acre under the project is being farmed and farmed well. The supply situation is the most critical in history. There will be some angry confrontations at the headgate this year. I hope nobody gets hurt.

Obviously the time has come to critically evaluate the benefits of putting more land under irrigation in Idaho. Some areas require such an extreme lift of water that the energy requirements outweigh the possible benefits. We must be careful not to over-appropriate the Snake River and other sources of water.

It is notable that the question of preserving the anadromous fish (salmon and steelhead) was not on the front burner then. Neither Arrowrock, nor another other major dam, could be built today.

Nothing excites a hunter more than the pursuit of the resourceful pheasant.

FEATHERS AWAY!

October 28, 1977

Wilder - It's that time of year again when we farmers expect an influx of pheasant hunters from the asphalt jungle in Boise. At least 75 percent of the hunters prove to have Ada county license plates.

There's no place to hunt pheasants in downtown Boise so I don't mind playing the host during hunting season. After all, I avail myself of the conveniences and attractions of the Big City many times during a year. The only other time Boiseans descend upon us en masse is during the asparagus-picking season.

But, even though I don't begrudge these urbanites the use of my fields in their quest for the wily bird, I am often amused and sometimes angered by the methods used in their madness.

It's not uncommon to see three or four elegantly appointed four-wheel-drive rigs going down the road in a convoy. CB radios crackle with terse reports of bird sightings or of finding likely looking cover. Guns bristle from the windows, making the vehicles take on the appearance of tanks. Hunting dogs lie at attention in their individual cages ready to charge like lions when the doors are opened.

When a pheasant is spotted close by the whole train screeches to a halt. Woe be to the unwary motorist who is tailgating one of these caravans. There is a burst of color as doors fly open, and splendidly attired hunters emerge. In a twinkling of an eye all nimrods are out of their vehicles and blazing away (often illegally from the road).

Sometimes the bird is not given even that much of a chance and is ground-sluiced from the car windows. I hasten to add, however, that this type of "sportsman" is in the minority.

Usually the farmer just looks on with a bemused smile, but sometimes one can't resist becoming a participant in this drama. A friend of mine found a stuffed pheasant in his basement and immediately hit upon a diabolical plan.

He placed his taxidermical masterpiece in an open field about 40 yards from the road and 200 yards from his house. The first group to sucker for the bait didn't even get out of their car, but fired away energetically from the road. Upon learning of the sham, they departed sheepishly. Several more parties came. They were all sportsmen. They sneaked on their bellies toward the prize rooster, before leaping up to blast it at the last moment.

My friend, of course, was beside himself with mirth. Finally, his sides hurting, he could stand it no longer. He waited until another set of city slickers was creeping toward the bird. Then he jumped into his pick-up, drove into the field and ran over the bird. He then stopped and thew it in the back, leaving his guests with their mouths hanging wide open.

We farmers really can't complain when someone sells us the Brooklyn Bridge. They're merely looking for revenge.

Alas, the birds are not as plentiful as they were in 1977, when this column was written. Pheasants Forever is a good concept. I hope it succeeds.

BIG PARTNER AND LITTLE PARTNER

November 11, 1977

Wilder - It was not your usual combination. He was tall, with the graceful bearing of a former professional athlete. I was short and dumpy and moved like a flea in a hot skillet. He was a Democrat who staunchly promoted the interests of the hard rock miners and of the unions that represented them. I was a flatlander Republican who thought anything not connected to farming was suspect. He was a gentleman who constantly tried to improve the decorum of the Senate. I was a gadfly who liked to give hotfoots to the sleepers.

I don't know why Senator Art "Pops" Murphy took me under his arm that first year of my Senate career. Maybe he recognized in me his own impatience with pomposity and unnecessary delay.

Looking back, I feel that I identified him with my late father - both were tall; proud of past physical accomplishments; possessors of limited education, yet eloquent in their own way; most of all inclined to urge self-improvement upon their compatriots.

At any rate, we struck up a common bond. He dubbed me his little partner, and we collaborated on various projects. A few were of real consequence, as in the repeal of the anachronistic oleomargarine tax. Many were of only potential importance, such as memorials to Congress, or revising and updating the Idaho Almanac.

He gave me only general advice at first. Namely, to assert my own independence and "stay out of cabals." As time went on, he took it upon himself to improve my knowledge and use of the legislative rules. He would encourage me to act as the presiding officer, and he always gave a thorough critique of my performance.

After several years of leadership, he changed my title to "The little giant," (perverted by some wags to "the big midget"). During that period, he made my life easier as Majority Leader. When we would come to a stalemate with the minority, he would lecture both sides on the futility of obstinacy. He reminded us Republicans that not one of our members had ever served in the minority. But he also told his own troops that, while the rules were made to protect the minority, they were not there to allow them to make public fools of themselves.

He became more and more obsessed with fine-tuning the rules. He told me that his ambition was to have the rules in a form where each member could understand them before he died.

His health started to fail badly the last couple of sessions. We counted him out on several occasions, but he would also battle back and, amazingly, would carry his own part of the legislative duties. He never failed to upbraid the entire Senate when he thought decorum was becoming lax or to correct me when he thought I could improve on my actions from the chair or the floor.

1977 was my first year as President Pro-tem. Art dropped into my office nearly every morning at 8 a.m. He would give his review of the past days activities and his suggestions for the daily session. He never stayed long and he was not offended if his ideas were not followed. He was merely following his life's pattern of seeking improvement in the procedures around him.

Senator Murphy died last week. Even the toughest of us will go sometime. Nobody will take his place because he was unique. The voters of his district had a man to match their mighty Coeur d'Alene mountains. Heaven will be a better place now that Pops is there.

Senator Murphy's heart was broken when the great mine disaster in his district took 91 lives. I wrote about it in another column.

Chapter 5—Batt'n the Breeze—Lt. Governor Years

One of the most unpleasant tasks of legislators is to act on questions for which there are no answers. The following from March, 1978 describes one such situation.

LAETRILE - GODSEND OR NOSTRUM?

March 10, 1978

Boise - They come from all stations in life - rich and poor, old and young, professional and blue collar. Some are highly educated - others have learned only in the school of hard knocks.

They are united by a common goal - they want laetrile. They demand that the state get out of the way and allow them the freedom to use this apricot derivative which they are convinced will aid in controlling cancer.

In most cases, they have a piteous tale to tell: A relative or close friend is being ravaged by cancer; he responds well to laetrile; restrictions are making treatments more difficult and expensive.

I have no way of knowing whether laetrile is an effective treatment for cancer, or if it is only a will-o-the-wisp, which is deceiving legions of victims. I don't have to know. I'm willing to let those sincere, desperate people have the substance in Idaho if they so desire.

But one part of their argument unsettles me. With few exceptions, they portray the medical doctors as a heartless, money-grasping group who are blocking their right to laetrile so that they may continue to kill their loved ones with chemotherapy.

I wonder which doctors they are talking about. Is it the one who eased my children from their mother's womb - who visited the hospital no

The "Little Giant", Senator Batt in 1970.

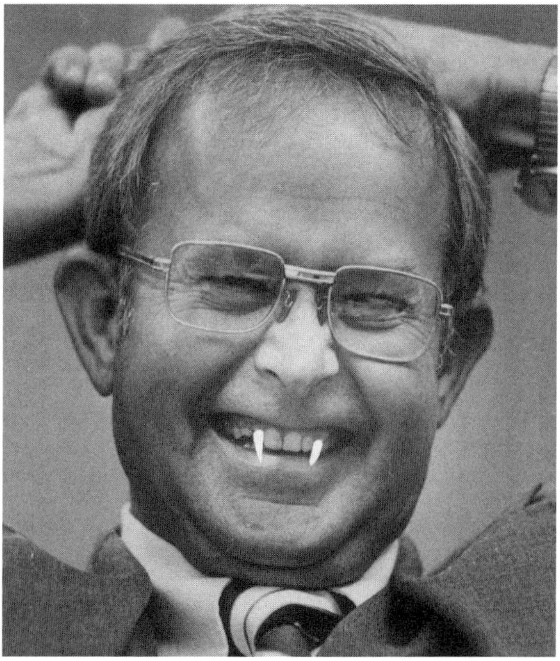

The "Little Giant", Senator Batt as seen by Democrat leader Senator Marguerite McLaughlin

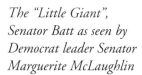

less than four times during a crisis night for my son - who drove fifteen miles to my home rather than have the sick occupants come to his office?

It can't be that sainted man who held unofficial Sunday office hours - whose last words were often, "Call me at home if you need me," and who

Woodstock aka "Birdie", singing "Down in the Valley". (See page 127)

had to quit his practice because he had ruined his own health from overwork.

Who then? Not his successor, who discovered and removed a malignant growth from my daughter's throat in time to cure her completely. He can't be the villain because he worked himself into a premature heart attack and is only practicing part time.

Maybe it's the one who worked all night on my foreman's hand when he ground it up in a hop baler; or the skilled surgeon who told me, with tears in his eyes, that he had just sewed up my mother, and that she would be dead in two weeks; or my friend, the innovative orthopedic surgeon, who has learned to restore mobility and usefulness, through replacing diseased or damaged joints and bones, to victims from all over the country.

No, they and other doctors are not the callous, arrogant, scheming individuals that the laetrile seekers are painting them to be. I haven't met one who would not admit his fallibility, nor have I met one who does not have pride in the knowledge he has amassed over many arduous years of schooling. All these superbly trained individuals are asking, is that they not be forced to refute that training and to treat cancer by a method that they don't believe in.

I have the deepest sympathy for those whose loved one is suffering from the ravages of malignant disease. They should not curse the medical profession, however. The physicians and surgeons are as outraged as are the victims about that immense sea of suffering caused by cancer.

Twenty-seven states eventually passed laws allowing laetrile to be used within their borders.

In 1980, movie star Steve McQueen attracted considerable attention when he was treated with laetrile at a clinic in Mexico. Although McQueen gave a glowing report when he began his treatment, he died shortly afterward. The National Cancer Institute conducted a scientific study on laetrile and found it to have no beneficial value.

Running for Lt. Governor in 1978 was my first venture into state level politics. Here is my summary.

HOW TO TAKE A POLITICAL DEFEAT WITH GRACE

November, 1978

Boise - It was about fifteen months ago that the idea of running for Lieutenant Governor started popping into my head at regular intervals.

The 1978 legislative session was approaching. I had the usual anticipation and hope of accomplishment that goes with the session, but I also had to admit to myself that my participation was losing its appeal. New blood in legislative leadership would be beneficial to the state. It was time to check it in.

As Lieutenant Governor I would be able to approach the state's problems from an entirely different viewpoint, and still be involved only part-time. The thought became attractive. I decided to make a run for it.

I had seen several politicians reduced to shambles by suffering an electoral defeat. The first question I asked myself was, "Can you get beat without having it ruin your life?"

My opponent made the answer easier. In no way should one's psyche suffer if the electorate chose to retain Bill Murphy in office. He is a competent, intelligent, capable man. He has run the office with dignity and patience.

I concluded that I could suffer defeat without serious damage to myself or my family and went about the business of campaigning.

For nine months of the intervening year or so, I had no idea of my chances. I vaguely assumed I was ahead but my fatalistic view toward defeat was unchanged.

After the primary, it became apparent that I was in trouble. Allan Larsen was not catching on [in his run for governor.] The early polls assessed my chances as somewhere between slim and none.

Finally His Highness, Mr. Schragg, announced in the Idaho Opinion poll that the odds were 99 to 1 in Bill's favor.

My determination to accept defeat stoically was intensified by these events. I was not only ready for defeat, but reciting to myself all the advantages of it. I could take winter vacations; play more music; write a lot; take part in organizations which I have reluctantly dropped for lack of time; improve my terrible golf game.

A few days before election night, the tide started to turn. Volunteers called asking for more assignments. My ads received favorable comment. Prominent newspapers endorsed me. People who had not called all during the campaign started telling me I was going to win.

By Election Day, my head was so big I couldn't find a hat that would fit. I began to believe my own press releases. How could the Idaho voters pass up a chance to elect a man of my unique qualifications?

The long election night began. I was ahead from the outset. As the cheers rang in my ears, the thought of losing became totally abhorrent. For one evening, I wanted the job so badly I would do almost anything to get it. I lost a balanced perspective of its value and the importance of any one person.

It was eight a.m. when the phone rang. It was Bill Murphy. "It looks like it's all settled," he said calmly. 'I congratulate you. Peg and I wish you the best.'

I made the long transition back to normal. For a few moments I almost wished that this competent, intelligent, capable man had retained the office and that I had accepted my defeat with the same dignity he was now showing.

Yes, I almost wished that - but not quite.

I'm still glad that I won, but we would have had a good Lieutenant Governor had I failed.

HUSTLING FOR LT. GOVERNOR VOTES

December 8, 1978

Wilder - I'm sure most Idahoans are thoroughly tired of campaign stories, but some of the highlights bear repeating.

There was the time when I called Dick Smith at Rexburg. I had departed from home at 5:00 a.m., bound for Eastern Idaho. As Dick was to meet me in Idaho Falls, I stopped in Bliss to notify him of my arrival time. He had been expecting a call from his wife so, when he lifted the phone he said, "Good morning, darling." I answered, "Well, hello sweetie-pie." The rest of the conversation is unprintable.

...

In preparing to MC the banquet at the Republican Convention in Pocatello, I bought a new pair of shoes. When I jumped up the morning of the banquet, I naturally put the shoes on last. Much to my consternation, they were both for the right foot. This necessitated changing into yesterday's dirties in order to match up with my remaining pair of shoes. But all was not lost. Butch Otter [who was running for Governor then] offered to take the unique pair off my hands to add to his right-oriented campaign.

The Battmobile (a vintage farm pickup painted in a bat theme) led a precarious life throughout the period. It's excessive oil usage necessitated frequent tune-ups. The used camper top stuck out further than we are used to on our farm. One day my son knocked the right clearance light off on an outhouse which borders one of our farm lanes. A few days later, I knocked the left one off on the same outhouse - going the other way.

But the trusty Battmobile made it through the entire campaign. . . I was driving it down to a repair garage to get assistance in starting an even older rig, when it coughed and died.... Maybe it's just as well to retire it. It's not worth a paint job and a person might get locked away if he consistently drove a pickup that's covered with bats.

Campaigns for lieutenant governor are more fun than running for a full-time office such as governor or congressman. Neither the candidates nor the public take the matter all that seriously.

As Governor, I often got standing ovations before I spoke. That's like buying a pig in a poke.

THE STANDING OVATION

February 16, 1979

Boise - The standing ovation has a long history. No doubt the Christians were afforded such an honor when they were successful in slaying a lion barehanded.

Samson was probably given several standing ovations for his feats of strength before he was shorn of his locks by Delilah. It seems safe to assume that spectators leaped to their feat and applauded when George Washington threw a silver dollar across the Potomac. A dollar wouldn't go nearly that far nowadays.

There never has been reason to object to proper homage being paid to persons who have given outstanding performances. But the current mania for giving standing ovations upon the slightest provocation has gone too far. A bunch of drunks once got on their feet and applauded Bill Hall [columnist for the Lewiston Morning Tribune.] They're even standing up for lieutenant governors.

You can see it wherever you go. Joe Hatfeather of the National Haberdashers Association comes to Boise to speak to the local merchants - he enters the room. You hold your breath. But as surely as night follows day, some dimwit stands up. The entire audience follows - only a few at first - then, as all sheep do, the whole flock becomes involved. Of course the routine is repeated after Joe's boring speech - he has at least done something.

Naturally, there are some occasions when a person should participate in a standing ovation, even if he feels in his heart that it is not deserved. These include those times when the boss gives a pep talk, or when the new daughter-in-law serves a burnt offering for the whole family, or when your child scratches out "O Sole Mio" on the violin. But we should not have to respond to every mediocre speech, musical performance, athletic event or chess match.

I know the government is short of money, but I would be willing to pay additional taxes to send an anti-ovation person to all public events. He would carry a long pole with a knob on the end and would bop anyone on the head who started to stand up. For those meetings where the folding chairs pinch your legs when you get up, I would send two pole-bearers.

Probably the best hope is to educate the public to the foolishness of profuse use of the standing ovation. We could give extra desserts to those who refused to stand at dinner. The best seats in the sports stadiums would be reserved "for sitters only." Best of all, if a person refrained from jumping to his feet and applauding for a period of one year, he could be rewarded by - a standing ovation.

By the end of my term as Governor, I often performed without ovations. Who says people can't learn?

Fruitless protests often do nothing but tarnish the image of the demonstrators. I didn't appreciate the farmer's march on Washington, DC, in 1979.

DON'T FARM THE CAPITOL MALL

March 3, 1979

Boise - We farmers have long touted ourselves as the last bastion of individual effort and economic freedom. We have endlessly extolled the virtues of independence of thought and action.

As one who has been particularly proud of this agrarian trait, I have been sorely disappointed by the actions of a collection of farmers in Washington, D.C.

I felt a deep resentment when I read several years back of the poor people's march on the Capitol Mall. I found it repugnant that some of them urinated in the reflecting pool and did serious damage to the grounds near the Washington Monument.

I find it no less distasteful when those of my own profession disobey the municipal laws of Washington, D.C., and wreck the greenery to the tune of a million dollars or more.

No one denies the seriousness of the economic dilemma in which many farmers find themselves. The need for a more effective marketing system for the individual farmer becomes more apparent each year. But the miseries of the farm economy do not give license to the plow jockeys to disobey the law.

The farmers in D.C. tipped over an old threshing machine, dismantled it, and threw some of the parts over the White House fence. For good measure they added a goat.

This may all be colorful but it does little toward creating public sympathy for farmers.

I wish they'd take their fancy, cab-enclosed, stereophonic-equipped tractors back to the south forty and resume producing crops more efficiently than anyone else in the world. Then all of us who till the soil can once again say, "I'm proud to be a farmer."

Farmers today are in worse shape than in 1979. But I'm glad we're not marching on Washington, D.C., and making fools of ourselves.

OH THE FLEETING WISPS OF GLORY WHEN THE GOVERNOR IS GONE

May 27, 1979

Boise -- How quickly they forget. Fame is indeed fleeting. Last week, when Governor Evans was in Washington, D.C., I served as

Governor of this great state. Now he's returned and I'm just another political hack.

When I was Governor, the aides would cater to any wish. I could summon department heads with the snap of a finger. Secretaries would record my every utterance for posterity and ask permission to bake me brownies.

Now, back across the hall, I watch the real Governor's aides go by. They titter nervously at the sight of me and hurry along.

Last week small children would toss flower petals in my path. Now they sic their dogs on me.

At the races, during my governorship, I was given the best box seats for my entourage and me. The ushers would ask if they could touch my robe. Now they hand me the scoop-shovel and say, "Follow the horses -- step lively."

Before, airlines would insist on giving me first-class accommodations. The pilots would whistle "Hail to the Chief" as I entered the plane, and the red carpet would be rolled out upon my arrival. Now they give me a parachute, and when we are over my destination, they boot me out the door.

Only a few days ago I had captains of industry and labor union moguls on hold on my 30 key telephone. Now, when I call, the other party says, "Phil who?" and then hangs up.

When I was Governor, the hotels always gave me the executive suite and insisted on writing off the bill. Now I have to pay in advance and share a toilet with three other rooms.

Last week I had to move into a larger room to accommodate all the press people and TV cameras. Now they make paper airplanes out of my news releases or use them to line their birdcages.

But there's always tomorrow to look forward to. Governor Evans is now in Lewiston. I asked him to drive over to Clarkston, Washington, and back so I might regain a moment of my previous glory and ease my withdrawal pangs.

Being the good fellow that he is, John agreed to do this. But it is not going to help for long. Can't we send him to Washington, D.C, again? He might even learn to like it and accept an appointment in Jimmy Carter's Cabinet.

What a difference a day made.

Jacque and I have always been garden fanatics. In order to be successful, you have to keep the fertility up.

ANOTHER WHO CAN'T RESIST A LOAD OF FREE MANURE

June 3, 1979

Wilder - Every year I have an enormous garden. Well, maybe you would believe a large garden.

The soil is blow sand. My homesite was a junkyard before we dozed it off and built here. Consequently, the soil is lacking in humus and tends to leach out nutrients.

It had been a few years since I fertilized the garden. I kept using the excuse that the tomato plants will put on more fruit if they're a little under-nourished.

Well, this year I decided it was time to pep up the tired soil. I wanted to start with peat moss but calculated that it would cost me $200 to put enough on.

While I was discussing this matter with another farmer at the Furrow Cafe in Wilder, he offered a better solution.

"I'm in the process of hauling manure to my hop-yard," he said. "You can have a load for nothing."

No politician can resist load of free manure so I readily accepted. Next day the manure truck appeared.... The driver emptied about half the load and then asked what to do with the rest. I instructed him to give me the whole load....

I ended up with a manure depth varying from 1" to 10" on my garden. I should have taken time to even it out but I didn't for a couple of reasons.

One, the roto-tiller man was on his way; and the other - my planters were coming. My family is willing to help at planting time and harvest, but very little in between. My wife is a pretty good soldier but the rest are like the ones the "Little Red Hen" talked about.

So, I smoothed down the rough spots and went to get chemical fertilizer. Instead of buying some of the expensive variety from the garden store, I dipped into some potent stuff down on the farm. The garden now had plenty of zing to it. My family arrived and we laid on the seed.

Unfortunately, when the shoots started up in some of the hot spots, they took one look and went back into their shells. I now have a polka dot garden, some lush and some bare.

Throwing all caution to the wind after finishing the garden, I gave the lawn a tremendous dose. Now, I have to water constantly to keep it from dying. I mow it every three days. I tried letting it go for a week but my little dog got out in it, and it took four hours to find him....

Politicians have a fascination with manure. I can identify the back end of most horses in Idaho from riding in parades.

Obviously, I didn't have enough to do when I was Lieutenant Governor. Here's one of my schemes.

"THAT WILL BE $600 EVEN, AND NO CHECK, PLEASE"

June 24, 1979

Boise - Firefighters are among those whose activities may be seriously curtailed when the One- Percent Initiative is fully implemented.

Following the lead of certain fire departments in California, it has been suggested that funding for fire control come from fees rather than property tax. The fees would vary according to the size of the structure and the potential costs which might be necessitated in order to put out a fire.

The Idaho Attorney General's office has now offered the opinion that such a charge would be illegal.

The firefighters are justifiably proud of their outstanding record in controlling conflagrations. They believe that large cuts in their budgets would seriously impair their effectiveness. Much of the public agrees, even though no one wants more property tax.

Yankee ingenuity being what it is, other funding avenues will no doubt be explored. As a last resort, it may come down to direct negotiations between the fire chief and property owner. I can see it all now.

Jones' house is on fire. The fire trucks come screaming up to the curb. The chief runs over to the lawn where Jones is anxiously waiting. Fortunately, he has been able to save a round table and two chairs. The chief and Jones sit down and start negotiating.

"Looks like a thousand dollar fire," says the chief for openers.

Jones laughs nervously, "Come on, let's be serious. I'll go a hundred bucks, plus coffee and doughnuts."

"You've got to be kidding," says the chief. "That won't buy a hose nozzle at today's prices. Besides, how would you like to have a rig that gets only two miles to the gallon of gas? Give me $850 and we'll get on with it."

Jones takes a quick glance at the flames licking at his garage eaves. "Have a heart," he says. "I just had to pay the orthodontist an arm and a leg and I'm behind on my car payments. I'll give you $300 on my Master Charge."

"My firefighters haven't had a raise in over a year," counters the chief. "You tightwads expect us to live on hot air. If you don't want to go $600 by check, we'll let her burn - but we won't cash it until Monday morning."

"It's insured," says Jones. "I'll let it burn before I submit to price gouging, but in order to keep your outfit going, I'll go $450."

"$500 and I won't use my fireax on your front door."

"$475 and I'll buy two tickets to the fireman's ball."

"It's a deal," says the chief, offering his hand. He blows a sharp blast on his whistle and hollers, "Turn it on Mac, and make it snappy. There's a factory on fire downtown and the owner's waiting to haggle."

What can I add to such a wonderful idea?

During my farming career, Mexican-Americans have provided a large part of labor. Here is a piece written late in 1979 about my favorite crew leader.

ADIOS, JOE, HASTA LA VISTA!

October 28, 1979

Wilder- Jose Perez Gonzalez is dead. For the past two years he disregarded warnings from his doctor that he must take it easy to protect his damaged heart.

He is a product of the migrant stream, and practiced a much-maligned trade -- that of crew leader for Mexican-American farm laborers. His family had him interred at Wilder, which was a proper choice as he had spent most of the last twenty years here. Nevertheless, he made the annual winter's trip to his native Texas to solidify his arrangements for next year's crew.

Joe had a large number of workers. I estimate that upwards of $100,000 passed through his hands during some years. Yet, little of it stuck there. There was always some special need for it: someone in the crew had a baby, or a family had to go to Texas to bury their grandfather, or a car broke down, or somebody needed some bail money.

The result was that Joe died leaving only a recent model van as any evidence of material wealth.

Each winter he would call from Texas with a request for an advance of funds. He put the touch on his former clients according to their prospective summer business--$500 here, $200 there, maybe $1,000 from one or two. The farmer was always assured that it was a loan, but both parties knew that unexpected misfortunes among the crew would eat it up long before the work season ended.

Joe had an annoying habit of calling me "Sir," or "Mr. Batt." He would say, "Don't take me wrong, sir, but I think you should use less water on your onions," or "Mr. Batt, your cultivating man is doing a lot better job than Mr. Johnson's."

As soon as he finished a job he would calculate the cost per acre and inform you, with considerable pride, that his crew had done it for much less than that of his competitors.

He was usually right and the main reason was because Joe would be out there in front of the group, flailing away at the weeds with one arm clutching a short handled hoe. A family argument had resulted in the loss of a limb several years previous. But, instead of making him less of a man, it only made Joe grow more compassionate and more determined.

He was no toady for the white establishment. When the campaign season rolled around, he openly showed his support for La Raza Unida, the activist Chicano political movement. And, while he was not a complainer, he helped call attention to sub-standard conditions at the old labor camp. He shared the community's pride when that relic of the past gave way to a modern housing development.

But his consuming interest, night and day, was the welfare of his crew. He was doctor, counselor, banker, and general ombudsman to all of them. He looked on each one as a special person with special needs. He was not so concerned with a person's age, or sex, or citizenship status, as he was with getting the work done by a productive member of society. In doing this, he used himself up.

Adios, Joe. Hasta la vista!

Fortunately, there is now less need for migrant labor among Idaho farmers. But those workers are still an essential part of farming. Farmers can be proud that they are now furnishing adequate field toilets, carrying worker's compensation insurance, and providing better housing. My small part in these improvements gives me satisfaction.

I'm out of my league in psychological analysis, but I tried it anyway in this column.

THE LAST SOLDIER OF CAMELOT

November 9, 1979

Boise -- I watched the recent television special on Ted Kennedy with unexpected results. As a conservative, I had expected to have my blood boil at his liberal fulminations. As a westerner, I was prepared to bridle at his environmental excesses. I intended to discount his tendency to drown factual discussion in emotional debate.

Well, to my surprise, at the end of the hour I found myself feeling sorry for this talented but flawed human. I saw an unhappy man, unwilling or unable to put his battered inner feelings on display for further public dissection.

Sen. Kennedy plainly wears the scars of the tragedies that have befallen his life: The assassination of his brothers; his faltering marriage; the unspeakable accident and his incredible explanation of it, which he can't change because it would brand him as a liar.

He seems locked into his fate. It is his job to pick up the fallen banner and move forward. He must always be tough -- always the leader.

What a price to pay! Every moment of his life is dogged by security men. Even his prized moments with the clan, all of whom he obviously loves, are programmed to fulfill the role of destiny which is cast for this lonely figure.

Since the tragic killings of his brothers his whole life is a play, and he must act out his part until the end.

Ted Kennedy loves and hates, and is sometimes sinful and sometimes noble -- but he cannot show emotion. It is his mission to lead; to win; to rule.

He is the last soldier of Camelot and he is not to be envied.

That column is 20 years old. Senator Kennedy's image on the pulp magazine covers has been replaced by younger members of the clan, but the tragedies continue and Ted is relied on to provide comfort and strength.

Here's an outlandish suggestion for bringing more meaning to Christmas.

XGIVING

Nov. 16, 1979

Wilder - Gangway, turkeys - here comes Santa Claus!

Did you think that the next holiday event coming up was Thanksgiving? Wrong -- it was the FairyLand Parade, which was held in Boise last Saturday, thirty-nine days before Christmas.

Already the TV set is being sprinkled with occasional Christmas commercials. This tiny volume will increase unabated until December 24th, when it will melt into an avalanche of January White Sales along with post Christmas clearances.

In the process, the Puritans and Indians will play a faint accompaniment as Thanksgiving whizzes by.

You really can't blame the merchants. Christmas sales represent a large percentage of yearly volume for all retail outlets and well over half for some. Their economic survival rides on a successful Yuletide season. It's sell or sink and that's the reason for the early hype job.

But it brings a twinge of sadness to the heart to see Miles Standish and Priscilla Alden trampled under by Comet and Cupid, and particularly red-nosed Rudolph.

Maybe we should invent Thanksgiving presents so that the shops would then promote that day of memorable feasting. A fellow could give his lady-friend a mink-lined Pilgrim outfit. Gentlemen could receive double-barreled Turkey guns and kiddies would be delighted with genuine settler and Indian trading games.

A bone-handled Thanksgiving carving set for your bone-headed cousin; John Alden's famous tips on courting for your unmarried, but aging children; a TV computer game attachment based on survival in the inhospitable wilderness -- the possibilities are endless.

The only disadvantage I can foresee is that the true meaning of Thanksgiving may be blunted and eventually lost. The traditional thanks to the Lord before the bountiful feast may be used less frequently. The name may be shortened to "Xgiving."

But we would be duly compensated. By losing some of its commercial appeal, Christmas would take on a deeper meaning. Gifts would be less ostentatious and come more from the heart. Old friends would be more likely to drop in to visit. More lovely carols would fill the air.

And the star of the show would return to the scene. The birth of Christ, the greatest gift of God, would be recognized as the reason for all the excitement.

Even Halloween isn't safe now!

A lot of folks said my public service was for the birds. They were right, but not after Woodstock died.

GOVERNOR EVANS MAY HAVE KILLED MY BIRD

January 11, 1980

Wilder -Woodstock has gone to that big birdcage in the sky. My intrepid Mynah bird, better known as "Birdie", expired shortly after watching the State of the State message on TV.

I don't know whether John Evans' pear shaped tones excited my feathery friend to an unbearable degree, or whether he spotted me sitting behind the Governor and decided I was being held captive.

Whatever the cause, he has sung "Down in the Valley" for the last time. Birdie was at least 12 years old. I received him as a present from my wife for our 25th wedding anniversary. That was seven years ago today. Some mynahs live to be thirty years of age. Birdie could have been much older than his previous owner reported (the bird always evaded the question), but he was not destined to set a record for longevity.

This is because he led the fast-paced life of stardom. He was the subject of TV interviews and radio talk programs; the life of numerous house parties with his one liners and infectious laugh; and a regular attendee at legislative leadership meetings (even though he was prone to release political secrets afterward).

He was an uncommonly robust pet. His only serious health problem, up to the time of his demise, was a spell of pulling out most of his feathers. The vet declared it to be a case of boredom, which he seemed to overcome as the political season approached.

My faithful little pal warmed many a maiden's heart with his loud wolf whistles; and his jaunty manner and unpredictable banter attracted fans of all ages.

Birdie traveled a lot. He spent most of each legislative session in the Statehouse where he amused countless school children with his colorful and extensive vocabulary. He once spent a week in the office of the Lewiston Tribune trying to get the hang of the reporting business.

One of the high points of his career was an interview in the Idaho Senate cloakroom by John Corlett of the Idaho Statesman.... Mr. Corlett reported that Birdie had mastered 35 or 40 sentences and concluded, "That's more than the average Senator knows."

All I could think of when I buried him in our garden was one of his everyday expressions -- "Bye-bye; go to bed."

Even now, though he's floating around in that heavenly ether, I doubt that the loquacious bird is keeping his silence. He's probably asking the angels, "You want a banana?" And helping St. Peter greet new arrivals with "Come in. What's your name?"

Bird-brains are better than no brains at all.

A public figure must always have an iron clad excuse, at the ready, for getting out of unwanted engagements. Mine failed me.

REFEREE EXTRAORDINAIRE!

February 29, 1980

Boise - A perverse tradition on the American political scene is that an office-holder should, among his other duties, hold himself out as a public clown.

The compleat politician can not only win the day with his skillful debate and rapier-sharp mind, but he can also kiss babies with a magnificent flair and can win, or at least compete well in, a pie-eating contest or a three-legged sack race.

This is the phenomenon that caused one of my least-wanted invitations. A certain individual was promoting a basketball game between the legislators and the Capitol press corps. He called upon me and generously invited me to be a referee.

Not one to be caught napping, I immediately decided to use the old ploy of having a previous engagement. As I reached for my appointment book, the promoter played his trump card. "Your administrative assistant has informed me that you have an open date that evening," he brightly intoned. My faithful assistant has since received forty lashes and a long probationary period, but I signed on as a referee.

I'm 53 years old. As a farmer, I stay in fair shape during the summer. But, after a couple of months of fried-chicken dinners on the speech circuit, and a sedentary exercise schedule consisting of walking upstairs to preside over the legislature, I am in poor condition.

They gave me a striped shirt and a whistle and turned me loose. Luckily I had a real referee for a partner, who did all the work. I limited my activities to slowly running up and down the floor and looking important. I couldn't hold the whistle in my mouth because it would interfere with my panting, so it hung, unused, around my neck.

I was on the horns of a dilemma. Which team should I cheat for?

There were arguments on either side. The news media, with their long memories and the power of the pen, represented a real threat. On the other hand, I didn't want to incur the wrath of my colleagues in the legislature.

I solved it by not calling a foul on any of them. As they wrestled for the ball, gasping for air while their spare tires bounced up and down, I concluded that it was all in good fun. Therefore, I let them continue without interference.

The legislators won, using sheer force of numbers and advantageous height, but the press put on a valiant show. The game probably set back the course of basketball several years. I hope so because I don't want to show off my incompetence again. I'd rather take part in a hog-calling contest. With my farmer - politician background, I should be a formidable competitor.

Still, that was more pleasant than playing King Kamehameha at a Republican convention or letting Miss Idaho sit on my lap and sing a suggestive ballad while my wife looked on.

SOMETIMES THE JOY OF FLYING WASN'T SO JOYFUL

March 7, 1980

Wilder - The cost of owning an airplane has become outrageous. Therefore, I periodically think of selling my half interest in a Piper Comanche. But then I take one of those glorious 32-minute flights from Caldwell to McCall, or the one-hour jump across the Sawtooths to Salmon. It is those road-straightening occasions, which make me happy I have an airplane.

Last weekend was a good example. I flew to Moscow for a belated Lincoln Day celebration. My three-year-old grandson, Ben, was my co-pilot. It was a magnificent flight. All you had to do was watch out for bluebirds and enjoy the majesty of Hells Canyon and the Seven Devils. I would have sold my dog before parting with the airplane.

But these things have a way of changing. Early Sunday morning I awakened to a gray dawn. A call to the flight service station brought the news that the weather was sufficient for visual flight but that it could deteriorate later.

Little Ben and I quickly started for home. The tentative feeler beyond Lewiston into the canyon resulted in a wall of obscurity.... I crossed by the west side of the Blue Mountains but couldn't see a clear route to LaGrande. After continuing nearly to Pasco, I returned to Walla Walla and landed.

An hour later, I was able to cross the Blues and follow the freeway to Baker in a light rain. Twenty miles short of Huntington, the ceiling lowered. With the canyon narrowing, I made a 180-degree turn while I still had room and returned to Baker.

After another hour of waiting, we were able to sneak through via Brownlee Dam and were soon over Caldwell.

Ben had been playing Star Wars all the way and it was too late when I discovered that he kicked off the alternator switch in the process. I had no gas gauges, no radios, no flaps, no landing gear power.

I flew around for 20 minutes in the futile hope that the alternator would reactivate and charge the battery. Then I gave up, put the gear down with an emergency hand procedure and landed. There was really nothing unsafe about the flight, but it was less than satisfying. Anybody want to buy an airplane?

Jacque and I had a lot of enjoyable times in our little plane, but I'm glad we're not flying any longer.

Is there a limit to the triviality of these columns? No!

OF BASS AND BUTTS

April 18, 1980

Wilder - There have been letters delivered to my mailbox over the years which bear numerous variations of my name.

Some handwritten ones tend toward the phonetic, such as Fil Bat or Mr. Filbat. Computers are inclined to brevity; thus -- P Bat. In an obvious tribute to my fishing ability, one letter was addressed to Bill Bass.

But most are less flattering, such as Sen. Blatt or Mr. Bratt or L.G. Bitts or Mr. Natt or Mr. Ratt.

What brings all this to mind was one mail delivery last week with two such missives. The first, a government wire, which wasted your money, was addressed to: Sen. Pillip E. Batt. There are many people who think I'm a "pill" so I merely shrugged and threw that one in the wastebasket.

The second presented more of a challenge. It was from none other than former President Gerald R. Ford and was "Registered for exclusive use by: THE H. BATT."

My daddy didn't name any of us boys "THE," so I attempted to deduce the proper recipient. I first thought it might be my cousin Harold, who would rather go by H. Batt than take a chance on being called "Hairy Batt."

But no, the mystery was deeper. Relying on other times when I have pitted my wits against a computer, I came up with the solution. The machine was not programmed to pick up more than one middle name. Therefore, it shortened "The Honorable Philip E. Batt" into "THE H. BATT."

I was so pleased with that knowledge that I sent that fund-raising appeal along with the other one into the basket.

Furthermore, it brought back memories of my own worst experience along this line. One time I received an invitation to a National Legislative Conference addressed to Senator Butt. I made the mistake of showing this to several of my colleagues.

During the last general election, I was touring the state stumping for Republican candidates. I invaded the territory of Representative Patricia McDermott, the capable but partisan House Minority Leader.

While speaking at a party rally, I made some rather unkind remarks about Ms. McDermott and suggested that the voters from her area send a replacement. The Pocatello newspaper reported: "Batt says - leave Petty McDermitt at home."

When asked for a reaction, Patty, who is never at a loss for words responded, "What do you expect from Senator Butt?"

Touché, Petty. If Jerry Ford had addressed my letter to "THE H. BUTT," I'd have known exactly what he was talking about.

Moving right along...

Things didn't go well toward the end of the 1980 legislative session. Here are excerpts from my assessment of the relationship between the Republican legislature and Democrat Governor John Evans. As Lieutenant Governor, I was the presiding officer in the State Senate.

A RAUCOUS SESSION

April 8, 1980

Boise -......Toward the end of the session, there was still time for another power play. Governor Evans demanded restoration of budget cuts suffered by his office. His club was a veto of the legislative staff functions, a million-dollar operation essential to bill drafting, auditing and budget preparations.

Raucous invective again took over the scene -- we will not submit to blackmail -- I will not be bullied -- we are the legislature charged with responsible law making -- I'm the Governor and I must have proper tools to work with.

With time running out, the chief executive broke out another bottle of his special red veto ink and wiped out the legislative aides.

Owls flapped furiously in their niches on the Capitol Dome. Coyotes howled in the foothills. Brass knuckles shone and shrill voices rang out in the Senate chambers. And the headless horseman galloped through the streets of Boise.

Well, it all turned out O.K.

Hollywood has its Oscars. Wilder has its point rating system.

ON A SCALE OF ONE TO TEN...

May 13, 1980

Wilder - The current phenomenon of rating performances and objects on a scale of 1 to 10 is a big improvement.

The old method of good, fair, or poor didn't allow for much precision and was not suited for instantaneous judgment. Obviously, Bo

Derek greatly enhanced the popularity of using the point rating system with her smashing hit in the movie "10."

I find this procedure useful in computing the number of points an object is worth as opposed to a previous time.

For instance, my little dog has improved considerably. Piglet, a circus-type mutt, is now 11 years old and had developed into an uncompromising house dog. No matter what the weather, Piglet would spend all of her outside time contriving ways to get back in, from piteous wails to fast-break dashes.

During the last legislative session, my wife and I moved Boise. We arranged for food and water for our pets, but no inside privileges. Except for a few rare occasions, Piglet was not allowed in our farmhouse for three months.

What a remarkable transformation! The little dog is now down from 15 to 11 pounds, and spends her entire day chasing rabbits. She performs her tricks as well as when she was a pup. Piglet's rating is up from a 4 last spring to 8, currently.

Last year, I dumped a huge truckload of manure on my garden. With a combination of excessive commercial fertilizer the results were a garden worth only 1 1/2 points.

This year, although the crabgrass is migrating from its usual confinement in the strawberry patch to the vegetable rows, the overall garden shows every indication of meriting a 7.

The homemade cinnamon rolls at the Furrow Cafe in Wilder have been gyrating between a 1 and a 9. At least there have been no reported deaths from eating this commodity.

The ability to tell tall tales continues to rate amazingly high in Wilder. We have several Furrow Cafe habitues who rate upwards of 8 in that category. One individual, who has not told the truth for least three years, deserves a flat-out 10 points.

The only real noticeable downtrend in Wilder, other than farm prices, is the tolerance for politicians. Whereas last year we scratched out a 3, we are now down to 1.5 and falling.

Cest la vie.

President Clinton has not helped our ratings!

I visited Taiwan as Lt. Governor, and came away impressed.

A LITTLE MEDICAL ADVICE

June 6, 1980

Wilder - Does the sight of Cubans disposing of their garbage by wrapping it in American flags give you an Excedrin headache? When the mob outside the United States Embassy in Iran chants, "Death to Carter," do you get an upset stomach? Do the French get on your nerves when they're chronically offended by not being consulted first? Are you suffering from that rundown feeling, caused by every tin-horn country in the world that is blaming Uncle Sam for everything from trade deficits to ingrown toenails? Is that what's troubling you, neighbor?

Then try some Taiwan tonic! It's good for everything that ails America. That tiny island republic, the sole remnant of free China, is a friend indeed. Free Chinese (Taiwanese) are encouraged by their government to buy American whenever possible and to continually work to strengthen the ties between the two countries.

When the communists completed their takeover of mainland China in 1949, the government fled to Taiwan. With the help of substantial U.S. aid, the destitute economic nature of the island has been transformed into a progressive, industrial society. Real growth in the national product has averaged about 10% in the last decade, compared with our 3%.

This small country of 17 million people now ranks seventh on the list of our worldwide trading partners. This feat is all the more remarkable considering that more than half the island is too mountainous for productive use.

There is less than one- percent unemployment. No welfare is provided except for aged and infirm. People in high and low stations seem happy, being prone to frequent outbursts of song or laughter. There is little hand wringing -- everybody works hard.

A recent buying mission of free Chinese purchased almost two billion dollars of U.S. goods in a month-long tour of America.

How do we reward such unusual behavior by another government towards us? By severing diplomatic relations with them.

When we normalized relations with Red China, one of the stipulations was that we would derecognize Taiwan, Republic of China (R.O.C.). Maybe that was inevitable given the fact that mainland China contains close to a billion people and that we could not forever ignore their impact.

However, the way we are going about it seems improper to me. The Reds are calling the tune. We now have informed the Taiwanese that they may no longer send goods into the U.S. which are branded Republic of China or R.O.C.

Secretary of State Muskie has proclaimed the we're going to help our friends and impede the progress of our enemies. I can think of no better place to start than sorting out which one of the Chinas we want to be kind to. I'll take my chances with our friends in Taiwan.

The dilemma of Taiwan remains with us today. I am still convinced that we cannot allow Taiwan to be bargained away in our zeal to please Red China.

North Idaho sustained a heavy dusting of volcanic ash when Mount St. Helens erupted. The fallout didn't damage much. The real hurt came from excessive reports of doom by the media.

THE FALLOUT FROM MOUNT ST. HELEN'S

June 20, 1980

Wilder - " It is curiouser and curiouser," as Alice in Wonderland said. The aftermath of the ash fallout in north Idaho continues to take new twists.

Tourist trade in that picturesque sector has been savaged by unduly adverse publicity. President Carter and Governor Evans have declared a disaster in the area. The Idaho Statesman has erroneously reported that 12 million fish died. Elaborate reports of the trials and tribulations of living with the dust have filled the airways and the printed pages.

It's no wonder that tourists have excluded the Panhandle from their plans. But it's also unfortunate and unfair, because the recreational value of northern Idaho remains undiminished.

Governor Evans suffered a substantial decrease in popularity when he took his time in responding to the eruption. He has since been busily attempting to make amends.

His latest move is to spend government funds to prove that there is no disaster. A free junket to Coeur d'Alene for some thirty newsmen is being offered. Payment will be made from $85,000 of Economic Development Funds -- 80% federal and 20% state.

The lucky newsmen are to be royally hosted; with the desired results being that they will go home and write glowing reports about the joys of a North Idaho vacation.

I have a lot of sympathy for the tourist-related businesses in the area. They are being punished because of overkill by government officials and newsmen. The tourism industry would've been far better off if the whole incident had been soft-pedaled.

But, it's really a weird sequence now. The same government people who rang the bells of doom too vigorously are now paying the same newsmen who overplayed the story to come to the same "devastated" Panhandle -- thence to return and write glowing reports about the exquisite quality of the water and the sky and tourist facilities encountered while there.

When the media and the government embark on a joint venture, it's best to grab your wallet and run.

As I had a deep desire to help all humanity, including politicians, I submitted the following observations on parades.

INSIDE THE PARADE

July 11, 1980

Wilder - Strike up the band! Line 'em up and head 'em out! It's parade time again.

Who can find fault with that universal attraction, the parade? With its colorful floats, high stepping drill teams, sheriff's posses, fun-loving Shriners, dressed up pets, and patriotic fervor, these annual affairs have widespread appeal.

At the risk of being a spoilsport, I must confess that politicians don't always have as much fun as the spectators.

The problem is maintaining an absolutely ecstatic visage, while traversing the entire route. The office holder or political aspirant is expected to present the picture of the perfect idiot, grinning from ear to ear and waving furiously with alternating hands.

There is a way to cop-out. That is to obtain a huge supply of candy and throw it to squealing youngsters along the way. That method gives you public exposure without testing your ability to have your smile and gestures returned by the crowd.

But the practice gnaws at the conscience. Does one really want to be responsible for bad dental check-ups or spoiled appetites? Furthermore, some of the little angels fight so hard for the candy that they narrowly avoid being run over by the next entrant. All in all, the candy throwing is a bad scene that has been outlawed at many parades.

A seasoned parade rider will check the float ahead of him for excessive exhaust fumes. Nothing is worse than creeping along on a 100-degree afternoon while inhaling huge clouds of exhaust smoke from your predecessor.

Well, there may be something worse. Some of us, when we are running for office, often decide to walk along, passing out brochures. That procedure can be extremely hazardous when you're directly behind the horses.

But the greatest challenge of all is presented by the waving and smiling department. Sometimes it is virtually impossible to get an acknowledgement from the crowd even with the best moronic grin and wildly gyrating hands. It becomes a contest. Did I make that lady smile just a bit? No, she was grimacing from the snowcone her kid dumped down her back.

But there's good old Joe, my neighbor. He'll wave back. Hi, Joe! Why is he turning his head away? Hey, Joe!

I'm sorry to announce that I'll have to miss all the parades this year. Scheduling conflicts, of course.

NOT WILLING TO GIVE THEM THE BOOT

"The weakest of all weak things is a virtue which has not been tested in the fire." -- Mark Twain

July 18, 1980

Wilder - It's always a question as to what a public official should accept from others as a perquisite of his office.

There is only negligible criticism leveled at the acceptance of meals or drinks proffered by lobbyists or concerned citizens. One past legislator laid down his definition of unacceptable gifts this way: "If you can eat it or drink it in one sitting, it ain't a bribe."

That limitation excludes such items as the boxes of meat given each state senator during the debate on federal meat inspection last session. A good number of solons refused the offering.

Most office holders are sensitive about accepting valuable merchandise because of the implication that a return favor would be expected.

I've certainly been careful in this regard. But it is hard to stay totally pure. I have refused items ranging from season passes to ball games and health spas, to a pair of jeans "to be custom fitted."

I did, however, come into the ownership of a pair of cowboy boots, and here's why.

One of the largest national theatre chains was opening a new three-part cinema in Boise. The chairman of the board, and the president, flew in from Kansas City for the ceremony. "Bronco Billy" was the featured movie. The three of us were fitted with cowboy boots and driven to the scene in Ford Broncos.

We then were allowed to place our footprints in cement, just like the movie stars at Graumann's Chinese Theatre in Hollywood. In order to keep me from being immersed in the cement, Mayor Eardley held onto me while I made my print.

The boots were quickly wiped clean. But should I return them? They were used and they were my size. I weakened and elected to keep the booty.

In fact, I was so carried away with that event that I returned later to check my footprint. I wish I had stayed home; all three of our cement foot signatures were filled with bubble gum and cigarette butts. Mine was the worst, however - a high-flying pigeon had dropped a messy message right onto my boot print.

Some people don't get no respect.

The best part of "Bronco Billy" was that Scatman Crothers was here on location. He came to the Idanha Hotel while I was taking part in a Tuesday night jam with Gene Harris and I got to perform with him.

The federal government can always be counted on to ride to the rescue. The 1980 ash from the Mount St. Helen's explosion gave them a rare opportunity to "tell you what to do next time."

THE GREAT PAMPHLET FALLOUT

August 1, 1980

Wilder - Now that the volcanic dust from Mount St. Helen's has settled again and all essential cleanup has been completed, the predictable has happened.

A new fallout of federal pamphlets has blanketed the Northwest. It covers a much larger area than the volcano did because the feds never want to leave anyone out.

The pamphlet starts out with this solemn warning: "Whether in a car, at home, at work, or play you should always be prepared." Shades of the Boy Scouts.

Anticipating possible intermittent ash falls for some time to come, our benevolent protectors tried to cover all the bases.

They really worried a lot about preparing your auto. Therefore, they suggest equipping it with a fire extinguisher, blankets, a road map and 18 other items, plus a survival manual.

In case anyone is too stupid to think of it, the pamphlet calls for providing quiet games and activities for children. Even the pets are included with the admonishment that they should be provided with extra dry and clean food.

But the publication and writers did their best work in instructing you what to do during an ash fall. No. 1 is positively brilliant - close the doors and windows. No. 4, remove ash from flat or low-pitched roofs and from rain gutters to prevent thick accumulation.

Here's a gem: "If you are engaged in ash cleaning, have your work clothes laundered at work." Not a bad idea even without an ashfall, if you can get away with it.

"You may eat vegetables from the garden but wash them off first." I wouldn't have thought of that.

"Keep your refrigerator closed." I guess most people usually leave it open.

"Bagging lawn clippings and mowing lawns when damp will cut down on dust." But, "blades will dull faster." Well, you can't have everything.

"Get clean water to livestock as soon as possible." A flash of genius!

"If pets go out, brush or vacuum them before letting them inside. Don't let them get wet or try to wash them." Now I'm confused. Do they want them clean or not?

All in all, in gives me a real sense of security to know that Mount Hood or Mount St. Helens may do their worst at any moment, but I am not afraid. My great protector from Washington D.C. has once again prepared me for any eventuality.

It's enough to make you blow your lid.

ON LISTENING TO OUR NATIONAL POLITICAL CONVENTIONS

August 29, 1980

Wilder - Both parties, upholding a long tradition, showed a genius for wasting invaluable time. For example, instead of answering the roll call forthrightly, a typical delegation chairman will pass the first three times and then say, "Mr. Chairman, the great state of Blarneystone, home of the double-jointed aardvark, within which resides the fourth cousin of our nominee for Vice President........... wishes to pass again for the purpose of polling its members."

It would help if each state chairman could be brought to the podium to vote. The presiding officer could demand a straight answer or hit the offender over the head with his mallet.

At the 1996 Republican National Convention at San Diego, I did the same thing on behalf of Senator Bob Dole. I deserve to be hit on the head with a mallet.

OF FARMS AND PHEASANTS

October 31, 1980

Wilder - There was only one good thing to be said about it.

The commotion caused by the opening of pheasant season resulted in politicians taking cover temporarily. It was the largest show of armed forces since World War II. How any bird survived at all transcends the imagination.

But survive it they did. You can still see small groups of rooster pheasants swapping war stories. They do keep a healthy distance between themselves and the roads. And, if you set foot in the same field, they immediately fly off. It's a tribute to the breed that they still thrive year after year.

More than ever before, the farmers in my community posted their places against the invasion from the east (Boise). When the four-wheel drive monsters arrived, a gun barrel protruding from every window, they found about 90 percent of the Wilder bench decorated with "No Hunting" signs.

Of course, that didn't stop some sportsmen(?) from firing from their rigs, or releasing a fusillade from the roadside. In fact, I saw one large vehicle parked in the middle of the road, and its occupants frantically firing from all positions around it.

I did not post my farm, with the exception of a small area around my house where the life and limb of my dogs required protection. The remainder of my place, due to heavy restriction elsewhere, attracted a lot of attention.

One of my farms is planted with sugar beets and has a large weed-filled draw meandering through it. It's ideal habitat for pheasants, and it was swarming with hunters. There were at least 50 guns poised on both sides of the draw. About 20 minutes before the noon opening hour, the first shot was fired. The whole scene soon exploded into a shooting gallery.

I estimate that there were 30 birds in the air at one time. The intrepid targets would wing down "Mig Alley" from one end to the other. Whenever, by some miracle, a rooster (or hen) would make it through and disappear into the distance, I felt like cheering.

Each year the hunters become more numerous and, too often, they exhibit carelessness and rude behavior. Yet, I must admit that there is another side of the coin. More and more of the farms are displaying "No Trespassing" signs and, in some cases, there is no compelling reason to put them up.

If there are unharvested corn crops, or livestock, or other vulnerable situations, the farmers should be protected. But if the owner is merely displaying his animosity toward strangers, it is poor strategy.

Even though we farmers hold title to these lands, nothing in that document crowns us as kings. Therefore, if we want to be treated kindly by our city brethren in the legislature and elsewhere, we should allow reasonable recreational use of our land. And the hunter should remember that a few rotten sportsmen are the ones who bring out those "No Trespassing" signs for everyone.

The birds haven't held up so well in recent years. The number of pheasants is way down and so, too, is the number of hunters.

RELIEF ON THE FARM

December 19, 1980

Wilder -- I'm not what you would call the number one fan of the Legal Aid people. It has seemed to me that these government lawyers often involve themselves in problems of doubtful merit.

However, I am willing to lend my support to a proposal that has been drafted by Legal Aid and which will be presented to the forthcoming Idaho State legislature. This bill would require reasonable field toilet facilities for farm laborers.

As a row-crop farmer, I have been faced with this problem over three decades. During most of that time I have provided passable facilities. As my farming interests have varied over the years, I have occasionally allowed my toilets to fall into disrepair or to vanish.

This is unfair to the employees who provide the vital services necessary for tending and harvesting the crops. A farm laborer, the same as anyone else, is entitled to the convenience, privacy and dignity of an adequate place in which to answer the call of nature.

At one time I purchased a couple of portable chemical toilets. I sold one after I determined that the other was sufficient. Alas, the remaining relief facility was stolen, due to its transportable nature. That problem could easily be avoided by locking a wheel when not in use.

The proposal itself is fairly written. Exceptions are made for operations working less than eight employees. If the crew works for less than four hours, no facility is required regardless of crew size. Amendments may be necessary after hearings are held.

The burden for furnishing the service is on the employer, who can be fined for noncompliance. As a matter of practical application, however, it would soon become the norm to refuse to hire a large crew unless the crew leader owned toilet facilities. Similar laws have worked well in other states.

Adequate toilet facilities are now required in other outdoor trades, such as construction sites. Agriculture has been exempted from these as well as many other labor laws.

But I believe it would be shortsighted to wait until federal law forces us to take action, as some of my agricultural friends advise. It seems only fair that toilet facilities be provided for our valuable workers as well as for any other. I hope the legislature will adopt the bill after examining it for needed improvements.

Everyone needs to know how to spell RELIEF.

This requirement passed the legislature and has worked out just fine. I know of no grousing about it by farmers these days.

"ORCHIDS AND ONIONS"

February 20, 1981

Boise - Is nothing sacred anymore? Are there no true value measurements left?

The Idaho Historic Preservation Council recently passed out some awards for the best and worst treatment of the state's historic buildings. The council labeled the awards Orchids and Onions.

As one who has long recognized the positive merit of onions, I naturally assumed that this marvelous vegetable (or herb) was again being recognized as a symbol of excellence.

Imagine my chagrin when I found that the onions were for the losers and were equated with ineptitude and destruction. In fact, one of the onion awards went to the elm beetle because it preys upon the historic trees of Boise.

How can ordinarily fair-minded people be so misled? The onion is a source of joy which lends a touch of excellence to all that it comes in contact with.

What soup would be worth sampling without onions? A salad loses all chance of sapidity if it is not graced by a touch of the tasty onion. All main dishes, from stews to steaks, are enhanced and embellished by onion salt or flakes or slices.

And, of course, the pungent bulb is a delight served by itself - baked whole on a barbecue or deep fried in rings.

If you don't like the looks of an onion, you can peel off a layer and find a whole new world. Furthermore, everyone's breath takes on character after the ingestion of onions. This phenomenon is so inviting that people will often eat onions immediately after smelling them on someone else.

Scientific studies have attached significant health benefits to the practice of eating onions. Circulatory ailments are alleviated and digestion is improved. Even claustrophobia is eased if a strong onion odor is carried on the person.

Adding insult to injury at the bad awards scene was the singing of praise to orchids. Can you imagine rating an orchid over an onion? An orchid is a parasitic plant that is such a pest in some parts of the world it is regularly sprayed with herbicide.

The orchid derives its name from an unmentionable part of the body. Although it has a certain beauty about it, its attractiveness is ephemeral. An orchid will soon wilt and return to the dust from whence it came.

An onion, on the other hand, has staying power. If you don't believe me just eat one whole and have someone check your breath later.

So I would implore the historic council, a group noted for its adherence to fact, to reverse the order of its awards when it presents them next year, for:

"Woe unto them that call evil good, and good evil." Isaiah 5:20.

The Idaho Historic Preservation Committee continues those misguided awards to this day.

Chapter 6—Batt'n the Breeze—Later Years

Even before I became a member of the State Transportation Board, I was free with my opinions about highway design.

HIGH-CLASS SIDEWALKS

March 5, 1983

Boise- "Come away with me, Lucille/ in our merry Oldsmobile"

What is more American than an enjoyable cruise in the family auto? Unfortunately, it's not so much fun when you hit a huge chuckhole, or find a highway impassable due to a dearth of road maintenance funds.

That's why we Idahoans have agreed to pay one of the highest gas taxes in the nation. Our state is large and sparsely populated and our roads suffer from geographic and climatic extremes.

It takes a pile of money to keep good roads and most of us are willing to pay what it takes. We are, however, entitled to wise use of highway funds and an equitable distribution of the tax burden.

A continuous argument rages as to what share of the highway budget should be paid by trucks. Some spokesmen insist that a heavy truck will cause as much road damage as a hundred light cars and, therefore, should pay accordingly.

The truckers vigorously dispute such figures and, further, point out that much of the cost of our highways has nothing to do with the roadbed.

Design, purchase of right-of-way, overhead, weed control, beautification, signing, and a myriad of other costs will occur with little regard to who uses the thoroughfare.

Our desire for good roads should not prevent us from reducing or eliminating wasteful procedures.

I'm merely a layman, but I can't believe that we have used common sense in designing the completion of Interstate 84 through Caldwell.

This is one of the last interstate projects to be undertaken in the State. The reason for placing it close to last was because a reasonably good 4-lane highway was already in place on the interstate route through the city.

The project was started back in the time of Methuselah and has proceeded with glacial speed since then. It has involved enough heavy equipment and vast seas of concrete to totally cover a smaller state. We look forward to completion sometime this century.

I'm sure most of this is necessary, but I'll mention a couple of items which baffle me.

One is a pedestrian or bicycle overpass, which extends across the whole shebang. One end of it abuts on an area populated by only a handful of residents; the other on a larger settlement of perhaps 50 houses within a quarter of a mile.

I've never seen any hardy soul attempt to cross this highway on foot. It would have required remarkable agility and bravado. But, more to the point, there never was any compelling reason to do so.

I don't know what something like that overpass costs but it's a lot longer than anything in Wilder. Let's say the price was $500,000. Let's further assume that a taxi would ferry a person across for $5. The taxpayer would be way ahead to provide 1,000 free rides a year for the foreseeable future.

The other part of this plan, which puzzles me, is the penchant for sidewalks. Several years ago, the road was widened from Caldwell to Simplot's french fry factory. The road was designed with anticipation of eventually hooking up with the interstate. The eyeballs popped out of us farm yokels when we noticed that sidewalks were laid some two miles from Simplot's to Caldwell. In addition to the cost of the walks themselves, extensive roadway drains were required.

I have yet to see a pedestrian using these walks. They do make fine runways for birds when they are teaching their young ones how to fly.

After the completion of I-84, there will be a great sidewalk network from Simplot's thence east 4 miles and across the freeway. It will be wonderful, but maybe the trucker is right. The pothole caused by his heavy rig is only a small portion of the problem. We need planners more attuned to basic transportation and less to sidewalks.

I saw a couple of kids on their bicycles using the overpass the other day. I haven't seen anyone using the sidewalks from Simplot's to town, but they probably do. I only have so much time for watching - thank goodness!

Some campaign events are fun and then there are others. You might say this one was not the greatest.

HOT TUB HAZARDS

March 12,1983

Political campaigns frequently produce the unexpected, so you learn to cope with almost anything. It's not often, however, that the candidate experiences a definite high along with an abysmal low the same day.

Jacque and I were being hosted by a prominent and charming couple at Elkhorn-Sun Valley. The fundraising event was held at my host's sumptuous home, located by the fearsome fifth fairway of the Elkhorn golf course. As my mediocre game had previously been destroyed by that 650-yard side-hill monster, I should have been prepared for disaster.

But the party was a smashing success. The host and hostess displayed a collection of paintings that would do credit to the Louvre. The guests, first class both in dress and political savvy, enjoyed the home and appreciated meeting Jacque and me. My political pitch was well received. A substantial boost to my war chest was assured.

When only my county chairman remained, we made plans with our hosts to have dinner at the Christiania. But wait; there were numerous social functions taking place within a few hundred yards. We should certainly drop in on at least one.

We decided to take a look at the newest and perhaps the most expensive of all the homes, where a party was in progress. The owner was a surgeon from out of state. He and my sponsor were well-acquainted, so we were greeted with enthusiasm. As a rough estimate, I'd say that vacation pad was worth at least $400,000. The doctor was understandably proud of it.

His friends and neighbors had been having a good time, and were not totally compatible with a sober politician. So, when the owner offered a tour of his home, we readily accepted.

A magnificent sunset was rapidly being devoured by the mountain darkness. Our guide urged us to hurry out on the deck and have a good look, before nightfall erased the view.

There was about a half-acre of barely visible deck around the house. I dashed through the sliding door, not wanting to miss anything.

The next thing I knew, I was looking up through water at the twilight sky. Being made of sturdy stock, I made it safely to the edge of a king-sized hot tub and scrambled out.

Needless to say my hosts, both old and new, were non-plussed. I was a waterlogged blob. It was out of the question to go back through the throng of guests. We opted for a plan to circumnavigate the house and meet at the end of the driveway. The lawn was brand new, and our route took us through an ocean of mud. It was as steep as a mule's face, but Jacque's acerbic comments concerning the incident gave us renewed vigor. We slithered to the top and, turning our heads from view, dashed by the doorway and on to my original patron's car.

That automobile was an elegant machine with posh and immaculate interior. As I was dripping like a Labrador retriever, I was reluctant to climb inside. But my benefactor insisted, and we decamped for the motel. My suit, Polly Ester, survived almost intact, but it was too wet to wear. I had brought only grubbies for the return home; therefore we tried to beg off for dinner. Fortunately, we were persuaded otherwise.

Replete with blue jeans and a farmer's shirt, we enjoyed a Christiania feast. The conversation was animated. It came to light that this was my first try at hot-tubbing. I may learn to like it.

I was all wet in estimating the cost of the doctor's house. Even in 1983, a million bucks wasn't that uncommon in Sun Valley.

I did a considerable amount of second-guessing as to why I lost the Governor's race in 1982. My local barber figured it all out.

RUNNING IT UP THE BARBER POLE

April 9, 1983

Wilder - There have been numerous theories advanced as to why I lost the election to Governor Evans. Some folks say that "right to work" was my downfall - others blame, or credit, the Idaho Education Association. One political observer says it wasn't too smart for me to declare in Payette (which borders tax-free Oregon), that our sales tax would probably have to be raised.

Some say I wasn't serious enough. A few claim that a short person with a squeaky voice is doomed from the start.

The "Big John" comic book elicits various opinions. I deplored the booklet, which I had nothing to do with, but defended the right of free speech. Still, Don Rollie, of the IEA, was partially successful in linking me with the instigation of that effort. Several critics say that, by defending the Governor as an honorable man, I blunted legitimate issues pointed out in the comic book.

One school of thought holds that I did most things right. After all, those people say, losing by one percent to a Democrat incumbent, in a year of spectacular gains for that party, was a creditable showing. They observe that only one sitting Democrat Governor in the entire nation lost his job in the 1982 election.

I decided to ask Clyde, my barber, about it. Clyde has an uncanny ability for correctly analyzing current events. He is shrewd at figuring out the odds on all sporting matches from frog-jumping to football, and he is also a student of the political scene.

Clyde was pleased that I asked him for his analysis. "You talked about the wrong things," he said. "Nobody really cares about selling public lands or financing schools. Deficits are boring to them. They're interested in the weather, the sports page, and the farm. If you can get the opposition on the defensive about those three items odds are 3 to 1 that you'll win."

"Supposing you are running right now. Here's what you should be doing," Clyde continued. "Point out that this lousy weather pattern has occurred only under Democrat governors. A few years back we had a drought that dang near ruined the farmers. Now it rains so much that no one can plant their crops or get in a decent golf game. You could claim that the Republican governors always provided good weather. That was so long ago that nobody could dispute it."

"Then don't forget the cattle ranchers. You could give Big John the rap for the brucellosis outbreak," Clyde went on. "It doesn't matter that it came in from Nevada. After all, they just elected a Democrat. If you get the farmers steamed up, they would tell their barbers and everyone else would hear about it and fall into line."

Clyde then delivered the clincher. "Where you really missed the boat was in sports. No Idaho team won a national championship last year. You should have called the governor to task for that. Furthermore, he should have been blamed for the imminent departure of coaches Monson and Criner. Of course, Big John did win a truck-driving contest with the Governor of Montana. You could have countered that by arranging for Vice President Bush to take a fall in a pie-eating contest with you."

Clyde had become so animated that he had given me a white side-wall cut. "It doesn't matter," he said. "With your lack of ability to focus on the vital issues, a classy haircut wouldn't help."

I remembered all that advice in 1994 and I won!

Ingenious solutions to thorny problems are commonplace among our farmer friends. Here is one of the most important.

BASKETFOOTING

April 30, 1983

Wilder - My neighbor, Killer Garrett, played football in college. To put it mildly, he is an avid sports fan. When he came into the coffee shop the other morning, it was obvious that he was depressed.

Pull up a chair, my good friend, and tell me what's bothering you," I said. It was apparent that Killer wanted to get a load off his mind, and he started right in. "We've got to do something about these sports events on TV," he said. "There's no break in the seasons anymore. Each of the sports is running all year long. First thing we know they'll hold the Super Bowl on the 4th of July. That would be downright unpatriotic."

"I went out and bought three TVs," he continued, "one for football, one for basketball and one for baseball, tennis, etc.. That helped a little but now you can't tell one sport from another."

"Last Sunday Tall Tree Johnson looked like he was competing for the Heisman Trophy with his open field running. But then Danny Ainge brought him down with a beautiful open field tackle. The strange thing, though, was that it all happened on the basketball court."

"Go on," I implored. "Get it all off your chest."

"Take the alley-oop pass," Killer said. "It used to be a football play. R.C. Owens started it at the College of Idaho and perfected it for the San Francisco 49ers. Now all the basketball teams use it. Why, if those Slamma Jamma guys from Houston ever get on a football field, they'll probably slam dunk the ball over the goal post."

"So what is your solution?" I asked.

"We'll do away with both sports," he replied. "Then, instead of boring the fans with a regular season, we'll just hold continuous championship playoffs between basketball and football teams and maybe throw in some wrestlers too. We could call it 'Basketfooting.'"

"The games will be held inside on the basketball courts in the winter and out on the gridiron in the summer. They'll go on all year long. The players, coaches and officials will rotate, but TV fans will stay glued to the set constantly."

"But what will they wear for uniforms?" I queried.

"Just plain basketball uniforms but with a football helmet," was his quick answer.

"Oh, to protect their heads when they hit the hardwood floors?" I asked.

"No, dummy, to keep the finger-biting to a minimum. A player would know his fingers were safe unless he stuck them through the nose guard. If he got his pinkies inside, they'd be fair game for mastication."

Killer was pleased with his solution to that thorny problem. I asked him if he had any further improvements.

"Another thing that gripes me," he said, "is the change in the tennis players. They used to have a fetish about being polite. Now they think they're experts in heckling the officials."

"I don't mind them spicing up the game," he went on. "It could use a change of pace. The thing that I object to is that Nastase and McEnroe think they're experts at needling the linesmen. Why, they couldn't hold a candle to some of the baseball managers."

"My idea is to have guest appearances of hecklers from one sport to the other. When a baseball player is called out, sliding into home, we'll call in Nastase or McEnroe and see how far they get nose-to-nose with those major league umpires. Their first obscene gesture would probably be their last."

"Then, at Wimbledon, when the official makes a questionable call about a service being long, we'll send Billy Martin in to let him know what for. If the official doesn't change his mind, Martin will punch him out."

Killer was warming to his task. "One more thing is bothering me," he said. There are now some lawyers on the golf pro circuit. They have all the advantage over the other pros when it comes to arguing about the rules. Regular guys like Arnie Palmer are at a disadvantage in presenting their case."

"Here's how each should be handled. Suppose that Nicklaus has hit behind a tree and wants a free drop. We bring in Judge Wapner from the 'People's Court.' The Judge is a quick study and could become an expert on the rules in minutes. Here's how it would go."

"The Judge arrives at the scene where the ball is behind a tree. 'I know you've been sworn, let's hear your testimony,' Wapner says to the two closest spectators, Joe and Mike."

"The ball bounced off my ear and came to rest behind that tree," says Joe. "Nicklaus richly deserves that bad lie."

"Not so," says Mike. "Joe and I have a bet on the match and he kicked the ball behind the tree. Nicklaus should have a clear shot."

"Someone's obviously lying," says the Judge, "and I think I know who. We'll take a short recess and I'll come back and give you my decision."

Killer finally relaxed after spelling out his suggestions. "We have to change with the times," he said. "If my plan is adopted, it will be a real pleasure to watch TV again."

Killer played basketball at 60 years old and still does a little calf-roping. But he mostly comes out with important suggestions like the ones above.

Everyone has his or her own fetish. Mine is mowing lawns. We had a hand push cylinder model when I was a kid, and I was assigned the task. So when power mowers came along, I became a mowing fiend!

MOWERMANIA

May 14, 1983

Wilder - I'm addicted to mowing lawns. The sight of a front yard in need of a haircut brings out a powerful urge in me. I've been known to offer my lawn mowing services to people who were only casual acquaintances, and my children know that their shaggy lawns will attract me like flowers beckon to a bee.

I've tried to control myself. During the gubernatorial campaign last summer, my timetable kept me down to a half-dozen mowings or so. I thought I could quit cold turkey this year, but after the first trip around my front yard I knew I was hooked again.

Lawn mowing is great for getting rid of your frustrations. If someone has given you a hard time, or if you're disgusted with the government, you can take it out on the offender with your lawnmower. "Take that and that," you can say, as you furiously attack the grass. Or, "Off with his head" as you clip the dandelions.

But usually I'm not mad at anyone, so I practice my skills and play them in the World's Championship of Lawn Mowing. The great Philip E. Mitty has reached the finals of the Kentucky Bluegrass Mow-offs. The next to the last heat has just been completed and the "Wilder Whirlwind" has posted some amazing scores.

"Nine point nine, nine point seven, nine point eight." One by one the judges announce their incredibly high ratings. I come out with a 9.7 in compulsory figures and 9.9 in speed and efficiency!

But will it be enough? An entrant from Africa who was trained on Sudan grass is nipping at my heels. The final heat will tell the story.

I have my own lawn down to a science. I can mow it in one hour and twenty-three minutes. My mower holds enough gas for one-hour, twenty-five minutes. If I run out of gas, it's impossible to start my machine again until it cools down. Because of my stellar record, my lawn has been selected for the championship.

So here I am, in the final heat, humiliating my challenger from Africa. My timing is perfect. I make the turns in a flash, everything is going my way.

Suddenly he appears. A salesman is standing in my driveway, motioning for me to stop. Would it be best to ignore him and have him plague my steps for an hour, or should I get rid of him?

I wheel over and idle back my mower. "I voted for you," he announces. That's the opening ploy for all the salesman these days. I yawn impatiently.

He is a callow youth of no more than twenty-three years and I don't have the heart to shout him back into his car, so I let him start his spiel.

It turns out that he is selling cancer insurance. With my red face and bulging eyes, along with my heavy panting, he should be able to see that I will die of a heart attack instead of cancer.

But he is undeterred. I shift from one foot to the other, devising a plan to get rid of him with a minimum of rudeness. I decide to promise him an appointment at my office, which he reluctantly accepts. That being done, I throw open the throttle.

The whole delay has not been more than four minutes, but my lead over the African challenger has been cut razor-thin. Using all the skills I perfected over the years, I plunge madly over the grass.

The finish line is now only a few rounds away and I have a clear lead. The world's championship will soon be mine.

Then it happens: pocketa - pocketa -pock-eta - pock... po... - the mower comes to a rest, out of gas. There's no way to start it for five minutes. My dreams of glory are gone. I resolve to make that salesman wish he had cancer.

But only for a moment - for my thoughts turn to the next mowing and the next and the next.

Now that I'm out of office I'm back in "high clover" again. Now I'm even beginning to like vacuuming. That's mighty odd.

Not knowing anything about foreign policy didn't keep me from offering my opinions.

FOREIGN FALLACIES

May 21, 1983

Wilder - I now plunge into the murky waters of foreign policy. To say the least, I'm not well informed and will soon be in over my head. A few generalizations won't hurt anyway.

First, the Russians are an implacable foe of the U.S. They are without honor or compassion in their dealings with foreign countries. This is proven in Poland, Czechoslovakia, Hungary and Afghanistan to mention only a few places. We should never delude ourselves into thinking that Russia will be reasonable on any foreign policy questions.

Israel is a staunch and courageous ally, certainly deserving of our concern in the Middle East. There are scores of factions involved in that tinderbox area. It sometimes seems as if we'd be better off to ignore them and let them blow themselves up.

But the Soviets would inevitably take advantage of such a vacuum and, indeed, are already up to their Red elbows in fomenting trouble there.

In addition, Israel could not survive without massive U.S. aid. We have, for several decades and under diverse administrations, determined that it was worth the price to give Israel our full support.

But we should be able to demand, from the Israelis, an all-out attempt at an accommodation with its enemies in return for this aid.

Instead, we find that nation rapidly building settlements in occupied territory, contrary to our well-reasoned advice. On several occasions, Mr. Begin, the Premier, has told us figuratively to go jump in the lake.

As much as I admire the courage and dedication of Israel, I believe that we must play hardball with its leaders when we believe that their actions are not conducive to peace.

In Central America, it's hard to find a government that is worthy of the title. Those in power seem about as inclined as the left-wing insurgents to violate the rights, safety and dignity of their citizens.

The example of Cuba clearly shows that we can't tolerate communist control of the area. Therefore, I believe we must keep the anti-Soviet factions from collapsing.

But we're kidding ourselves if we think model governments will emerge from our efforts. The only real cure is long-term economic development of the area.

I believe that our strongest efforts should be concentrated on building Mexico as an economically powerful ally. Most of the population is there. The best chance for true democracy is there.

Our relationship with our southern neighbor has too often been of a condescending nature. Canada often complains of that type of treatment too. We should treat these two countries as if they are essential to our economic health and security because they are.

Israel is important, El Salvador is important. But our closest neighbors should be our first concern.

It's hard to believe now that Russia was such a menace only sixteen years ago. Ronald Reagan, with help from a lot of others, reduced that cruel tyrannical system to a non-functional jellyfish.

After losing the 1982 election I had too much time on my hands as you can see.

JUNQUE

July 2, 1983

Wilder --It's one of those things that happens gradually. You don't realize the magnitude of it until it's all-around you.

I guess there have always been yard sales. They used to be called garage sales when only a few "white elephants" comprised the whole inventory - they were junk sales when they amassed a whole array of goods.

Now they are everywhere. One man's trash is another man's treasure - and thousands of people, rich or poor, are getting in on the act. Some people make professions of inspecting the various sales, snatching up the bargains for resale later.

Of course some permanent secondhand operations go under the guise of "yard sales." Some lowlifes even rob Salvation Army boxes and vend their ill-gotten pelf at yard sales.

There was recent talk of imposing a sales tax on such functions. One city council, personifying the modern trend toward taxing everything, is proposing licenses for these events. The police can then let the speeders and drug runners go while they close down yard sales for lack of a permit.

I had never gone to a yard sale until my forced departure from politics gave me some extra time. A close relative recently put her "pre-owned" material up for sale and I sat in.

There was a perfectly good plumb bob for $1, but it was a slow seller. When I left it was still going begging - likewise for a non-descript mallet and an old-time whiskey bottle, both priced at 25 cents; a magnetic knife rack, asking price $1; plastic curtain hooks, 50 for one dollar; and a hamburger cooker for $5.

Used clothing sold well. In fact, an expensive sweater coat fetched $25. But ugly neckties at 3 for $1 were a slow item and wigs didn't go at all.

The buyers were wary of defective merchandise. A clock radio was presented in which the clock worked but the radio didn't. No sale at $3. A seltzer bottle, which leaked, bogged down at $5.50. A tape deck priced at $7.50 attracted no interest when shoppers discovered it didn't work.

There was a "free" box in which the owner had placed items of extremely dubious value. As far as I know, nobody took anything.

I tried to remain aloof from the process; after all, who needs that junk. But my eyes kept wandering to some used tomato frames. They had been in use for so long that the legs were rotted off and parts of the tops were broken. But, as the afternoon wore on, I concluded that some masking tape would make them perfectly acceptable for at least a season.

"No," I said to myself. "It will take an extra trip to Boise to get them all home and that will cost at least ten bucks."

It was no use, I had to have them. I got the whole lot for ten cents. It was a steal.

Those good old tomato frames lasted about five years.

When I sent the following column out to the newspapers in Idaho, I included this note: "I recently drove my auto to eastern Washington. On the way over, I noticed two stray dogs on the freeway near Baker, Oregon. On the return trip, only one dog remained. Here's how I reconstructed the story."

HEAVY TRAFFIC FOR DOGS

July 9, 1983

Wilder - Tige flopped down beside the freeway, all four paws underneath him. He'd been standing for 30 hours now, and his short legs could hold that massive head up no longer.

"I hope my master comes back soon," he thought. He was hungry. At least he'd had a few licks of water from the dirty puddles that formed during the overnight drizzle.

Tige was what some people call an ugly dog - a mixture of terrier, bulldog and shepherd with a dirty gray coat. The orange and yellow stripes didn't do much to enhance his features, the most prominent of which was a sharply receding jaw.

Why his master had dumped him and Blackie out on a roadway eleven miles from Baker was a mystery to Tige. "I know he doesn't pay much attention to me, but I don't think he hates me," the exhausted dog mused.

Blackie had lasted less than five minutes. It wasn't the truck driver's fault. He tried his best to miss that ball of fur, but you can't tip over a loaded semi to avoid hitting a dog.

Tige's mother wasn't much to look at either, but she was attractive enough to get pregnant, and two months after she had her pups, her owner took them all down to the humane shelter. His mother had loved him a lot, and Tige missed her when they took her away.

But he did get one lucky break. His master came in to the shelter to find some pups. Even ugly dogs are cute when they're puppies. Tige and Blackie were chosen.

They were treated pretty well for the first year or two. But then the master's kids became young adults and moved away. Blackie and Tige spent the long days in their pen, suffocating from boredom.

Sometimes his master would give Tige a little kick if he got too close, but usually he would just feed him and ignore him... at least the ride out here had been a change of pace. And probably his master would be coming back soon.

Tige struggled to his feet. "I'll just move across the road and wait over there," he decided.

It all happened so fast. There was no time for pain - it was more a sensation of vanishing.

Tige's body was tumbling beneath the truck wheels, but he was no longer in it. He was nipping at his mother's heels in a boundless pasture where no human being could decide what dogs must do. He was no longer ugly. Tige was free - free at last.

The Oregon State Police checked out the situation and doubted that either dog was killed there. I hope they were right.

ROUGHING IT

July 23, 1983

Wilder - Off, in search of the wily crappie! I have this boat, of an obscure vintage.

My wife, Jacque, and my daughter, Leslie, delight in poking fun at my boat. It has high sides and those two hunker down so no one can see them when they're riding in my boat. But I think the square cut gives it distinction. As a matter of fact, it looks almost exactly like the one in the picture where George Washington is crossing the Delaware.

It's not your cleanest boat. It seems as if the gasoline-motor oil mixture mysteriously spreads itself all over the life preservers and anchor ropes. It has a few minor leaks and these contribute to a permeating goo. My boat is always up for loan but few people take advantage of the opportunity.

Therefore, when it was decided that we should go crappie fishing at Owyhee Reservoir, I took a look inside the boat. It was immaculate. I hadn't used it for a couple of years, so I assumed that the borrower, Mr. Clean, had put everything in ship shape.

I inspected it no further. I bought a boat license and a decal and a trailer license and two fishing licenses and a lot of tackle and groceries and away we went.

The question to be decided was whether to put the boat in at Cherry Creek, at the dam or Leslie Gulch, on the upper end of the reservoir. Cherry Creek has a fine restaurant, a bar, repair facilities and even a motel. A good paved road would get us there in an hour. Leslie Gulch has a pair of outdoor toilets and a place to launch your boat. It's nearly three hours driving time on a rutty, dusty dirt road to get there. The choice was obvious - we'd take Leslie Gulch - because the rumor mill reported slightly larger catches there.

It was a jolly trip to the reservoir, filled with high expectations of record size crappie catches. Only when the boat was in the water did I discover the bad news. The clod who used the rig previously had snipped off the rubber connector tube to the gas tank. We were approximately 50 miles from the nearest repair station.

So, the challenge was mine. I took out my trusty toad-stabber and made a clean cut on the remainder of the line. It then fit onto the motor nicely, but left the problem of two fuel valves that shut off the flow when the connector is not in place. I broke off the end of a butcher knife and used it as a shim between the line and the valves, in order to hold them open.

Eureka, the engine roared into life. But, just as abruptly, the jerry-built arrangement flew off from the pressure of the carburetor. Again and again I pulled on the rope with the same temporary results. A couple of observers from the shore became concerned about my condition. As I panted faster and faster, one fellow yelled, "You're liable to have a heart attack."

"Bug off," I muttered under my breath. While a heart attack was not out of the question, my immediate concern was the mass of blisters resulting from the gasoline-soaked rope.

The futility of the effort soon became apparent. Handing Jacque the good paddle (she is much more skillful than I at the oars), I took the broken one and we rowed over to a small cove.

After an hour of desultory effort toward catching a fish where we could be certain there weren't any, we paddled back, loaded up and hit the trail.

Jacque was stoic about the whole venture. "I knew all about your boat before we came over here," she said. Then she went back to her crossword puzzle.

I finally gave the boat away, but the recipient would take it only on the condition that I wouldn't give him the motor.

SUNRISE, SUNSET

October 7, 1983

Wilder - In the early fifties, we spent a couple of years homesteading north of Rupert. Our children were small; the youngest was born there.

It was a little primitive. There were no telephones or TV's. The roads were dirt and, if it rained or snowed, you waited until they dried up before you ventured out to civilization.

So we weren't too formal in our dress, and protocol was fairly lax. The kids were inclined toward comfortable attire and, in the hot summertime, that meant as little as possible.

The motor was going out of our Chevrolet sedan and it became necessary to trade it off. Fancying myself as a shrewd dealer, I prepared the old car for haggling.

It had not been so clean for a long time, and the motor chugged along pretty well as we drove the ten miles to town.

It was hot, and the kids were down to the bare essentials. But even then they needed additional coolant, so we stopped for ice cream cones on the way.

The new auto was all anyone could want. The price was right. All we needed was to set a value on the old one. The new car man climbed inside. It was then that my two-year-old daughter decided to rub her ice cream cone over the upholstery. A few shrill commands put a stop to that practice, but then things got worse.

The little urchins weren't used to seeing anyone else in the car and, as the salesman settled in, my darling daughter began shouting: "Get out man! Get out man!"

We got the car traded with little further difficulty. I only mention it to show how things change over the years.

We always had trouble with our offspring littering up our cars. It only got worse when they reached high school. First, they would squander their savings from a whole summer's work on some terrible vehicle such as a GTO (goat) jacked up in the rear-end. Then they would fill it to the gunwales with hamburger wrappers and Coke cups. Only the sternest threats would bring forth an occasional cleanout.

But the world turns. After returning to the farm from the political wars, I still had a perfectly good Ford compact car. It was my Battmobile in the 1982 campaign. I had the decorative paint removed, and now drive it on the farm. After 120,000 miles, the car and I are old friends, so we don't need to be formal. Therefore, I drive it through the fields and collect lots of dust. If farm machinery breaks down, I throw the old parts in my car and head for the repair shop. If a candy bar wrapper falls to the floor, I don't always pick it up immediately. My little mutt, Piglet, likes to go along too, and he's not your cleanest dog.

I went to Boise the other day. My car was unusually dirty, but that matter did not weigh heavily on my mind.

I stopped to see my son, the new lawyer, and it turned out that he needed a lift for a few blocks. Resplendent in his black lawyer's suit, he opened the door to get in.

"What a pit!" he exclaimed. But being a good sport, he settled in. After he got out, I tried to brush him off. It was no use. His suit, which had just come from the cleaners, would have to go right back.

I was the new owner of the dirty car championship. Sunrise; Sunset. How quickly the years go by.

That was a mighty fine automobile. It has now gone to that great garage in the sky.

SHAGGY DOE STORY

My heart's in the highlands
My heart is not here
My heart's in the highlands
A-chasing a deer.
Burns

HUNTING MADNESS HITS IDAHO

October 19, 1983

Boise - The 19th of October having arrived, deer-hunting madness pervades the Idaho citizenry.

The Congress of the United States is furiously debating as to whether our economy can stand another holiday. But our Fish and Game Commission, a non-elected group, has effectively forced a one-week cessation in work activities on Idahoans.

By opening deer hunting on Wednesday, the commissioners have destroyed a whole workweek. There is a fair amount of devotion to duty on Monday, but, by the time Tuesday morning rolls around, the true aficionado's thoughts are "in the highlands." As Tuesday wears on, job depression mounts and, if the boss does not give in, the hunter breaks out in a cold sweat by five p.m.

Occasionally, an extra conscientious employee will struggle back in time for work Friday. But he is of little use. His eyes are glazed from all-night poker around the campfire, and his body aches from tramping up and down mountainsides.

Back in the good old days, the general deer season opened on Saturday. There was considerable absenteeism Friday afternoon, but that was of little consequence to the employer. All he had to do was announce that, when the day's work was done, everyone could take off. Productivity would soar and by 11 a.m. the hunters could depart.

They then spent the weekend firing at those big-eyed deer, or at each other, and made it home in time to go to work on Monday. There were lots of hangovers and resulting inefficiency but that was little different from an ordinary Monday.

The old system was not only better for employers, but also eliminated an unfair advantage for the affluent. Now that the season opens Wednesday, George Gotrocks, who owns his own business, has no trouble finding time to go. But Dan Deerhunter, who works in a supermarket, can't take off without losing his job.

The commissioners claim that the middle-of-the-week opening reduces the pressure on the game animals. There must be ways of doing that (i.e. shorter seasons) without giving an advantage to rich people over poor ones. We should go back to a Saturday opening and give everyone an equal shot at those smelly deer.

At least the sport has bridged the gender gap. Noting that my neighbor was eating his meals out, I inquired about his wife. "Oh," he said, "my dear's in the highlands, chasing a hart."

Oh, dear!

ON GOD AND THE LOCKER ROOM

February 17, 1984

Wilder - This whole country could use more religion and I'm certainly not against bringing God more closely into our daily decisions.

However, I've never felt it was fair to ask the Lord to intervene in a sports contest. Why should we ask Him to take sides? There are good guys and bad guys on both teams so why seek divine intervention?

The Washington Redskins are the practitioners of the most prominent locker room prayer. Not satisfied with their own skills, they want to bring down the wrath of God on the other team.

Of course, they're proud of their own talents too. Joe Theismann was insufferable the two entire weeks before the Super Bowl. He was not only cocky about his football exploits, but he would also have us believe he was the shrewdest businessman, most talented speaker, etc. One reporter, trying to conclude an interview, told Joe he was out of paper. Theismann asked him to turn the notes over and continue.

After reading about and listening to a great volume of boasting and crowing by the Redskins, I concluded that the Lord certainly wasn't going to favor that outfit, in spite of their frequent entreaties to Him.

I therefore laid a small wager on the L.A. Raiders with my friend Richard. Those Raiders occasionally praise God also, but that doesn't keep them from playing pretty rough football. While the Redskins were basking in self-praise for hundreds of reporters, the Raiders generally kept to themselves. If a reporter asked an L.A. player who was going to win, the Raider would grunt, "us," and go back to eating his raw meat.

Well, you all know what happened. That Redskin line, composed of 300-pound musclemen called "hogs," turned into sausage meat. Theismann threw the ball like an old lady when he wasn't getting sacked, which was often. Los Angeles won it 34-9.

The Raiders play dirty, but they hide it well from the referees. They only got penalized twice as much as the Redskins, and that was for brass knuckles and a blackjack. I wish they wouldn't show those instant replays of my team cheating. If it becomes too obvious, the Lord might be tempted to intervene.

There's one thing worse than the prayers. That's when the President has to hold up the celebration with his phone call. Who started that anyway? I think it was Dick Nixon. I love President Reagan, but his jokes about the MX missiles were really bombs. I say let the players and owners get on with pouring champagne over each other. After all, they just struck it rich.

A short public thank you to God afterward is quite appropriate. Marcus Allen did that nicely. Then he followed with a few cuss words just to keep things in perspective.

I don't believe God will give you more than your share of help in some situations. For instance, if your golf ball is lost in the woods and you have dropped another one with a clear shot to the hole and you holler "Lucky me, I found it" to your opponent, you can't expect God to give you a super next shot.

But, chances are He won't penalize you either. Our God is a wise God and I believe that He lets us fail or succeed at card games and sport matches on our own. Of course He is there, and He cares about all of us, but sometimes He's a non-interventionist. Take note, Redskins.

But a little prayer never hurts anyone, either.

HONOR BOUND
AT THE SHILOH CIVIL WAR SITE IN TENNESSEE

March 2, 1984

Wilder - The whole battlefield couldn't have been more than five thousand acres in size. Yet it was strategically located, adjacent to Pittsburgh Landing, on the Tennessee River. 70,000 Union troops had been massed there for months. It was no secret that the 40,000 Confederate soldiers nearby were considering an attack on the post.

Soon after General Johnston started marching the Rebels from 10 miles south, he was informed that the Yanks were onto his plans and that success was doubtful. But he had planned this assault for a long time; and he had to continue, because to back out now would sully his honor as well as that of his troops.

So the slaughter began. The battlefield was so dense with smoke that friend and foe were identified only by their flags and bugle calls. Brother or neighbor or former countryman sighted in upon his counterpart, and blew off his leg or sent him to oblivion. A small pond became a neutral zone, where both sides washed their wounds until the waters turned red.

When the carnage ended, some 23,000 men lay dead or grievously wounded. Those novice gladiators didn't have much against each other. Most of them were young farm boys. It was not certain that the question of slavery was at stake. Not everyone felt strongly about it on either side. What was clearly understood was that the South wanted to choose its own destiny, and that the North wanted to preserve the Union. That main issue translates into the motive which fuels all warfare - HONOR.

I walked along the battlefield trying to sense a feeling of honor worthy of the anguish brought about by these killings.

But now, only 120 years later, all a visitor can feel is sadness. The vision that is conjured up is that of grow-up boys running between the trees, grabbing the flag from their fallen comrades, clutching their breasts and calling out to their mothers as bullets tear the life from them. There is no honor to be felt from Yank or Rebel - only a tragic permeation of loss and waste and despair.

In "The Mysterious Stranger" Mark Twain put it this way: "(We) have made continual progress. Cain did his murder with a club; the

Hebrews... with javelins and swords; the Greeks and Romans added protective armor; the Christian has added guns and powder; a few centuries from now he will have so greatly improved the deadly effectiveness of his weapons of slaughter that all men will confess that, without Christian civilization, war must have remained a poor and trifling thing to the end of time."

Mark Twain did not divine that Christianity has no bearing on the matter. Today, the experts are the godless Communists with their poison gas in Afghanistan, or the Arab religionists who kill with suicide bombs under a wide array of beliefs.

Nowhere is that omnipresent banner of honor held higher than in the Middle East. Twelve-year-old Lebanese or Syrians are asked, "What is your goal in life?" Their answer - "To get a gun and kill the enemy," even though they cannot define who the enemy is.

All through history men have fought duels and murdered each other and engaged in wars for honor. Most wars are started for no good reason. And when they're over, they haven't settled anything permanently. But they have provided a pretense for honor, so that man can go about his bloody ways.

The Iranians held our embassy people for a year to enhance their honor. The Red Chinese can't leave Taiwan alone, because it is their honorable duty to keep their version of China whole. We couldn't pull out of Lebanon as soon as it was obvious we were doing no good, because our honor was at stake. We now have two or three hundred corpses to prove that we are honorable.

In all but a handful of cases throughout history, this killing, in the name of honor, has been done by the male of the human species. The female has used markedly superior judgment by tempering violence in the pursuit of honor. I am for equal employment, comparable pay, and other opportunities for women. There are, however, some facets of man's nature which are of doubtful value. Women would be well-advised not to demand full equality in the protection of "honor."

General Sherman was right - war is hell. There are no exceptions.

ON THE DEFENSE

April 6, 1984

Wilder - I was fourteen years old when the Japanese bombed Pearl Harbor. By the time I reached my seventeenth birthday and signed up for a chance at the aggressors, the atom bomb had been tested. The war was soon to be concluded.

At fifty-seven years of age I now can qualify for some senior citizen discounts. A lot of water has gone over the dam since the surrender of the axis powers. Most people in the U.S.A. were not born until well after that event.

Yet, in our military mind-set, it is as if it were yesterday. We are carrying almost the entire defense load for our allies, as we were forty years ago.

We have also cheerfully assumed the cost of defending our erstwhile enemies - Germany, Japan and Italy. From all appearances, we are going to carry out this chore in perpetuity.

West Germany and Japan, freed from costly defense outlays, have made us eat their economic dust for the past couple of decades. The Italians seem incapable of forming a productive government, and the Germans are losing steam. But Japan, capitalizing on our slow-wittedness in trade negotiations, continues to drub us economically.

What has all this gained us? We have contained communist expansion only to a degree. The free world is certainly not more secure than it was four decades ago. But worse, in carrying out our mission, we have become the international whipping boy for "friend" and "foe" alike.

The United States is regularly being criticized by the French. If we sneeze, they are insulted. Let them build their own defenses. Maybe they can improve on the Maginot line.

The Italians deride us. We are the "Great Satan" in Iran. Anti-American demonstrations are commonplace in India. The Lebanese government, after watching our Marines die in Beirut, now chastises us for abandoning that hopeless situation. High officials there advocate breaking relations with us.

The Philippines, Chile, Brazil, Argentina and Zimbabwe have a lot in common. If anything goes wrong, it is blamed on America.

Israel, which would not exist without billions of dollars in aid from us, often thumbs its nose at advice from Uncle Sam. We all admire that tough-minded nation, but it is hardly our duty to finance their religious claims as well as their defense. The Israelis create settlements in the Palestinian area in direct defiance of our considered demands. We should respond by cutting off half a billion until they get the message.

There are a few countries that seem to appreciate our efforts. The Taiwanese contribute substantially to their own defense, and make heroic attempts to buy American products. Britain keeps a stiff upper lip and, with few exceptions, seeks and applauds our friendship.

Most of the rest leave a lot to be desired. The next time the rabble is whooping it up with "Yankee go home" rallies, we should consider doing so. Jesus' admonition to turn the other cheek surely did not mean that we must bankrupt ourselves by defending the dubious national causes of the entire world.

We have now abandoned NATO's assigned role as a defense mechanism. If that is to be the case, let the Europeans furnish the manpower for bringing peace to the Balkans. After all, it is in Europe.

HORSING AROUND

January 31, 1985

Wilder -- *"...Back in the saddle again - out where a friend meets a friend."*

A common thread, for those who wish to communicate with members of the legislature, is to host a "legislative reception." These affairs are generally held from 5 p.m. to 7 p.m. or so. The format typically includes substantial hors d'oeuvres accompanied by soft drinks and sometimes the hard ones too.

I have gone to about a million of these and there have been a dozen or so already this session. They are o.k. It's moderately useful to see all the legislators you worked with all day again in the evening. And the hosts, more often than not, have something worthwhile to talk about.

But enough is enough, so I decided to call a halt to this. *Wild horses* couldn't drag me to another one. It was the *end of the trail* for legislative receptions.

With great determination, I started thumbing through my invitations. I would throw out all the remaining cards. *Whoa!* What's this - a reception provided by the *Horse Council.* Deeply intrigued, I immediately changed my mind and decided to attend.

... Ridin' down the canyon where the evenin' sun goes down ...

I could see it all now. The horses would stand in a circle and have their council. Would they all vote *neigh?* Only time would tell.

When Jacque and I arrived we noticed that there were no *horse blankets* on the racks - only ordinary overcoats and ten-gallon hats. O.K., so it would be horse people and not real horses. It would still be interesting.

... I can't get off my horse - all day and night I roam among the cattle. I can't get off of my horse, 'cause some dirty dog put glue on the saddle . . .

Horses and I never hit it off well. They like to step on me or bite me, so I've held my riding to a minimum. It probably cost me the governorship. If I'd only been an expert horseman, I could have ridden into all the rodeos, tall (short?) in the saddle, to the cheers of the multitude. Instead I was towed in last by the mule wagon to the accompaniment of jeers and catcalls.

Anyway, the Horse Council was a good affair. We *dallied* around the bar and were served a couple of *snorts.* I didn't get *roped in* to talking with any boring people. The speeches were short.

After a brief stay, Jacque and I *saddled up, dug in our spurs and hit the trail.* The Horse Council had restored my faith in legislative receptions.

. . . Drifting along with the tumbling tumbleweeds . . .

Some of the Horse Council people took offense at the article. They should develop a thicker skin - maybe like a horse.

ACROSS THE CONTINENT - AT LEAST PART WAY

March 6, 1985

Wilder - There are some chores, so ghastly in nature, that they should not be thrust upon young people. Let the grizzled old veterans do them, and give youth a chance to enjoy life before facing the worst. That's the way they do it in old war movies and that's the way it should be.

Thus, when it came time to drive an old farm truck across Oregon, I declined to delegate the chore to my son-in-law. He's barely thirty and not ready for such hazardous duty.

Eastern Oregon trains state police, and they are ever at the ready. I had a farm near Vale for awhile, and we commuted daily. But we stopped sending the trucks in. Marker lights, mud flaps, signal arms, loose chains, windshield wipers - whatever decided to temporarily fail, would immediately catch the sharp eye of the Oregon State Police.

But in the spring of 1984, it became apparent that a farm truck trip was in order. I ordered some grape plants from a nursery located some 40 miles south of Portland. To insure that the plants would arrive in prime condition, it was necessary to go get them.

I would be the driver. I chose, for my vehicle, one very fine 1973 Cornbinder (International) truck. I took it down to Wilder's premier service station. It's the only one, and they went over my truck with a fine tooth comb. I noted also that the homemade mud flaps were pretty well intact.

I loaded up eight large onion bins and threw on a brand new tarpaulin. Well, maybe it was a year or two old, but it looked good. I also took enough rope to tie up a battleship.

An early morning departure set me winging. I'm a radio freak; I soon discovered that the radio alternately blared and went mute, unless the ignition key was in a certain exact position. That gave me something to do, as I had to move it every few minutes. The rest was routine, except for numerous gas stops caused by the Cornbinder's five miles-per-gallon gas consumption.

I wanted to get loaded up and return to Portland by dark - trusting the headlights would be stretching my luck too far. This was accomplished, but not without difficulty.

The nursery owner also had a small winery, of which he was justly proud, and he insisted upon a tour. But the plants were finally on the truck, packed in sawdust and watered down. Then I found that their sharp stalks would be sticking out above the crates and poking into my tarp.

Well, whatever. I made it about ten miles back toward Portland before the first rip appeared. With darkness gathering, I ignored it and stepped on the gas. After threading through a harrowing maze of freeways, I found a motel. It was late twilight - the canvas was well shredded.

Next morning at daybreak I took a taxi to a building supply, and sat on their doorstep until they opened. In possession of a hammer, a bundle of lath, and a box of nails, I then became a human fly. I didn't think the old bones had it in them, but I covered each square foot of exposed area, nailing lath to the onion boxes and securing the tarp.

Then down the road. What a great feeling. I had triumphed over the vagaries of fate. All I had to do was to keep adjusting the radio and pour on the coal.

I passed various policemen along the way but, in that truck, you can't speed much. They paid scant attention. Then, outside Pleasant Valley, a state trooper gave me a quizzical look as I passed by.

My pulsating radio had informed me that the wind was blowing 35 miles-per-hour, gusting to 45. It was at my back then, and I was afraid I had slipped over the speed limit.

But when he turned on those blue lights and pulled me over, that wasn't the complaint. My good homemade mud flap had been blown over the wheels by the wind.

The policeman was a gentleman and a fine fellow. I thought, for once in my life, I was going to get by with a warning. I might have, too, except that he wanted to see my driver's license. It had been expired for two weeks.

That's the best luck I ever had with a farm truck on a lengthy trip.

FORGET CATTLE - LET'S HERD THE 'HOPPERS

They're full of protein and crunchy, too

June 28, 1985

Wilder - I would never have believed it. And I wouldn't yet if it hadn't appeared in a leading Idaho newspaper. As we all know, that makes it true.

"Seven grasshoppers consume as much as a single grazing cow..." Gadzooks! This calls for some calculations.

The same article reported concentrations of grasshoppers up to 1,800 per square yard. But let's be conservative - we'll say 700. That's 100 cow-equivalents per square yard. There are 4,840 square yards per acre. The federal government plans to spray 5,000,000 acres. By our new grasshopper formula, we find that we are spraying an area with - let's see - [100 x 4,840 x 5,000,000] equals 242 billion cow-equivalents.

The Bureau of Land Management has been saying for years that we have been over-grazing our public land. That theory is now shot. We could have been grazing 242 billion head of cattle without doing any more damage than the grasshoppers.

The trouble with trying to graze 100 cows on a square yard is that their heads keep bumping together, so we'd better stick to grasshoppers. We have a potential bonanza here. All we have to do is find enough grasshopper herders.

Names will be a problem... In naming cows I'm partial to "Bossy," but there are a lot of good ones. With grasshoppers it's more difficult. "Hoppy" is good, or "Legs" ... "Jiminy" is excellent, but it's more of a cricket name.

The amount of protein we could generate each year staggers the imagination. Just looking at a grasshopper, you can tell that he is bursting with protein.

Market potential is unlimited. What's crunchier than popcorn? Deep-fried grasshoppers. We could sell to every movie house in the world. When I was a kid we used to squeeze grasshoppers to get "tobacco juice." This nicotine-free substitute would have the tobacco-growing states begging for mercy while millions of dollars would pour into Idaho.

If this enterprise catches on, Julia Child will no doubt write a "Grasshopper Gourmet" cookbook. This would probably spawn a whole new generation of diet books. Richard Simmons could dress up in a grasshopper suit while leading his group of overweights through vigorous routines.

We could also tag some of these hoppers and put them into an open-topped enclosure. Then we'd hold a lottery. The ticket-holder whose grasshopper jumped out first, over a ten-foot wall, would win the jackpot. The proceeds could be used to double the salaries of our teachers.

There would be so many hoppers left over that we'd have to find other uses for them. Maybe we could use them for livestock feed. I'll bet a cow could eat at least seven.

Predictions are that we'll have hordes of hoppers next summer. We must act fast.

In July 1985, I represented Idaho at a Republican National Committee meeting in Atlanta, Georgia. The politicians were OK, but I was more interested in onions....

THE SWEET SMELL OF A SCAM

July 6, 1985

Wilder - National party meetings are full of hyperbole, but the most outrageous con job Jacque and I saw was not in the political arena. It was at the Farmer's Market.

As an onion grower, I always head for the market when I get in the city. Atlanta has a world-famous one. The wholesale area is accompanied by approximately 1000 retail stalls.

Vidalia, Georgia has a national reputation for its sweet onions. Along with Walla Walla, and Maui, they are able to demand huge premiums for the product.

Vidalias are a delicate onion, with a very short shelf life. This year the area suffered almost a total wipe out from winter freezes. Therefore, the onions are in extremely short supply. Large ones are almost nonexistent.

But Vidalia onions were in conspicuous evidence at nearly all the retail stalls. They ranged in size from small to gigantic. They had one feature in common. They were all priced at the $50.00 per hundredweight, or higher, which supply and demand would indicate.

Obviously some fakery was going on, so I engaged in a spirited conversation with one of the most expert salesmen. He was on the elderly side, evidently with long experience.

"How can there be so many Vidalias when the crop was wiped out?" I asked.

His honesty was refreshing. "Any onion from Mississippi east is a Vidalia, son," he said.

I started examining the tags. The "official seal" guaranteeing that they were Vidalias, was produced in about fifty different styles. The lack of uniformity plainly proved that they were bogus.

My informant told me that most of the onions came from Texas, at a price of around $5.00 per fifty-pound bag, and then were resold as Vidalias at $12.00 for 10 pounds.

Not a bad business. But it was not limited to onions. "All these spuds are Idaho's," he said, with a wink. The empty cartons told the story. Most were grown in the South, including one brand labeled "BULL'S HIT."

A few Washington apple cartons were in evidence, but not enough to account for the voluminous displays of "genuine" Washington apples. There were mountains of watermelons. Fortunately they were locals, and were not being foisted off as California's.

So free enterprise reigns in the "Athens of the South." And, if imaginative marketing will do it, Atlanta will be a hard place to compete with.

The state of Georgia subsequently gave its Vidalia growers some muscle to deal with bogus imitations. If you buy a buy a Vidalia today, you can be reasonably assured it's the real thing.

In the farm crisis of 1985, a major cause of bankruptcy was high interest rates. It's hard to believe now that 15-20% interest rates were common. Here are some excerpts from a column I wrote then.

THE FARM CRISIS

Wilder- Recent monetary events have dealt a death-blow to some farmers.

For those of us farmers who were lucky enough to be reasonably liquid when the crunch hit, it has been a matter of casting off an illusion. Our net worth, on paper, has decreased substantially.

A nationwide study, conducted several years ago, depicted Idahoans as having the highest number of per capita millionaires of all the states. But a more recent one found a much different picture. Instead of 24,000 millionaires, Idaho now has 2000. That's no surprise to close observers of the agricultural scene.

It is hard to over-emphasize the tragedy that has befallen those farmers who were over-extended. But, for the remainder, we can appreciate even more the true rewards of farming.

Our wealth is in taking up a handful of soil and contemplating its productive potential; it is in being able to look at rows of young plants, visible only in the early dawn; it is to marvel at God's awesome power to radically change the weather and to gain the humility to adapt instead of fighting it.

And it is to watch a vine grow a foot a day from nothing but soil and water. Our wealth is to set our own hours, even though they are often from daylight until dark. We have the good fortune to work in an outdoor laboratory where the heat and the wind and cold may sometimes be severe, but where the beauty of nature is unsurpassed and the air is sweet and clean. We are a privileged lot. We mourn for our comrades who have been forced to bite the economic dust.

Each periodic crisis reduces the ranks of active farmers. I don't know when, if ever, the numbers will stabilize.

I am a San Francisco aficionado, having. visited there annually for 40 years. Therefore, I felt free to offer this critique

A SURPRISING SMOKE SCREEN

1985

Wilder - I gave up smoking those nasty cigarettes about 20 years ago. I reckon they're hard on your health and they're an irritant to non-smokers.

I still puff on a stogie now and then, which is even more obnoxious, but I try not to offend others. I certainly have no objection to non-smoking sections in public facilities and usually take that option if there's a choice.

Nevertheless, it left me breathless when the San Francisco City Council decreed that private office facilities must be segregated between smokers and non-smokers. I doubt that much of a problem existed, except in a handful of cases. Those could surely have been ameliorated under existing labor safety laws without adding the expense and turmoil, which will result from the ordinance.

The strangest part of the episode is that it occurred in San Francisco. That city, sometimes known as Baghdad by the Bay, has been stubbornly tolerant of every kind of human excess that can be dreamed up by its ever-changing populace.

San Francisco is a diamond among the fake gemstones which make up most large cities. Its unique bay, set against redwoods and lush greenery, gives it an almost unworldly beauty. The climate is stimulating but comfortable. The whole setting breeds creativity.

But some of this creative thinking has resulted in pain and degradation. I walked through Haight-Ashbury when the drug culture was enjoying its most favorable publicity. The toll on those pitiful young people was incalculable.

There were some notable artistic accomplishments by members of the dropout society but many paid a high price and some are still paying.

The city looked the other way, exhibiting its determination to accommodate any and all life styles.

Homosexuals found San Francisco's tolerance to their liking. Persecuted elsewhere, they have concentrated in the city. Approximately one in four San Franciscans now admits to being gay.

The effect on city government has been pronounced. Gays have demanded their wishes be met on a wide variety of issues.

Crime has taken a frightening leap in the Bay City. It's no longer as much fun to visit as it was when you could walk around the town night or day with relative safety. Our entire society has experienced a loathsome increase in crime but San Francisco has had one of the sharpest run-ups of all.

I believe the major cause is the tolerance factor. Guilty consciences are not in prevalence in the city. Doing one's own thing seems to include a wide variety of subjects both legal and illegal.

When Mayor Mosconi was gunned down in his office by a former city supervisor, the jury found the killer innocent of murder. They convicted him of manslaughter. The reason? He had been eating too much junk food and was, therefore, not responsible for his actions.

Law and order candidates regularly aspire to the San Francisco City Council and to the mayorality. They are just as regularly defeated.

That's why it seems incongruous that San Francisco, of all places, should segregate smokers in private offices. You can do about anything you want in that town. You can go see dozens of square flocks of strippers with no limit on outlandish sex acts. You can find and join every kind of a weird sect or cabal known to mankind but, by golly, you'd better not fire up a cigarette next to someone who doesn't have that vice.

I can just see the hardrock miners, fur traders and pirates who walked that ground a few generations ago. They're rolling over in their graves. "The city has gone to ruin," they say. "Just wait until the earthquake. That'll straighten "em out."

I've long since dropped the cigars too. I reckon the whole tobacco scene is bad for your health.

I was really angry when the Idaho Education Association threw me in with the Nazis and the Ku Klux Klan.

I'M NOT A NAZI

January 23, 1986

Wilder - I've developed a thick political hide over the years. When I'm attacked, I usually ignore it unless some good can come from a reply. I guess I could shut up and take this one. I'm not going to, however, because the teachers of Idaho deserve better representation, and the leaders of the Idaho Education Association seem to have a political death-wish.

The IEA has prepared an "education" film designed to show how unfairly it has been attacked from the "far-right." The film has been shown to teachers and community groups across the state. I requested, and was granted, a chance to view the hour-long program.

Right off the top, I was lumped in with George Hansen, "a convicted felon" and Tom Stivers, a man who opposed capital punishment by lethal injection because it was "a mere slap on the wrist." My qualification for joining this duo was the "Big John" comic book.

The film then went on to compare us with the Aryan nations, Ku Klux Klan, Nazis and Moral Majority, plus a potpourri of other real or imagined scalawags. Jerry Falwell doesn't deserve all that either, but he can fend for himself. I'm concerned now only with the lies and insinuations, concerning me, which were used in the narrative.

I'm particularly incensed with being included in the same barrel with racists. I'm a conservative and I have advocated a tight-fisted monetary policy for the state throughout my political career. But I've hardly been a bigot.

I authored Idaho's first comprehensive civil rights act and helped form the Human Rights Commission. This law and this agency have dramatically abated overt discrimination in Idaho. I've served on the Idaho Advisory Committee to the U.S. Civil Rights Commission. And I'll be a speaker at a ceremony commemorating Martin Luther King, Jr.'s birthday.

I've written a weekly column, on and off, for 20 years. It has a conservative fiscal tone, but a moderate social one. I've promoted field toilets and bargaining rights for farm workers and helped eliminate lie detectors as a condition of employment. My IEA critics know this, yet they choose to include me with Nazis and tub-thumping evangelists who get rich from TV.

All this could be excused as obtuse and pea-brained lobbying. It's not the first case, nor will it be the last.

What can't be excused is an outright lie. In this case, the film shows the "Big John" comic book, which became an issue in my campaign for the governorship against the incumbent, Governor John Evans.

Display of the booklet is followed by the ominous declaration that I refused to disassociate myself from it. Further, even though I was defeated for governor, I was still in the Idaho Senate.

Either the IEA officials can't read or they don't care about the facts. When the comic book was published, I said: "... I deplore, condemn, and disavow this type of campaigning."

Don Rollie, the Wizard of the IEA, called a news conference before I ever saw a copy of the book. He blasted the publication and predicted, sneering, that the next step would be for me to disclaim any association with it. Rollie, therefore, branded me as a mudslinger before I could even comment on a booklet I had not seen.

The poison spread through the IEA by Rollie and associates was effective. One straw poll I ran showed 105 teachers for Evans and five for me.

What did this infamous book contain? Parts of it depicted Evans as a helpless creature being manipulated by big labor and educators. Although overblown, the gist of the cartoons was accurate, at least as much as other cartoons. However, it wasn't my style, and I said so. In fact, the Republican State Newsletter had published 10,000 copies of an issue which contained one of those cartoons. I asked that they be destroyed, and my party complied. The book survived, and I'm convinced that it hurt me, particularly with a little help from my IEA friends.

The sad part of the whole story is that the teachers are entitled to fair and effective leadership. They're a large group, depending heavily on governmental actions, and they deserve strong representation. They're not getting it from the leaders of the IEA and they will not until the general membership demands it.

Gross distortions, such as this film, only weaken an organization which has plenty of troubles already. Who suffers? Thousands of able, competent educators who are distracted from their occupation and legitimate goals. Inevitably, the real losers are the school kids.

Oh well, politicians are fair game. I came out all right. We finally came to sort of a truce. I addressed their state convention. They apologized for past actions. They still back mostly Democrats.

AN ARID SITUATION

September 21, 1988

Wilder - One of the nice things about living on a farm is that you have your own water supply. If everything goes well, you can use unlimited amounts of water at little extra cost.

However, when the pump breaks down, you don't have any water - not even a cupful. This results in great inconvenience and, sometimes, a cranky wife.

When we built our house, we also drilled a giant irrigation well. Our domestic well put out only a puny amount of incredibly hard water. The irrigation well, on the other hand, yielded a copious quantity of reasonably soft water.

The irrigation well sanded in, and we were forced to tap into a drain ditch, half a mile away, to get water for the farm.

But every cloud has a silver lining. We moved the domestic pump 800 feet to the irrigation well where plenty of culinary water could be pumped without disturbing the sand. This required a remote electrical apparatus, plus a lot of pipe and underground wire, which the mice and gophers like to chew on.

So, if the water goes off, there is a smorgasbord of possible causes.

Last November, I rose at 6:30, which was a little late. I was chairing a legislative meeting at 9:00 a.m. in Boise, an hour away. I'd have to keep moving in order to get there on time.

But first - a nice shower. I turned it on full force. Not a drop. Cold sweat broke out. This called for fast repair.

Donning only the bare clothing necessities, I grabbed a flashlight and screwdriver, and bolted out the door. First I reset the magnetic switch - no action. Then into the service pit to brush aside the black widows and check the pressure switch. It was okay. Next the fuses; ok.

I jumped into the pickup for the short trip to the well house. Black widows galore. I stuck my hand through the web and pushed the capacitor reset - nothing.

Back to the house, I disassembled the magnetic switch, being careful not to drop the parts into the Russian thistles. In the light of my flashlight, the contacts looked corroded so I scraped them with my knife. The reassembled unit still didn't perform.

It was 7:45. The jig was up. I took Jacque's hairspray and plastered down the ducktails. An old electric razor wrenched off part of my whiskers.

With my slicked down hair and pepper-colored stubble I looked like a combination of Junior Samples and Yasser Arafat.

I arrived at the meeting almost on time. A TV station had called. I phoned back and assured the reporter that this would be a deadly dull session. No pictures desired.

The State Personnel Administrators had invited us to lunch at the Ag Building. I tried to sit in a dark corner with little success.

The meeting droned on. By the time I got home, darkness was approaching. The pump had been fixed by a smart fellow, who had filed the points. I decided to go dirty until morning.

At 6:00 a.m. I enjoyed a luxurious shower and shave while Jacque got a few more minutes of sleep.

I fluffed up my sparse hair, stepped out of the bathroom and struck my best Tarzan pose.

"Ah, back to my old handsome self, again," I cried.

Jacque squeezed further down in the covers and pulled a pillow over her head. It takes a lot to impress some people.

Now that I'm a city slicker, I miss the farm somewhat, but also somewhat not.

Meryl Streep scared the country to death by demonizing apples treated with Alar. Later studies showed no health risk whatsoever was posed by that coloring agent. There is an understandable desire among consumers to refrain from ingesting any injurious substance, thus the interest in "organics."

"ORGANIC" FARMING

November, 1988

Wilder -- Everybody considers ditchbanks and roadsides fair game for chemical weed control. Farmers spray them with everything from moss-killers to brush defoliant. The ditch company and the highway people join in with anything they can legally use.

Thus, when the city folks descend in hordes to pick wild asparagus, they expose themselves to more chemical residue then they'll ingest in a lifetime of commercial fruit and vegetable consumption.

When Dad is laying on the ant powder and spraying the crab grass with soil sterilants, he's picking up a dose of high-powered chemicals. In the meantime, Mom is giving the flies an extra shot of insect spray. The close, inside quarters insure a toxic exposure thousands of times higher than it would be possible to obtain from eating produce.

Commercial fruits and vegetables are raised under a strict set of Food and Drug Administration rules. The resultant product is pure and nutritious. All objective medical studies have concluded that Americans would be healthier if their diet contained not less, but much more, fresh fruits and vegetables.

Yet, the question of raising commercial produce without chemical additives is worth considering. I am in the onion business. The chemicals I use are costly. I would be perfectly agreeable to saving $250-$400 per acre by eliminating them from my program. Here's what would happen if I went pure "organic" in my business.

I use large quantities of nitrogen, phosphate and potassium fertilizers. I often leave test strips with no fertilizer. The results leave no question. My yield would dramatically decline without them.

I apply herbicides at three different stages. If I eliminated these weed-killers, the weeds and onions would come up in one solid cushion. We would not be able to get domestic workers who would crawl on their knees to separate them. If it could be done, the cost would be horrendous. The remaining onions would be sparse and damaged.

We place organic phosphate powder along with the seed when we plant. Without this chemical, the onions would be heavily infested with maggots. The yield would be decimated and the storage quality debilitated.

Onion thrips attack the plant all during the hot, dry summer. Without pesticide control, the onion plant would shrivel and the bulbs would be small and deformed.

We raise a storage onion, which we market all winter. We apply a sprout inhibitor before harvest, which generally arrests sprouting until late March. Without this dormancy-inducing product, the onions would be unmarketable by December 15th.

We now produce 500 cwt. of beautiful onions per acre. The average is over three inches in diameter. They pass all purity tests. They have been touted by the medical profession as beneficial, not only in nutrition, but also in reducing heart attacks and circulatory problems.

Without chemicals, we would probably end up with 50-100 cwt. of scraggly, wormy 1 1/2 inch onions per acre. They would not store properly and they would sprout soon after going into storage. They would be produced at enormous cost.

The farmer receives about four cents per pound now for onions. After sorting and grading, they eventually sell in the store for 20 cents to 49 cents. Under strict organics, the farmer would probably need one dollar per pound and the retail store, because of high cullage, would need four to five dollars per pound. Domestic onions would be available only a short period of time. For the rest of the year, they would be imported from another country, which would probably pile on the chemicals at a much higher rate than we do.

Meryl Streep can afford $5.00 onions. She can also fly off to Australia and pick up a supply if domestics run out. But the average buyer can't, and we should not be deluded into the belief that the product we now use is unsafe. America's fresh fruit and vegetables are a tremendous bargain and they are also a healthful, tasty food, which should be enjoyed in abundance. The FDA should keep its strict tolerance rules, and everybody should eat a lot of fresh produce.

Do I eat the wild asparagus, too? But, of course. It's delicious.

Our Idaho farmers now average 600 cwt., instead of the 500-cwt. twenty years ago.

There are some good organic products and they are achieving increasing popularity. Our difficulty comes in defining "organic." The whole exercise benefits consumers by making us more aware of the need for edible products that are safe.

When I was 65, I was unduly pessimistic about my physical prognosis.

GRANDPAS AND FIVE-YEAR-OLDS

1992 -- Anna is five years old. She's a bright, affectionate child. She likes to sit up on Grandma's or Grandpa's lap. We read to her and she reads to us.

But, what she likes best is to have me carry her when we are outside. Always the picture of politeness, she will look up at me and ask in a soft voice, "Grandpa, will you pack me?"

Last summer, I developed a severe back problem. The doctor finally ordered me to complete bed rest. After I recovered somewhat, he forbade any substantial lifting.

Anna and her family came visiting again. The usual question was earnestly posed - "Grandpa, will you pack me?"

"I'm sorry Anna, I can't," I replied. A look of disbelief, followed by disappointment, crossed her pretty little face. She took my hand, and we had a nice walk, but it wasn't the same.

Next spring I'm planning to have the doctor whittle on my back, and maybe I'll be in good shape after that.

But Anna will be six by the time I recover. She'll be heavier, and she won't be so fond of being carried. She's the last of our grandchildren. I've packed them all, but I guess I'm through.

Where do the five-year-olds go? They're only here for a shining moment. What a wonderful age.

And, where do the Grandpas go? Over the hill, to be replaced by younger and stronger ones. They're entitled to their turn, too.

Well, I finally had the operation two years ago. I woke up pain-free and my back is as strong as that of an ox.

I could pack Anna just fine now but she just turned 13 and no teenager wants her Grandpa carrying her around.

Chapter 7—Potpourri/Jokes/Eulogies

Although I've spent an inordinate amount of time concerning myself with governmental policy, I've never believed that it was the most important thing in my life nor should it be for anyone else.

Oliver Goldsmith had it right: "How small, of all that human hearts endure, the part which laws or Kings can cause or cure."

So, in addition to applying myself to my family and farm, I've pursued a wide variety of other interests.

"Jack-of-all-Trades - Master of None" seems a fitting description for me. I've dabbled in poetry, composed songs, emceed a wide variety of functions, written newspaper columns and given several funeral orations. None will ever capture a prize, but they've been well received.

Music, in particular, has been a mainstay of my life. I wrote the following piece for Boise Music Week 15 years ago:

MUSIC

By Phil Batt

Music soothes the savage beast; yet, the bugle call, or the fife, or the jungle drum can lead men to almost certain death in battle.

Music is the nectar of the Gods; the food of love; the life of the party.

The human memory can seldom accurately recall what was said a decade ago, a year ago, even a month ago. Yet, it's common to remember, for a lifetime, the moment and place you first heard a song, complete with the exact arrangement and artist. This impact on the memory is not duplicated by any other stimulus.

Musical training is one of the most valuable of all assets. I had a complete high school career—including academics, student politics, and athletics. It was easy, at that age, to think that the success of our football team was the highpoint of our lives. Now it means nothing.

But what was it that lasted? I was lucky enough to get some excellent musical training. I played in dance bands and performed elsewhere.

I abandoned the clarinet for 25 years.

It's like riding a bicycle. Once you learn it you can bring it back throughout your life. Scientists now believe that music has a direct physical effect on the brain, separate and apart from other auditory impacts. I believe it. It's magic.

Dance band at University of Idaho, 1947.

Campaigning, 1982.

With Chet Atkins at inaugural event, 1995.

At Lionel Hampton Jazz Festival, University of Idaho, 1997.

With Jazz Angels playing for weary Boise airport travelers at Christmas, 1997.

Miner's Memorial, Osborn, Idaho.

Idaho's Centennial celebration, in 1990, included a song-writing contest. I didn't participate. They came up with a good song for a winner.

Nevertheless, I didn't think the historical significance was highlighted enough by the contestants. One day an idea came to my head.

I wrote "Centennial Idaho." It has since been performed by scores of grade school choirs around the state. It's a good song and the kids love it.

CENTENNIAL IDAHO

1

Moderately

By: Philip E. Batt

Centennial Idaho 2

2. In the footsteps of Chief Joseph we have come,
Though no longer do we hear the warrior's drum,
Yes, we owe our native friends a princely sum,
For they shared with us this land called Idaho.
Chorus

3. In the hills of Boise County gold was found,
And at Wallace precious ore was underground,
Miners' picks played sweet music all around,
And the sourdoughs found wealth in Idaho.
Chorus

4. As the pioneers cleared sagebrush from the plain,
And they found that on the desert it won't rain,
Mighty reservoirs were built to retain,
Cooling water for the crops in Idaho.
Chorus

5. Now our wild west mode of living's not the same,
City lights have made the frontier life more tame,
But there's still high adventure in our name,
For the next hundred years in Idaho!
Chorus

As my campaign for governor headed down the stretch, I reflected upon the contributions of my dear wife, Jacque, and wondered how I could show her my appreciation. I wrote the "Jacque Elaine Waltz." It was played at our inaugural ball and in various other venues. Herewith, I present it:

JACQUE ELAINE WALTZ

By: Philip E. Batt

Jacque is pronounced "Jack" and is used thus in this song, although she also goes by the pronunciation "Jackie." This song is reproduced in the key of "C." However, it is much easier to sing in "F" and I will send such an arrangement upon request.

My hearing has steadily deteriorated. I'm worthless without my hearing aids and even when I'm using them I miss a lot of subtleties in sounds emitted at natural levels.

I like to get in my car (alone), and turn the volume up. Whether it's a Chopin piano interlude, or the booming bass guitar of "Hot Rod Lincoln," I play my favorite passages through 10 times, nay 20 or more, until I've savored every last nuance of the music.

Last year, I started working on a musical play based on Idaho's history, particularly the Lewis and Clark expedition. Laziness has set in, and I'll probably never finish it.

I've written limericks and other doggerel since my high-school days. Most of it was mercifully destroyed upon receipt by the person to whom it was presented.

But before subjecting my readers to the surviving examples, I want to present my best effort in the field of poetry.

On May 2, 1972, a disastrous fire exploded in the Sunshine mine at Kellogg. Ninety-one men lost their lives that terrible day. The tragedy affected me profoundly, as it did most people in the state. One of the hardest hit was Senator Art Murphy. Senator Murphy represented the district where the mining disaster occurred.

When I entered the state Senate in 1967, as a brash flatlander freshman, I immediately struck up an alliance with Senator Murphy. I don't know why he took me under his arm...maybe he sensed that I would take a leadership role in the Senate.

Whatever the cause, Art named me his little partner and set out to teach me the rules of decorum and to care more about people.

He was the elder Democrat statesman and I was the impatient Republican lieutenant. We teamed up on several legislative matters and it was mainly through our efforts that the regressive tax on oleomargarine was repealed. He also helped me immensely in getting a reasonable civil rights law put upon the books.

Senator Murphy gave me a daily grade as to my progress in presiding over the Senate and in other leadership matters. He finally promoted me from "Little Partner" to "Little Giant."

Art's health was failing rapidly and I yearned to repay him for his kindness to me. Then I thought of the disaster and of Art's love for his lost friends.

A few mornings later I woke up and the framework of the poem concerning the fallen miners was complete in my head. God had given me my present for Art Murphy. I wrote it in less than a half-hour and presented it to Art on the Senate floor.

I was humbled more than I can say when it was added to the miners' memorial. That memorial, at Osburn, Idaho, is a huge replica of a miner and his drill. (A smaller version is on display in the Capitol building.) It is awesome and beautiful. Widows and mothers of lost miners sold charms to tourists in order to raise enough money to pay for the plaque, which is etched with my words:

Our tongues have not tasted the bitter dust
The roar of the drills has never reached our ears.
Unfelt to us is the darkness of the shafts.

Yet we are Idahoans
    And we were miners then.

We are farmers

    We run the water from melted snows
    Onto parched desert soil.

    The planted seeds take root and grow
    The harvest fills our granaries

The pits are strange to us
But we are Idahoans
And we were miners then.

We are loggers

We are your neighbors
We share the high country with you

But we sing our song
To the buzzing of the chainsaw
And do our dance on the spinning logs.

There's no room in the mine
For our trees to fall
But we are Idahoans
And we were miners then.

We are cattlemen, innkeepers, merchants,
Men of the law and men of the cloth
Ours are a thousand trades
But only you go into the bowels of the
Earth to do your daily chores.

Yet we are all Idahoans
And we were miners then.

Yes, we were miners;
We waited in spirit at the mouth of the pit
Ached in unison at the news of the dead
Joined the jubilation at the rescue of the living
Marvelled at the poise of the tiny community.

And we became strong
The flux of the widows' tears welded
Your strength into our bodies.

And we were all Idahoans
And we were all miners
And we were all proud.

Ten years later, I gave a short talk at the memorial site. I reflected on the history of the incredibly rich but challenging mines in the Silver Valley of North Idaho. This is some of what I said.

What pain this valley has suffered!

The immense wealth under these mountaintops has spawned mining activity for nearly a century. But the earth has never yielded its treasure without exacting a price from those who work it.

Fortunes have been made and lost within the confines of the Silver Valley. Small investors have become millionaires through pyramiding purchases of penny stocks. Ironically, large national corporations have sometimes had to throw in the towel because their enormous investments failed to turn a profit.

It is a gamble for the hard rock miner, too. Those who tear at the ore seams and labor in the tunnels receive their rewards. They also pay with sweat and toil and sometimes much more - - - even with their lives.

The earth's surface groans and creaks and changes with the activity below. In this respect, much improvement has been made. Decades ago the greenery withered and expired from the discharges of the smelters. Now, most of the landscape has been restored and prospects for further gains are good. The river, which once lay dead from mine tailings, has made a remarkable recovery and will likely regain most of its vigor.

For the men who work the pits, progress has also been made. The labor is still hard, but not as difficult as in the early days. Safety has improved both in regulation and in practice, although our ceremony today sends us the chilling reminder that we have not done well enough.....

Twelve years ago, during a visit to San Francisco, I picked up another California craze, "Califinitions," which I used in one of my 1987 newspaper columns.

'IDANITIONS'

The San Franciso Examiner has been running some "Califinitions," in which the names of California cities are used to define certain nondescript things.

For instance, Topanga: That span of time between stubbing one's toe and feeling the pain. Or Cucamonga: A home for mentally disturbed dogs.

Whatever the Golden State does, the Gem State can certainly imitate, so here goes.

ACEQUIA: What I do when I'm "it" in hide and seek.
BURLEY: Feed grain with a Southern accent.
CALDWELL: A place to get a cool drink.
CATALDO: Second part of an alley quartet.
CULDESAC: What you do when the potatoes go bad.
GOODING: The best place for a bell factory.
HAGERMAN: A gent dressed in fancy jeans.
HOMEDALE: What you shout at your dog, Dale, when he chases your car.
JULIAETTA: What Julia did at dinner.
MALAD: Milady's mate.
MOSCOW: That part of the herd that belongs to Mother.
PARMA: Father of that cheese you put on spaghetti.
PICABO: A game ending with, "I see you."
PRESTON: A brand-new antifreeze.
SHOSHONE: Past tense of shoeshine.
WEISER: A two-pack-a-day man.
WILDER: Homedale is wild, but the next town is Wilder.
WINCHESTER: What you shout at your horse, Chester, when he's coming down the stretch.

I mentioned that all "Idanitions" contributed by readers would be gratefully appreciated. I received several replies. These are among the best:

RICHFIELD: Better than Fairfield.
EDEN: Garden of bliss.
BLISS: Lost out to Eden.
HOLLISTER: Cattle van.
POCATELLO: Push button telephone.
HORSESHOE BEND: Smithys at work.
INKOM: Stamp pad necessity

About 1967 I became fascinated by Ben Franklin's "Poor Richard's Almanacks." When I thought back on the many arguments that had taken place in the 39th Session of the Legislature, several of his sayings seemed appropriate. But, as always, there are two sides to every question.

For instance, "A Spoonful of Honey will catch more flies than a Gallon of Vinegar," but, "The Cat in Gloves catches no Mice!" By the same token, "He that would catch Fish, much venture his bait,"...but, "Necessity never made a good Bargain."

One must exercise some discretion in debate. You might say of your opponent that, "He has changed his one-ey'd horse for a blind one,"...but remember that, "Tho' the Mastiff be gentle, yet bite him not by the lip."

Being rather an impatient man, I do not care for undue debate on a matter. Consequently, I was reminded of 'Poor Richard's' sayings including: "Great talkers should be cropt, for they've no need of ears," and, "Here comes the ORATOR! With his Flood of words and Drop of Reason,"...On the same line, "Clearly spoken, Mr. Fog! You explain English by Greek,"...or, "A Word to the Wise is enough, and many words won't fill a Bushel."...Also, "Silence is not always a Sign of Wisdom, but Babbling is ever a mark of Folly." But 'Poor Richard' had a solution, as follows:

"The Tongue offends, and the Ears get the Cuffing," yet, "A Pair of good Ears will drain dry a hundred tongues."

Hasty decisions, or careless debate, can result in disastrous consequences. I have been reminded that, "He that lies down with dogs shall rise up with fleas"...or, perhaps more pertinent, "He that falls in love with himself, will have no Rivals." But, if you have done what you feel is right, at least you may have the consolation of, "He has lost his Boots, but saved his Spurs,"...or, "A hundred Thieves cannot strip one naked Man, especially if his Skin's off."

It is well, also, to avoid the bars, even though part of the action takes place there, because 'Poor Richard' advised, "Take Counsel in Wine, but resolve afterwards in water,"...and then admonished that, "The Royal Crown cures not the Headache."

Many bills are debated with righteous indignation. Proponents of certain legislation are looked upon by some as being immoral, or worse. But remember that Ben Franklin said, "There is no man so Bad, but he secretly respects the Good," and, "Clean your finger, before you point at my Spots." But, probably more to the point, "Many have quarrl'd about Religion, that never practis'd it."

If you have ambition for higher political office, you will probably be found out because, "Nothing is humbler than Ambition, when it is about to climb." Also, don't overrate your power of persuasion if you don't have the vote because, as 'Poor Richard' so aptly stated, "Don't think so much of your own Cunning, as to forget other men's: A Cunning Man is over-match'd by a cunning Man and a Half."

But, when the debate is over and the votes are in, "'Tis more noble to forgive, and more manly to despise, than to revenge an injury."...and, when you come home and the constituency asks why you were so obstinate, you can quote 'Poor Richard's Almanacks' as follows:

"To serve the public faithfully and, at the same time please it entirely, is impracticable."

What a man! Ben Franklin was a bedrock participant in forging our Constitution; a prolific inventor; gifted writer; and European diplomat. A lot of his accomplishments took place between 70 and 85 years of age. There's hope for me, yet.

But, let's get on with the doggerel:

For forty years I lived across the road from the Wilder Rod and Gun club. It had a much longer history than that and a fine tradition of camaraderie among trap shooters.

The gun club only operated in the dead of winter when no farm activity was underway. We would cook our own hamburgers and warm our frozen fingers and behinds in front of a roaring open fire.

In addition to competing for turkeys and other prizes, we would practice on a run of 25 targets. None of us were experts and it was a rarity when a shooter would break 25 clay pigeons in a row. Therefore, when one of our gang would reach 15 or more without missing, we'd all come outside and cheer him on.

Shaky Harris is a smart and affable fellow and a pretty good marksman.

He gets his name from his nervous mannerisms. When he converses with you he will impulsively grab your sleeve or poke his finger into your chest while making his point.

He's an astute card player but his excitable nature makes it hard for him to maintain a poker face. He's a great favorite among all his fellow trap-shooters.

One memorable day, Shaky was hot on the trail of a perfect shooting score. This poem tells the tale:

SHAKY AT THE TRAP

By
Phil Batt

'Twas the 19th of December
and a dark and stormy day,
when the Wilder Rod and Gun Club
put their trap house into play.

The wind howled like a banshee
and the snowflakes beat the door.
Shaky Harris ate his burger
and then ordered up one more.

Soon he fitted on his earmuffs
and his face became a frown.
He arose and left the TV
and he plunked his money down,.

For his shooting had been lousy
and his average was poor.
Only half a dozen shooters
could not say that they had more.

Now his eyes became determined
and his jaw was firm and set.
He muttered lowly to himself
I'll get those donkeys yet.

He stepped up to the firing line,
yelled "pull" and fired his gun.
The bird flew into pieces
Mr. Harris had begun.

Right and left the angles widened
but he gave them sheets of lead.
And the scorer sat in wonder
as he said "that bird is dead."

The others often missed their mark
as Shaky blasted on.
He beat Howard, bested Hoadley
passed up Richard, Bob and Don.

The targets turned to powder
and he soon had twenty-four.
All the others watched in silence
for he needed just one more.

As the bird came fleeting upward
Shaky aimed with eye so bold.
and he squeezed upon the trigger
with his finger numbed by cold.

Every eye was on the target
but there wasn't any doubt.
The bird was flying onward
mighty Shaky had struck out.

Ron Beitelspacher entered the Idaho State Senate from Grangeville at age 34, one of the youngest members on record. Ron is an intelligent person, conscientious and a little over-intense. He was a parliamentary expert and a stickler for the rules. We became friends and I felt free to salute him in poetry.

Thus, when his 40th birthday rolled around, I presented him with the following:

LIFE BEGINS AT FORTY

O Time in thy relentless flight
On Beitelspacher's shoulders light.
But gently touch our birthday friend
And happiness and mirth please lend.

At forty years, a youthful age,
'Tis time to start another page.
So give Ron wisdom, courage, wit
Life starts today - make well of it!

Senator Beitelspacher's penchant for strict adherence to the rules subjected him to unwelcome scrutiny when he inadvertently shot a bear out of season. He was, and is, a great outdoorsman and hunter who now makes his living as an outfitter. But his geographic sense failed him when he rationalized that his house was in a nearby area where bear season was open during this infamous incident:

BEITELSPACHER AND THE BEAR

Beitelspacher rose from sleep,
And looked out on his yard.
"Criminey!" He said, "I think
a bear I do regard."

"An insult to my hunting skills -
There's no doubt in my mind;
I'll grab my trusty firing iron,
And blow off his behind."

The mighty hunter aimed his gun,
And Bruin bit the dust;
Then entered in a pesky thought -
"Bear season's on, I trust?"

But 'twas not so, and Ron could see
His future in the jail;
"I'll sin no more, "the solon said -
They let him out on bail.

The jury members licked their chops,
And sent out for a rope;
To hang a politician, well,
'twas more than they could hope.

The judge, a lifelong Democrat,
Seized then the opportunity -
To give the hapless Senator:
Congressional Immunity.

By Philliam Battspeare

Ron Beitelspacher ran for the governership in 1994. He would have been my opponent, had he not lost to Larry Echohawk in the primary election.

When I was in Senate Leadership, one of my main duties was to bring the over-long legislative session to a merciful end.

A permanent issue was state regulation of daycare facilities. It was always a balancing act between affordable care and a safe environment for the children.

The question lengthened many a session. One year I wrote the following:

What's the issue of the week?
Day care; Day care

The main concern of strong and meek?
Day care; Day care

Right to Work may come and go
Firemen want the right to know

Investment credits may survive
College Presidents will arrive

Budget problems now subside
Successful lobbyists swell with pride

But Lo, one issue yet remains
It still is plagued with growing pains

Does this dilemma have an end?
Or will it once again extend

...The session - you unwelcome friend
Day care; Day care.

The struggle continues today. Now Idaho wisely requires more supervisors for infants. The other ratios generate hot opinions on both sides.

Sometimes I'd correspond with constituents by poetry. One of my favorites was Mel States, a disabled retired policeman.

I introduced Mel and his poetry in one of my columns:

SENACOTT OR NOT

November 9, 1988

The ravages of old age affect each and all of us, if we're lucky enough to live that long. Therefore, it's best to accept the inevitable infirmities with some good humor.

Among my long-time correspondents is a former police officer. He was wounded while on duty, and now suffers from various ailments.

He writes that he takes a laxative nightly, because he is partially paralyzed. Sometimes he forgets to take it. My friend says that his son thinks it's pretty funny when he wakes up at night and sticks his thumb in the cup to see if the laxative is still there. "Usually is," he adds.

The writer continues: "I do a few other things that make me wonder, too - like forgetting to unplug the heater cord on the truck. It's too hard to get back out of the truck, so I try to pull it out by backing slowly away. What really makes me upset is when the house comes along with me."

The best part about my philosophical penpal is that he has a great talent for poetry. Thus, he set his troubles to verse:

GETTING OLD I THINK

It's two o'clock when I wake up,
I think - Did I or not?
My thumb I stick into the cup,
And there's the Senacott.

I drink it and the cup I break,
My mind's completely dead.
Tomorrow with my bellyache,
I'll lay here on my bed.

I wonder, did I go to town;
And if I did, what for?
Now am I up or am I down,
And did I lock the door?

But all's not lost, I think I ate,
Tho' I'm not sure of that.
I'm either early or I'm late,
Now I can't find my hat.

I start the truck (forgot the cord);
Think I can pull it free.
The sparks sure flew, the engine roared,
The landlord yelled at me.

I think I went to get the mail,
At least I went to Star.
But I'm not sure 'bout heads or tails,
Came home without the car.

I wonder if I took my pills,
I think I ate my egg.
My body's full of aches and chills,
There's spasms in my leg.

I think that's what I did today,
But couldn't say for sure.
I guess I did or didn't. Say;
Did I write that before?

My poem-writing friend went to his reward during my last year as governor. I hope I can match his positive attitude as I advance further into old age. He was sometimes carried away with his opinions but they were colorful, to say the least. Another example of his poetry:

When I was just a little tad
Was probly eight or nine
My Pop and I we worked the farm
And really done just fine.

Now Pop was small but very strong
And also pretty wide
The cow step't on his big sore toe
He threw her on her side.

She "takend" out across the grass
Her tail straight in the air
And I went out to hed 'er off
I shouldn't have been there

The old fool ran right over me
And made me black and blue
And Papa couldn't stop the horse
So he ran o'er me to

I finly staggered to my feet
Sed go on I'm not hurt
He finly caught the ratty cow
And threw her to the dirt.

John Greenwad Snakespear

Then my reply:

Dear Mel:
As always, your correspondence is like a ray of sunshine.

One guy, who with me really rates
Is correspondent Ol' Mel States.

Though time has made his body frail
His pen can still tell many a tale.

Ill fortune only makes him smile
His sense of humor helps a pile.

When my good health has gone to pot,
One thing I'd really like a lot.

Is just to write like good Ol' Mel,
Instead of tolling a gloomy bell.

Very truly yours,
Phil Batt

It helps a lot when people write you a poem or a song because you know they care. When Sniffer, the first dog of Idaho, died during my term, my daughter Rebecca and her husband Randy wrote us the following song to the tune of "Sweet Betsy from Pike":

SWEET SNIFFER FROM ARMADA STREET

Oh, do you remember Sweet Sniffer from Armada?
He was so good, he did what he ought to
He was so funny and faithful and true.
Now Sniffer's in heaven and everyone's blue
Oh, do you remember Sweet Sniffer so fine?
Now he's playing with angels, all is sublime.
He's a young party poodle and feels no pain.
Goodbye, Little Sniffer, 'til we see you again.

He was 16 when he left us. He was a good doggie except once when he made a pile on the carpet in the governor's office.

I often marvel at the resiliency of our beloved country. Our governmental structure undergoes monumental changes to accommodate new technology - new problems and opportunities.

Yet the framework of freedom laid by our founders and zealously guarded by every succeeding generation has survived intact. In recorded history, no nation has ever duplicated our system. We live under the oldest truly free governmental framework and it is as strong now as ever before.

Our founders were unbelievably wise. They were also brave and selfless. Sometime during my legislative career, I delivered the following remarks to a group of inductees into the National Honor Society. As this later date, I don't know how much of it was original. The message is the same in any case:

SPEECH TO NATIONAL HONOR SOCIETY

I hope you will flash back in your minds to over 200 years ago, when this nation was being founded, under God, with liberty and justice for all.

Thomas Jefferson told us in his writings that on the day of our nation's birth, in the little hall in Philadelphia, debate had raged on for hours. The men gathered there were honorable men, hardpressed by a king who had flouted the very laws they were willing to obey.

Even so, to sign a Declaration of Independence was such an irretrievable act, that the walls resounded with the words, "Treason, the gallows, the headsman's axe," and the issues remained in doubt.

Then a man rose and spoke. Jefferson described him as not a young man, but one who had to summon all his energy for an impassioned plea. He cited the grievances which had brought them to this moment, and finally, his voice failing, he said, "They may turn every tree into gallows; every home into a grave, and yet the words on that parchment can never die. To the mechanic in the workshop, they will speak of hope; to the slave in the mines, they will speak freedom. Sign that parchment! Sign if the next moment the noose is around your neck, for that parchment would be the textbook of freedom, and the Bible of the rights of man forever.

The man then fell back, exhausted. The 56 delegates, swept up by his eloquence, rushed forward and signed the document, destined to be as immortal as a work of man can possibly be.

Fifty-six men, our Founding Fathers, were a little band so unique, we have never seen their likes since. They pledged their lives, their fortunes, and their sacred honor. Sixteen of them gave their lives in the war that followed, and most of them gave their fortunes.....Thirteen years later, those remarkable men we call the Founding Fathers had formalized their concept of government with a Constitution.

Probably the most important bargain between man and government incorporated into this document is the one that has been less appreciated and less talked about than the others. This is the overall concept that government exists solely for the benefit of the people; that government's only excuse for being is to guarantee that each individual will be protected by the collective might of his fellow citizens, if, at any time, his God-given, inherent rights are imposed upon, either by another individual or an outside force. If our leaders in government ever lose sight of that ideal, our people may lose their loyalty to our government.......

We are loyal to our government because our elected officials still respond to our wishes. Our government is still the servant - not the master.

Over the years, I made some frank, but complimentary, observations about the deceased whenever I spoke at a service. I hope I get the same treatment when I go.

Aside from my parents, the elder who probably influenced me most was my Uncle Percy, or P.G., as he was always addressed.

There were three brothers - my father John, Uncle Roger, and Uncle P.G. Roger and my father didn't attend school beyond the 8th grade. P.G. graduated from high school and received further training in the military. He even taught school for a while when farming was too tough.

He later returned to the farm and, in fact, became a wholesale vegetable packer (my chosen profession).

P.G. was a great philosopher and would gladly give you the benefit of his knowledge. I was honored that, during his final decline, he asked me to speak at his funeral.

Here are some excerpts:

You know the old folk song - when I first came to this land/ I was not a wealthy man/ but the land was sweet and good/ and I did what I could.

P. G. Batt was dirt poor when he came to this land. He lost his first farm and taught school in order to pay off his debts. But he came back to the soil and it was sweet and good. He did what he could and he became reasonably wealthy in monetary terms. But the gains he brought to others and to himself were mostly in the form of improvements - to the economy - to the quality of life - to the enhancement of the soul.

It is not correct to call P. G. a farmer - nor a businessman, because he was first and foremost a teacher. I already mentioned that he taught in the classroom (his pupils included his future wife Cornelia.) But he also taught farming; taught produce packing; taught banking and commerce; and - most importantly - taught self-improvement.

He and his brothers relished the new and untested and the smell of sagebrush excited them considerably. They were all pioneers, but P. G. was the strongest disciple of motivation.

He was in great demand as a performer at local functions, and he didn't waste the opportunity to motivate. One of the vivid memories of my childhood is an IOOF lodge program where P. G. gave a rendition of "The Little Train Who Could." P. G. gave an animated performance as the "I think I can's" became "I know I can" and Little Toot scaled the mountain.

He scaled many a mountain. When he decided to do something it was time to get out of the way because no obstacle was going to stop him. P. G. took charge of a struggling insurance venture and turned it into a large, healthy company. He was a pivotal member of the Board of Directors when Idaho Power Company changed from a sleepy local business to a corporate giant.

I benefited the most from P. G. when he had his office in Wilder. I stopped in regularly, sometimes daily, in order to solicit wisdom and advice. It was a teacher-pupil relationship. Oftentimes he'd throw his feet up on the desk and expound about the topic of the day. While he was free with his opinions, he expected input from the student also. I put in my share, and sometimes we argued with great vigor. But it was always objective, interspersed with gales of laughter. He was a happy warrior and he practiced his own advice to be constructive and cheerful. Sometimes we'd give a third party a going over, but he insisted on looking at the good points as well as the warts. Then we'd have another good laugh.

P. G.'s activities in the produce business are legend among the old-timers. "His word was as good as gold" is a phrase I often heard to describe him. Krackengood lettuce and Idaho Pals potatoes were big names in the trade during his packing days. What I liked best though, was that he always had a lunch stand in his shed and I could buy a hamburger with half a cow in it for a nickel. When packing season was on I never had to take a lunch to school.

Uncle P. G. had his formula for the correct way to spend the stages of your life. First you raised your family - then you tried to make money

- then you entered civic and political life - lastly you reflected and contributed toward a better society.

He ran for the Idaho House of Representatives one time. "They elected all Democrats," he told me. Not wanting to waste time dealing with what he considered bad judgment he dropped the matter, but he maintained a keen interest in politics and served as an avid rooter for me. He didn't mine giving me a good lecture, however, when I voted for a power plant siting bill contrary to Idaho Power's position. When I sent out my first fundraising letter in the gubernatorial campaign, he promptly returned $25. I sent another letter, telling him I had large expenses and that we had a thousand-dollar club. Within two days I received another check for $975. He wanted to be in the game, he just had to find out the stakes first.

I visited him at his home a few months back. He gave me some valuable advice. When we got around to his status, he had absolutely no complaints. He did say however, "When you reach my age, you fade into insignificance." It's true that the poor vessel of a 91-year-old body is rather unimportant, but there is nothing insignificant about the impact P. G. Batt has had on Idaho. His intelligence, his wit, his constant goal of progress and improvement, have enriched all our lives. Thanks, P. G. Thank you, teacher.

Let me offer this anonymous prayer.
Loving God, hear this plea to Mother Earth:

Dear Earth, remembering his long toil on thee
Let Percy George in thy lap recline.
In thee he planted many a tree,
Filled thee with corn, and dressed thee out with vine.
His water channels too to thee he led,
Whence fruit and herbs thy soil in plenty gave.
Then, in return, lie soft on his gray head,
And let spring's flowery herbage deck his grave.

Amen

My friend Willie Stevenson met an untimely death. His horse reared up and rolled over backward, crushing the life from Willie.

I started his eulogy with a quote from Edna St. Vincent Millay:

Down, down, down, into the darkness of the grave
Gently they go, the beautiful, the tender, the kind;
Quietly they go, the intelligent, the witty, the brave.
I know. But I do not approve. And I am not resigned.

When I heard of Willie's death, I wondered why. I did not approve. I was not resigned. He was my friend. Why did he have to die?

But after some reflection, I not only can accept it, but also see the wisdom of it. Death is merely a phase of eternal life and Willie is now with God.

The youngest babe will certainly perish from this earth. If it were not so, most of the worthwhile aspects of life would have no meaning. There would be no reason to marry and have a family, to obtain an education, to care for the old and unfortunate, to earn a living, to tend a garden, or care about one's parents.

Life on earth would have no value without death. Therefore, our concern should be with the quality of one's life, no matter how many years it covers........

It's much easier to accept death when the departed has lived a full life span.

Bill Norberg was my neighbor. I submitted these remarks for his funeral:

....Bill was an impeccable dresser. In his younger days he had a flair for bow ties, occasionally set off by a decorative shirt stud. This led to me giving him the title of Daddy Warbucks and its shortened version, Daddy-O. Some of us used that term to address Bill for many years. Of course, my children used it also, until Bill pulled little daughter Leslie aside one day. He said she really should not call him that, lest people get the wrong idea.

Bill Norberg did not suffer fools gladly. A certain con man came to Wilder and took over the newspaper. The Wilder Herald had only used banner headlines for such events as Pearl Harbor. But now, week after week, three-inch headlines announced such doubtful events as "Cat killer roams Wilder." Feature stories included a drive to raise money for Christmas lights for impoverished Wilder, and the exciting news that a large shopping center was about to locate here. To top it all off, the publisher was going to build a mansion in Wilder, complete with all the trappings of royalty and five bathrooms.

Bill Norberg and Bob Bushnell pondered this nonsense for awhile. One dark Saturday night, a troop of acquaintances descended upon Wilder and, at the main intersection, left a replica of the mansion - a picket fence - a mailbox - and an outdoor toilet with five fur-lined holes. The publisher flummoxed on for a few weeks, but it was clear he had been exposed. He departed Wilder, leaving debts and proof of his deception behind.

Bill was a conservative. But he did not just preach it - he practiced it. He was deposed from a County Commissioner's seat after he refused to accept wasteful suggestions for depleting the County treasury. Later, he was appointed head of the Farmers Home Administration for Idaho. When some clients did not repay their loans, Bill held them accountable. He did not believe his job was to loan your tax money to impossibly risky borrowers. Furthermore, when advocates for the defaulters took him to task, he held his ground. He was a man of great compassion, but firm principles. He did not view government as a grab bag for special treatment.

I'll see you on the other side, Daddy-O!

To my dear sister, Emma, at her funeral:

.....Emma was a delight to all. Smart, pretty, affectionate, helpful. She made a multitude of friends wherever she went.

She advanced two grades in one year - ended up Valedictorian of her class. She was a Maypole Dancer, and May Day Queen. She was Emma May - everyone's favorite person.

Although her adult life had some tragedy, she was a dependably positive person. She took whatever turns life gave her - and made the best of them.

She was the consummate sorority sister, maintaining close ties with her classmates until her death.

She was a gifted teacher; a superior editor; and a prolific and interesting writer.

While not prone to pick a fight, she also could hold her own during an argument. She would politely grant you the validity of your point, but then proceed to show you the error of your reasoning.

She was kind to all of us - protective of her family and concerned about fair treatment for all mankind.

The world is better because of the life of this wonderful person.

Sleep well, Little Sister.

Edith Miller Klein was the first full-time female practicing attorney in Idaho. She was a key member of the Legislature and had already staked out her territory when I entered the House of Representatives as an obnoxious freshman.

Speaking at her funeral I recalled testing her during my early days in the Legislature.

Some of us weren't very nice to Edith and poked a lot of fun at her. When Dean Summers and I were irreverent, Edith was good-humored to a point; then made sure we offenders paid the price. I soon recognized the error of my ways and eventually Edith and I became good friends.

She was a most effective feminist but despised the baseness practiced by some women's rights advocates. Her work inspired hundreds of women to take up law. She was a small woman, but fearless. When she led the Judiciary and Rules Committee in the Senate, if the panel voted differently than her wishes, she swiftly asked them to start from the top and take the debate all over again.

She was a great booster of mine and rescued my faltering gubernatorial campaign. I was running short of the cash needed to maintain my momentum. I had invited 18 supporters to the Arid Club, mostly giants of industry, to see what we could do. Edith had already given far more than she should have. But she stood up and said she was doubling her contribution. Then, looking them in the eye, she said: "And I expect the rest of you to do the same." They were taken aback, but eventually they did.

As Velma Morrison said at Edith's funeral: "Farewell to a great lady who embraced death willingly with peace, serenity and courage."

Jacque's brother, Bill, was a U. S. Forest Service supervisor and, as such, served in various parts of the country, including Washington, D. C. He died in Missoula, Montana last year.

To Bill:

Bill Fallis was a kind, gentle, positive and helpful man. He never seemed to hold any animosity toward anybody even under mild provocation.

He didn't show too much mercy, however, for fish and game. He spent a sizable slice of his life in pursuit of the wily deer and elk, or casting a line for various kinds of fish.

Bill's appetite for the outdoors extended far beyond hunting and fishing. He liked to camp out for extended periods of time. He and some friends contracted to remove an entire cabin from the wilderness on foot and by horseback.

He had a permanent love affair with horses - some were fine animals - others were worthless, but he patiently cared for them all. It is ironic that one horse bucked him off in the mountains, causing serious injuries at the outset of his decline into bad health.

His travels, as part of his job, took him to various parts of the country, including Albuquerque, Spokane, Missoula, Richfield, Utah and Washington, D.C.

In Richfield, Bill, Dorothy and kids were among only a handful of non-Mormons. There was even some polygamy practiced there - not by Bill, however.

In Washington, D. C., Bill never got used to the bureaucracy but served loyally, as always.

He spent all of his young adult life devising ways to cut down trees efficiently. Then the mission changed to emphasize conservation. When I questioned that early on, Bill told me, "Maybe the environmentalists have a point." He was, of course, correct.

One time, in Washington, D. C., Dorothy, Jacque, Bill and I started looking up all the past Presidents. Then we toasted each one with a sip of wine. When we ran out of Presidents, we started on the Vice Presidents. It was a good time.

Bill was a role model, a mentor, and an inspiration for Jacque. He trained her in track and she ran like a deer. She shared his love for horses. She adored him as most of us did who were privileged to know him. His ravaged body is now at peace.

You've served us well, Bill Fallis.

Percy George Batt. Uncle P.G. taught me about many things.

My sister, Lt. Emma Batt Kurze, U.S.N., widowed in the Big War

Jacque's brother, Bill Fallis, U.S. forest manager extra-ordinaire.

My handwriting isn't the greatest. My signature is not bad, but it should not be sent for interpretation without letterhead accompaniment.

Programs in the Dodge National Circuit Finals Rodeo in Pocatello carried a message from the governor. I had sent a cover letter along with my message but it didn't make its way to the printers.

Therefore, they merely had my signature, which they made out to be PHILIP E. SATO. (See Below.)

Try printing name next time, Gov. Batt

Idaho rodeo guides read 'Gov. Sato'

By Tim Woodward
The Idaho Statesman

Introducing the governor of Idaho, the honorable . . .

Philip E. Sato?

Forget Phil Batt. To rodeo fans across the country, Idaho's governor is Philip E. Sato.

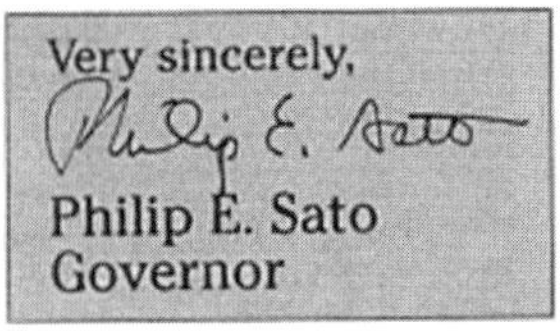
Very sincerely,
Philip E. Sato
Governor

dent of the Pocatello Frontier Rodeo Committee. "Batt sent his on a piece of paper with no letterhead or anything. It really does look like Philip E. Sato."

Gov. Batt

Amy Kleiner, Batt's press secretary, said the signature was accompanied by a cover letter, which apparently wasn't forwarded to the printers.

I received a lot of good-natured flak over this event. So much that I researched the signatures of a lot of folks, including several governors. Mine is among the most legible.

I learned the hard way that a Governor should not throw his weight around, even when it seems a practical thing to do.

Two volunteer firemen were trapped in a terrible range fire near Kuna and lost their lives when their truck stalled.

All of southwest Idaho was in mourning and I thought I should attend the funeral of these good men. A large outdoor ceremony was planned. Firemen brought their pumpers and other vehicles from all over the Northwest.

I wanted to get there in plenty of time so as not to divert any attention to myself because of a late entry. Therefore, I planned to leave at noon for the 1 p.m. ceremony. I figured the ride to Kuna would take no more than 25 minutes.

But it was one of those days when you couldn't just up and leave the office. Important decisions had to be made and a Russian diplomat was arriving at 11:30 a.m.

I didn't usher the Russian into my office until 11:40 a.m., and instead of the usual half hour visit, he wanted to give me the whole load, talking about the Aral Sea and coal mining in Siberia.

At 12:25 p.m., I finally made it out the door. I usually drove myself to my appointments, but on this occasion a loyal member of my staff was at the wheel.

I instructed him to proceed without delay. That's when I made my mistake. If we'd merely sped down the freeway, the troopers probably would not have pulled over my car, with its #1 license plates. But I foolishly got on the police radio and asked them to cut us a little slack.

We arrived about 10 minutes before 1 p.m., and I took my seat for the ceremony. They were waiting for some relatives and the service didn't start until after 2 p.m.

Later that day, I got word that a TV station had been monitoring the police radio and that the evening news would carry my request for special treatment.

I was caught and I had no good excuse. All I could do was admit I was wrong.

I wrote the following poem, which The Idaho Statesman dutifully reproduced for the public.

WHILE RIDING IN YOUR CAR

As Governor, you'll quickly learn
That you weren't elected czar.
So you must follow the rules of the road
While riding in your car.
If nuclear waste is on your plate
Discussion of it will have to wait.
For the Governor mustn't be running late
While riding in his car.
If a Russian official lengthens his stay
And the next appointment is far away
You had just better grab the wheel and pray
While riding in your car.
The people are fond of making jokes
If the Governor calls the dispatch folks.
So leave that radio set alone
If you're over the limit, you're on your own.
You can't ask the troopers to turn away.
If they give you a ticket just shut up and pay.
So do better work in planning your day
While riding in your car.

The whole affair was embarrassing but I brought it on myself. Excerpts from a Lewiston Tribune editorial are accurate and appropriate:

Look! It's a bird! It's a plane! It's a speeding Batt!

.....The speeding laws exist to keep your speed under control because you could hurt somebody.

But Phil Batt knows that. He just wasn't thinking Thursday when, uncharacteristically, he tried to pull a little rank to cover the fact his driver was speeding. They were late for a funeral, a funeral for two Kuna firefighters. The governor was apparently concerned that it would be rude to barge into the middle of the service. He didn't want to be a distraction. He didn't want to make a scene. His good heart was showing.

But the same is true of practically everyone who has ever been late for a funeral. That is no license to press your luck and the luck of everybody else on that road.....

As a rebuttal to the activities of the publicity-seeking members of the Hitlerite Aryan Nations located in Coeur d'Alene, a Human Rights Commission was formed.

It was called the Kootenai County Task Force. They held a celebration in April 1988. I was invited to speak and gave the following remarks:

"Where is Sid Dunagan's grandson?

He's not here. Sid Dunagan was piloting a bomber over Germany when Nazi gunfire hit him from below. He landed back in England, but he was dead when they removed him from the cockpit. He was 21 years old. He never had a wife and so his grandson is not here.

Where's Jack McGoldrick? He died in the Battle of the Bulge. So he didn't make it here tonight.

Where are the families of 15 of the finest of tiny Wilder, Idaho's high school graduates? None are here because all of those young men gave their lives in the Big War.

Why did this happen?

Because an evil maniac named Adolf Hitler hypnotized his country into a doomed battle for world conquest that eventually embroiled most countries and cost 40 million lives in battle and civilian casualties.

Where are the grandchildren of Dresden? There are few indeed because that city was consumed in a firebombing raid by our forces retaliating against the Nazi war machine.

Where are the 6 million Jews?

They were savagely removed from this Earth in a thousand ways. The gold was pried from their teeth. Their skin was used to make lampshades. They were shot at random by guards who were afforded the pleasure of target practice. They were stripped of their dignity and stripped of their clothing in the most disgusting fashion. Their children, grandmothers and friends were wrenched from their grasp, after which all parties were subjected to torture and mass extinction.

And now, here in Idaho, we count among our residents the Aryan Nations - and those who make up this wretched group wanted to celebrate Adolf Hitler's birthday with a public display of support.

What motivates these people? Do they think Sid Dunagan deserved to have his buttocks blown off? Do they think der Fuehrer was correct in subjecting Dresden to its fiery destruction? Do they think millions should have undergone the Holocaust because they made the mistake of being born Jewish?

Instead of marching, why doesn't the Aryan Nations give us the answers to my questions?

This city of Coeur d'Alene has unequalled natural beauty. When an eyesore occurs, there are plenty of volunteers to clean it up.

We have one eyesore that is resistant to improvement. That is the presence of irrational hatred and bigotry in our midst. We invite and we challenge the practitioners of this intolerance to come forward and explain their behavior.

Idaho and America have much in their history that cause some shame. Each one of us knows about incidents involving the native tribes, the Chinese workers, the interned Japanese, the African Americans, and more recently, the Hispanics. The history itself is not as important as what we choose to learn from it, and those are the lessons we draw on every day in thousands of ways.

Maybe the Aryan Nations is just another lesson. But it feels different, somehow.

Perhaps that is because it forces us to weigh our fundamental commitment to freedom of expression, however unpalatable that expression seems, against an equally fundamental belief that what Adolf Hitler stood for, and what he did, was evil.

The idea of a march celebrating evil is repugnant and it is not what Idaho stands for.

Coeur d'Alene, North Idaho and, indeed, the entire state are on a campaign for self-improvement. We want to know how we can convince this small group of malcontents to move on.

Maybe they could give us some answers.

I think Sid Dunagan and Jack McGoldrick and all those other guys from Wilder would want some answers, too."

Never one to refrain from voicing an opinion, however unpopular, I submitted the following column to the media regarding the controversial Military Training Range expansion near Mountain Home:

Training range part of price of freedom

Idaho is proud of every square inch of this state, and I am happy that various interest groups will go to great lengths to protect it from deterioration.

Nevertheless, we should be willing to do our share to defend this great nation. Idaho cannot exempt itself from its collective responsibility with the rest of the country. We cannot defend ourselves alone against aggression, which arises inevitably and regularly, from runaway foreign powers.

Therefore, in a state with our huge geographical mass, we should be able to accommodate some military activity. We now devote one-half of 1 percent of our land to the military. Washington has twice that rate, or 1 percent; New Mexico is 15 times or 7.5 percent; Nevada and Arizona are 10 times the rate, or 5 percent.

Sure, we want to protect our bighorn sheep and other wildlife and to keep the serenity of this peaceful region. But I have spent a lot of time in Owyhee County. I have watched cows and wild animals not even bother to look up when the occasional jet sweeps over. The bighorn sheep have done well in the Owyhees since their introduction several decades ago. There have been low-level flights all during that period.

I watched training maneuvers at Saylor Creek range in the summer of 1997. A very large antelope ambled up to our observation tower just as the Warthog airplanes screamed by, opened up with loud cannon fire and dropped their dummy bombs. The old boy drank from a nearby trough and ambled off, oblivious to the action.

The Air Force has negotiated every complaint and objection to the best of its ability. It has moved, reduced and kneaded its proposed range expansion whenever possible.

Now it comes down to whether the territorial objections will prevail or whether this reasonable expansion will be allowed. We love our freedom. We are part of these United States. We should do our part.

The late 1970's were some of my best legislative years. I was moving up in leadership and served as a negotiator for agreements between the two Legislative Houses as well as working through political discussions with my Democrat counterparts in the senate.

These lawmakers took their duties seriously. Practical jokes were in abundance, however. Here's one letter that showed up in my mailbox.

THE REVEREND ELTON JAMES RESCUE MISSION
534 West 11th Avenue
Mankato, Minnesota 56090

March 1, 1976

Dear Mr. Batt:
Perhaps you have heard of me and my nationwide campaign in the cause of temperance. Each year, for the past fourteen years, I have made a tour of Idaho to deliver a series of lectures on the evils of drinking.

On these tours, I have been accompanied by my young friends and assistants, Mr. and Mrs. Clyde Lindstrom. These young people of good family and excellent background are a pathetic case whose lives were ruined by excessive indulgence in whiskey, gambling and immoral couples.

They would appear with me at lectures and sit on the platform wheezing and staring at the audience through bleary, bloodshot eyes while I would point them out as an example of what drinking would do to a person.

Last summer, unfortunately, Clyde and Mary died. A mutual friend has given me your name, and I wonder if you would care to take their place on my spring tour?

Yours in Faith,

/S/

Reverend Elton James

I've never been the greatest orator, but I could usually hold a group's attention long enough to get my message across. I kept it short and direct and I often warmed up the audience with an old chestnut-type joke.

I called them farmer jokes, and most of them were. A lot of folks had heard them before, but that made them laugh all the louder as I built them up to their outrageous conclusion.

Sometimes I'd start by saying: "Just as I left home Jacque said, 'I hope you don't tell any farmer jokes,' or 'I walked over here with so and so and he said, 'Please, no farmer jokes today.'"

Then I'd say, "But, what the hell, I'm going to tell one anyway." That put the group in a great mood.

A few farmer jokes:

A farmer was taking his produce to town. His wagon was being pulled by his faithful old horse. The cart was filled with squash and melons and tomatoes and corn - the entire year's crop. The farmer and his dog rode on the top of the heap.

A city slicker, in his shiny red car, ran through a stop sign and - **WHAM** - there was a terrific collision. Produce, farmer and animals went flying in all directions.

As these matters often do, it ended up in court. The farmer was on the witness stand. Counsel for the defense said - "I'm only going to ask you one question - Is it true that, immediately after the accident, you said you never felt better in your life?"

The farmer shuffled around, looked down, and answered: "Yes that's true."

His own lawyer jumped up. "What are you saying? That was a serious accident."

The farmer replied, "Well it was like this. An officer showed up to investigate. He walked over to my dog - the dog was writhing in pain. The officer pulled out his service pistol and - **BAM** - there went the dog.

He then looked at my horse - the horse had a broken leg and other mortal injuries, the cop pulled out his pistol and - **BAM** - there went the horse.

Then he walked over to me and asked, 'By the way, how do you feel?'" ...That's when I said, "I never felt better in my life."

A little boy, caught in mischief, was asked by his mother, "How do you ever expect to get into Heaven?"

He thought for a moment, and then said, "Well, I'll just run in and out and keep slamming the door until they say, 'For goodness sakes, either come in or stay out!', then I'll go in."

Butch Otter and Cecil Andrus are great hunting companions. They've gone to the same place in the Owyhee Mountains for many autumns in a row. The farmer has always welcomed them because they take good care of the property - always close the gates, never make ruts, etc.

This past fall, they went again to the same place. It was Butch's turn to ask for permission. He went to the door; the farmer was gracious as usual.

"You folks are welcome here, but I'm asking you for one big favor," he said. "See that old gray mare over there? She's thirty years old, got the spavins, she's swaybacked and crippled. I can't bear to shoot her. Won't you do it for me?"

Butch replied, "Gosh, I couldn't do that, I'm too tenderhearted."

But the farmer pleaded and coaxed and finally prevailed. Butch reluctantly agreed.

On his way back to their pickup, Butch decided to play a trick on Cecil.

He jumped into the driver's seat and bellowed "Would you believe that after all these years when we've come here - took good care of the place and all - he won't let us hunt."

He spun around the barnyard, slammed on the brakes and stopped. "That makes me so mad I'm gonna shoot his horse," he said. He jumped out, leveled his rifle and -**BAM** - down went the horse.

He heard three shots behind him - **BAM** - **BAM** - **BAM**. "I got three of his cows," Cecil shouted.

A certain gent stayed at the bar too long. He wisely decided he shouldn't drive, so he called his wife.

"Honey, would you please come get me?" he asked.

"Where are you?" his wife impatiently queried. The man looked around and finally replied, "Well, right now I'm at the corner of Walk and Wait."

One blistering hot day when guests were present for dinner, a mother asked her four-year-old son to say the blessing. "But mother, I don't know what to say," he protested.

"Just say what you've heard me say," she told him.

Obediently, he bowed his head and said, "Oh Lord, why did I invite all these people here on a hot day like this?"

My hometown, Wilder, is full of great fishermen. But one fellow always came home with the most and biggest fish.

A game warden moved to Wilder. He did not reveal his identity. At the coffee shop, he became acquainted with the famous fisherman and arranged for an outing.

They pushed their boat out on Lake Lowell and found a likely spot. The fisherman pulled out a stick of dynamite, lit it up and tossed it into the water. After a terrific explosion, a great number of dead fish floated to the surface where the fisherman scooped them up.

"I'm sorry to tell you this," said the officer, "but I'm a game warden and I'll have to take you in."

The fisherman lit up another stick of dynamite, handed it to the warden, and asked, "Now are you gonna fish, or just sit there?"

The minister was walking down the street when he recognized the town drunk tottering along.

"Drunk again!" remarked the pastor.

"Me, too!" said the drunk, tipping his hat.

Two boys were riding a train for the first time. They took out their lunches shortly before the train entered a pitch-black tunnel. "Have you eaten your banana yet?" asked the first boy.

"No," replied the second. "Why?"

"Don't touch it!" the first exclaimed. "I took a bite, and went blind."

A burglar broke into a house. The parrot called out, "Jesus is watching."

The burglar started searching about for valuables - the parrot repeated, "Jesus is watching."

The burglar continued, "What does a stupid parrot know about Jesus?" he said.

"Sic 'em, Jesus," the parrot said to the giant watchdog behind the sofa.

An old hillbilly was driving down the road too fast and a highway patrolman pulled him over. "Do you have any I.D.?" he asked. The hillbilly replied, "Any idy about what?"

The golfer's ball rolled into a bunch of anthills. His first swing hit six inches ahead of the ball - the second six inches behind. Two ants popped up and one said to the other, "We'd better get on the ball or he'll knock the hell out of us."

A book agent, selling scientific agricultural books, called on an old farmer. The farmer thumbed through his wares and told the salesman he didn't want to buy them.

"You should buy them, sir. If you had these books you could farm twice as good as you do now."

"Hell, son" he replied, "I don't farm half as good as I know how, now."

Each day the children tried a different kind of meat, after which the teacher asked them to identify it. One day it was deer meat and no one could guess. "I'll give you a hint," said the teacher, "it's what your mother sometimes calls your father."

"Don't eat it," screamed a little boy. "It's Jackass!"

The golfer had reached the seventh hole when another of his foursome keeled over and died of a sudden heart attack.

Upset from the incident, and thinking of his own mortality, he later initiated a serious discussion with his wife.

"Honey, if I were to die, would you marry again?" he asked. His wife hesitated, deep in thought, and then replied. "Well, I'm young, I suppose I would."

He went on: "Would you live in this house?"

"Sure, I love this house."

"Would you use our bed?"

"I guess so," she said.

"Would you give him my golf clubs?" he persisted.

"Of course not, silly," she answered, "he's left handed."

Three hogs were lying in the sun on the hottest day of the year.

"I never sausage heat," said the first. "Me, either," replied the second, "I'm really bacon."

"I ham too!" added the third.

There's a bar out in the country, and some of us ride up to it on our horses. My friend, who thinks he's pretty tough, tied up his horse and went in and tipped a few. When he came out, he found that his horse had been painted yellow.

He charged back into the bar and shouted, "Who's the rotten, no good skunk who painted my horse yellow?"

An enormous, rough-looking cowboy rose from his stool - "I did," he bellowed. "So what?"

"I just wanted to let you know the first coat is dry," my friend lamely replied.

Two brothers lived in San Francisco. They were the owners of a cat, which was their prized possession.

It became incumbent upon brother #1 to travel to Hawaii on business. Shortly after settling into his hotel, he placed a call to brother #2. "How is the cat?" he asked.

"I'm sorry to have to tell you this," brother #2 replied, "but the cat got on the roof. In trying to rescue him, he fell off, and was killed. He's dead."

Brother #1, totally devastated, hung up the phone.

Next day he called San Francisco again and remonstrated his brother. "That was a terrible thing to do," said brother #1. "You should learn the art of communication. On the first call, you should have said: 'The cat's on the roof, we're doing our best to get him down.'"

"On the second evening you could have said: 'During the rescue, the cat fell off the roof and was grievously injured.'"

"On the third call, you could have said: 'The cat seems to be sinking, but we are giving him the best possible care.'"

"Then - on the fourth night you could have said: 'In spite of the most extraordinary veterinarian efforts to save him, the cat has, unfortunately, died.'"

"That's the proper way to communicate," said brother #1 - "and, by the way, how is mother?"

The reply came after a long pause. "Well, right now she's on the roof."

Butch Otter and I have done a lot of campaigning together. Last fall we were working the streets. We asked a lady for her vote.

She looked us up and down and then said, "Butch Otter, I wouldn't vote for you if you were St. Peter."

Butch, never at a loss for words, came back - "Lady, if I were St. Peter, you wouldn't be in my district."

Butch and I know that you can't quit campaigning early in the day. So, in the evenings, we register voters.

We were out one night registering voters. We were in the cemetery. I was holding the flashlight, and Butch was registering the voters.

"Look here, Butch," I said, "Henry David Thomas. We can get several names off this one - Henry Thomas, Thomas David, and so on."

"No," said Butch, "we've got to be fair - he gets one vote - just like the rest of them."

Three ladies were bragging on their adult sons. "My son is an accountant, and makes $85 per hour," said the first.

"My boy is a lawyer and charges $150 per hour," the second lady chimed in.

"Well," said the third, "my son is a preacher, and it takes four men to gather up the money after he talks for just one hour."

Three preachers were visiting with each other about the economic perils of their profession. They all agreed that their low salaries required a supplement from the collection plate.

"I have a very good system," offered the first. "I take the collection plate into the anteroom. I've drawn a line on the floor. I throw the contents of the plate into the air. Whatever comes down on one side of the line is the Lord's, and whatever comes down on the other is mine."

"That's a good system," said the second, "but I believe mine is superior. I take the plate into the anteroom. I stand on a chair and throw the contents into the air. Whatever stays on the chair is the Lord's, and whatever hits the floor is mine."

"Excellent, excellent," said the third. "I've refined it even further. I go into the anteroom. I toss the contents into the air. The Lord takes what He wants and what hits the floor is mine."

My son is a lawyer, and a good one, too. I have many lawyer friends. They're a fine bunch of humans. Nevertheless, they're fair game for jokes.

Pat and his wife Molly were out for a stroll. They wandered through a cemetery and started reading the tombstones. "Look at this one," said Molly - "Here lies a lawyer and an honest man."

"Shure and Begorrah," Pat replied, "They're buryin' em two at a time!"

The heirs were suspicious about their father's death. They hired a lawyer and he was interrogating the attending physician on the witness stand.

"Did you check to see if his breathing had stopped?" asked the counselor.

"No," replied the M.D.

"Did you check to ascertain that there was no heartbeat?"

"No," the physician continued.

"Do you mean to say that you signed the death certificate without checking for vital signs?" the lawyer pursued.

"Well," said the doctor, "his brain was sitting in a jar on my desk - however, I can't be sure he wasn't out practicing law somewhere."

The General, a West Point graduate, was skilled in military tactics. Nevertheless, he had enough faith in his shiny new computer that he consulted it on various and sundry occasions.

It became time to go into battle. The General inserted a question into the computer - "Shall I attack from the left or the right?"

Lights flashed, whistles blew, bells rang, and out came the answer - "Yes".

The General was impatient and angry. He submitted a second question - "Yes, what?"

Bells rang, whistles blew, lights flashed, and the reply came forth - "Yes, Sir!"

Back in 1970, when phone calls were only 10 cents, a certain candidate took his campaign to the streets.

He suddenly remembered that he had to make an important phone call. After determining that he had no change, he stopped the first man he saw. "Can I borrow a dime to call my friend?" he asked plaintively. The man gave him a sharp once-over, then reached down in his pocket. "Here's 30 cents," he said, "Call 'em all."

"Nurse, why are the shades down?"

"There was a fire across the street. We were afraid you'd wake up and think the operation was a failure."

Election night returns - the incompetent is ahead.

When I was Lieutenant Governor and John Evans was the Governor, he was not much for giving me important assignments. However, one day he called me into his office and said, "Phil, you've been going around saying I don't give you anything to do. Well, I'm tired of hearing that, and here's what I want you to do. Go out and count all the cattle guards in the state and report back to me, as soon as possible, what that number is."

I hustled right out and counted the cattle guards, and ran up the statehouse steps as fast as I could to report back to him. "Governor Evans," I said, "there are 14,382 cattle guards in the state."

"Golly, that's way too many," John responded. "Fire half of 'em." (That's just a joke, folks.)

A priest asks a dying man whether he had made his peace with God. "Yes," the man says. Has he renounced the devil, too? the priest asks.

"Father," the man responds, "in my position, I can't afford to antagonize anybody."

I'm an ordinary-looking fellow and I've had a substantial number of men report that we are look-alikes.

A man approached me one day and said, "I get people coming up to me all the time telling me I look like Phil Batt. You kind of look like him, too, does that ever happen to you?" "Yes", I said, "that happens a lot." He quickly came back - "Well, doesn't it make you mad?"

I hope I haven't made too many people mad. Most of us have had a good time together.

Epilogue

Mother Earth turns on her axis and every revolution brings change to each of her six billion inhabitants. All of these people have their own stories to tell. I'm pleased I've had the chance to review mine. The sun has passed over me more than 25 thousand times. I've been most fortunate to live in the finest state of these blessed United States and to have had a smorgasbord of opportunities throughout.

If I've had a constant in my life, it's assuming the role of a pupil. Here are a few samples of my learning processes.

When I was a small boy Santa Claus brought me a BB gun. I liked to shoot at paper targets but my limited funds were almost always exhausted after I'd purchased my BBs.

So, I sighted in on tin cans and small birds. There were millions of sparrows and a generous sprinkling of exotic varieties such as wild canaries. If I bagged an unusual specimen, I would strut into our house and show it to my mother. She'd dutifully admire the deceased bird, but would occasionally ask me if I didn't feel bad about killing such a beautiful creature. I learned to spare the exceptional varieties but continued to mow down the sparrows.

When I was older, my friends and I would go "sparrow batting." After dark, we'd shine a flashlight on the hapless birds while they roosted under eaves, or in granaries, then roust them out and dispatch them with ping-pong paddles while they flew toward the light.

The rationale was that they were damaging crops. Whether that was right or wrong is debatable. In any case, the birds have gone into serious decline from lack of habitat. A sparrow-batting expedition nowadays would not yield very many carcasses.

In high school, our agriculture class sponsored a pest-killing contest. Sparrows (bring in their heads) counted for one point, gopher tails fetched two points and a small payment from the government watermaster's office. Jackrabbits counted for several points when their fluffy tails were presented.

I had a good 22 caliber single-shot rifle. I have sent many hundreds of jackrabbits to their reward. Arena Valley, an area west of Wilder, was still covered with sagebrush and the rabbits flourished. They chewed on the crops surrounding the area but actually didn't harm them much.

In any case, I pursued sparrows, gophers and rabbits with great vigor and won the contest hands down. Rabbit hunting honed my rifle skills. I later qualified as an expert marksman in the Army Air Force.

In my later high-school years, I turned almost entirely to the shotgun. In the 1940s the daily bag limit for Chinese pheasants was four roosters and one hen. It was no trick at all to fill that quota after school.

As a young adult I continued pursuing pheasants, chukkars, ducks and geese. But they were increasingly hard to find and less of a thrill to shoot. When I brought down my last wild goose, the wounded bird flapped its wings, desperately attempting to become airborne. Its mate swooped down and tried to lift the large bird. I never shot another.

This is no indictment of hunting. It's a wonderful sport and builds character in thousands of young Idahoans.

Am I saying that the question my mother asked about killing those pretty things finally overshadowed my desire to do so? No, I'm just too lazy anymore. If a pheasant or chukkar jumped up right in front of me and my gun, I wouldn't hesitate to blast the bird. My mother would approve. She loved to eat pheasants!

Our Fish and Game Commission has a tough job. They must maximize fishing and hunting opportunities while respecting private property and protecting endangered species and non-game creatures. They usually end up pleasing few people. During my campaign for governor, I heard a veritable torrent of complaints about the way that our department was being run.

Looking back on it now, I can see that this was a fairly normal state of affairs. Each person who buys a license becomes an expert on fish and game management and nothing can please them collectively.

But I took the complaints to heart and promised improvement. After I got in office, I did a foolish thing. I asked each of the commissioners to submit his resignation. (I had that power under the law.) I had no plan to install my replacement members prematurely, but I thought that I could force those incumbents to address the complaints. There was no way they could effectively do so as there was little consistency to all the griping. Asking for those resignations was probably the worst mistake I made as governor. I quickly recognized it, withdrew the request, and apologized to the commissioners.

Bill Coors gave me some valuable lessons in the proper way to run a business. I started my relationship with Coors Brewing company at what was probably the most exciting time in the history of that great firm (see Life Story). They were only a year or two into an explosive expansion from a million barrels of production annually on their way to over 21 million barrels today.

The Coors family adhered to a hallowed tradition. The oldest male of the oldest living generation was in charge until his demise.

Adolph Coors II, at 90 years of age, still had veto power over all business decisions. Adolph III, his eldest male child, had recently been kidnapped and murdered in a tragic, senseless encounter. Bill Coors and his brother, Joe, the remaining sons, divided the duties between them with Bill in direct charge of the brewery.

As their first rapid expansion took off, Coors beer became a prized status symbol in many parts of the country among young people. It was distributed in only a few states, and a case of Coors would fetch an astronomical price at a college located in the eastern states.

Bill Coors was a perfectionist. The plant was immaculate - the ingredients were raised and prepared for brewing under the strictest quality control - the advertising was tasteful - the marketing strictly limited only to those consuming states that could be properly supplied.

There was a Spartan atmosphere surrounding the firm. There were no corporate airplanes - in fact, highly placed employees rode with me in my puddle-jumper to look at their high-country barley-growing area.

Bill Coors religiously attended each barley growers' meeting, emphasizing the need for quality and backing it with high premium payments for crops with outstanding brewing characteristics.

The venerable Adolph II looked upon domestic hops as decidedly inferior. The German Hallertaus had a distinct aromatic character not to be found in American hops.

But the German supplies were deteriorating in quality. Most came from tiny plots and by the time they were pooled for packaging, they often contained sticks, stones and other foreign material.

Bill Coors was convinced that the company should make the transition to American hops. But how could he do it without changing the unique flavor of Coors beer? Equally as important, how could he overcome the reluctance of his father to reduce the percentage of German hops in their brew?

Bill Coors, the innovator, included me in his solution. Along with his experts, I went to Germany and closely examined growing practices. Our conclusion was that the German varieties would have to be duplicated in America to obtain the desired characteristics.

This was no small chore. Obtaining authentic German roots and getting them to the United States was accomplished by means unbeknownst to me. Propagation of sufficient plants to populate a commercial hop farm involved some large and complicated greenhouse procedures as I've detailed in my life story. But Coors prevailed, even though we had to move the operation to northern Idaho. The University of Idaho experiment station developed new aromatic varieties. The Coors organization got its dependable hop supply, protected the integrity of its product and satisfied the big boss, Adolph II.

All through this arduous episode, I admired Bill Coors' patience and determination to succeed. I've tried to apply his teaching methods to my own business and political activities.

From Ernie Stensgar, Chairman of the Coeur d'Alene Native American Tribe, I learned that one should weigh circumstances before setting on an absolute course of confrontation.

My aversion to legalized gambling is thoroughly detailed elsewhere in this book. But, unusual facets of history merit a second look at tribal "gaming." It's only been a few generations ago that the tribes were herded onto the reservations. They were given certain guarantees in their treaties and the rest of us have not been consistent in honoring these promises.

Central to any discussion with the Native Americans is the question of sovereignty. Rightly or wrongly, the treaties give American Indians the right to regulate their own internal affairs. It's a gray area that is continuously refined by the courts. In general, where there is not undue oppression of non-Indians, sovereignty has been upheld.

Therefore, the U. S. Congress and federal courts have decreed that tribes will be allowed to carry out whatever gambling activities are legal for others in any state.

Nearly all the states, including Idaho, have initiated their own lotteries and the question most often posed is this: "What forms of tribal "gaming" can be carried out in comparison to a lottery?"

Advertising for our state lottery, and that of most states, highlights casino-like games. We also dispense lottery tickets by machine. Therefore, the tribes argue, their slot-machine-like devices are in conformance with the law.

Only a few years back, Idahoans voted to amend our Constitution to prohibit electronic devices in gambling. There is no question that this initiative was aimed at tribal gambling and it was easily adopted.

I doubt that it would pass today. The improvements in life for the tribes have been dramatic and negative effects on other Idahoans seem to be minimal.

But, back to Chairman Stensgar. Ernie is not a polished speaker. Yet, he is eloquent in his own way. He is not afraid to bare his inner feelings. They reveal a sense of outrage that tribes find themselves in such desperate straits. But he also exudes politeness and hope and a desire to cooperate in any constructive fashion

He informed me that his son was in jail. And, while he didn't excuse it, he said that the squalid circumstances and lack of opportunity prevalent on the reservations when his boy was growing up led to serious drug abuse.

Soon after its gambling enterprises took hold, the Coeur d'Alene Tribe started putting money into improvements. They gave, not only to their own schools, but also to other public schools. They set up additional scholarships, allowing tribal members to attend college. They improved their police departments and upgraded tribal facilities. As far as I know, no profits have been allotted for anything other than public improvements.

All this could change, of course. But I see no selfishness emerging at this point. I'm willing to leave it alone for the moment. And I'm sure Ernie Stensgar is, also. His son is gainfully employed at the casino.

What's it like being a governor? It goes without saying that it's a fascinating position to find yourself in. It provides an opportunity to push the state in a direction that you think will be beneficial. It's scary, too. You're expected to make hard decisions from the moment you set foot in the office.

The power of the governorship varies with the occupant. I had no desire to obtain any kind of royal status, so I downplayed the ceremonial aspects of my service.

I believe that my forte is in management, and I concentrated my efforts there. I kept close tabs on the directors of the various departments through personal visits and frequent cabinet meetings.

The public probably overestimates the power of the governor to direct day-by-day policy. Public employees are protected from any executive pressure that would violate regulations or law. Budgets are set by the legislature and the governor's authority to change legal expenditures is small, indeed. That is a good thing. It's the public's money, not the governor's.

But the governor has immense power in one area - the bully pulpit. If he so desires, he can affect nearly any topic by publicly stating his views. That is a two-edged sword. The governor is also expected to have an opinion on everything from ingrown toenails to endangered salmon. I sometimes felt as if I were regarded as an expert on matters of which I had little knowledge. I tried to make it clear that I was not all-wise.

I automatically became Chairman of the State Land Board. The other members were Attorney General Al Lance, Secretary of State Pete Cenarrusa, Controller J. D Williams and Superintendent of Public Instruction Anne Fox. This board oversees the state's assets, which are valued at some $3 billion. That group of elected officials is charged with maximizing financial returns from state-owned timber, mining and grazing lands and various other properties. The board also handles a wide-ranging variety of questions such as regulating the use of our streambeds and lakes.

The Land Board had its first meeting six days after I took office. I was green as grass and quite unfamiliar with the questions before us. I was also impatient with the interminable debate that customarily comes with each Land Board decision. I once stated that they didn't call it the Land Board (Bored) for nothing. But, serving on that panel taught me a much-needed lesson in patience. It also brought me a valuable camaraderie with the other board members, which I'll always treasure.

It was exactly 30 years between the time I was first elected to the legislature and the time I won the governorship.

One would think that I would have developed a thick enough hide to shuck off unfavorable editorials. But I found that difficult to do.

I never objected to any critic pointing out my errors in judgment or other human frailties. What bothered me was the assertions or insinuations that I was taking certain actions because of campaign contributions, or that I was a slave of big business, or that I lacked compassion for poor people or others needing help, or that I didn't care about those sections of the state that are a long way from Boise.

I resented such charges because they aren't true. But, when you're governor, you're probably better off to shut up and take the heat. I did a better job of that later in my term. I still couldn't resist an occasional turnabout column in rebuttal.

While I'm still the same person I always was, my election as governor changed my life permanently. It caused me to sharpen my perspective on all facets of our daily existence that can be affected by government.

But, it also bolstered my belief that most important things in life are independent of official rules and laws, and should remain that way.

A politician striving for a high office works feverishly at increasing his or her public visibility. Unless a candidate is negatively viewed by the electorate, the more he or she is recognized, the better chance for election.

But one must realize that all privacy flies out the window when you're elected governor. I don't mean this as a complaint, because it's a highly flattering aspect of the job.

You can't expect to go to church or go shopping without being recognized if you've served as governor. But nearly all encounters are friendly. Personal acquaintances and perfect strangers alike will come up to me, thank me for my service, and tell me I did a good job. Even though that can be debated, I tell myself it's true. Most of the public has a genuine affection for Jacque and me.

So, if we lost some privacy, we gained some warm feelings. It was cetainly a good bargain on our part.

For three and a half decades I've been allowed to influence public policy in Idaho. During my 72 years on this earth I have watched our nation finish its era of homesteading and have shared in its pride at becoming the envy of the entire world. What a privilege it is to have lived here in these times. I hope to enjoy them for a while, yet. After all, my Grandpa was 97 when he died.